MY BEST STUFF:

21st Century Sermons for the Dawning New Age of Faith, Hope and Love

Rev. John T. Crestwell, Jr.

CONTENTS

REV.JOHNT.CRESTWELLJR.

ENDORSEMENTS

Rev. Dr. Brock Leach, Unitarian Universalist Minister, Community-Builder and Social Entrepreneur: *"Rev. John has been clairvoyant in envisioning ours as a faith that places love at the center--a place where every person, no matter who they are where they come from, can find belonging, meaning and spiritual wholeness in the company of a whole community. In this beautiful collection, he invites us all to join him, shows us how it's done, and encourages us to demonstrate the Beloved Community in a world that's thirsting for it."*

Dr. Sharon Welch, PhD., Retired Professor of Religion and Society, Meadville Lombard Theological School: *"Rev. John Crestwell offers profound wisdom and a call to action for our shared work in justice and spiritual growth. His words are a powerful blend of inspiration and challenge, inviting us to live with courage and compassion."*

Rev. Dr. William Sinkford, Former President of the Unitarian Universalist Association: *"Rev. Crestwell speaks to the heart of what it means to live a life grounded in faith, justice, and love. His sermons inspire action and reflection, offering a much-needed compass for our times."*

Dr. Cherie Carter-Scott, PhD., Bestselling Author and "Mother of Coaching": *"John's insights remind us that true leadership comes from within. His message of transformation and courage offers readers a roadmap for living their best lives."*

Diana McNab, Performance Enhancement Coach, Olympic and Professional Athletes: *"Rev. John is a brilliant fusion of spiritual wisdom and personal growth. His message resonates with anyone committed to pushing the boundaries of their potential and living with purpose."*

Elizabeth Kinney, Founder LightHouse Shelter; Social Entrepreneur with LightHouse Bistro and Rise & Shine Bakery: *"Rev. John's dedication to social justice is truly inspiring. He recognizes that building a more equitable world and uplifting the community starts from within. Authentic and impactful love for others begins by nurturing and discovering the treasures within one's own*

2

REV.JOHNT.CRESTWELLJR.

heart."

DEDICATION

For my family, faith, and the Unitarian Universalist Church of Annapolis—my beloved congregation. You have given me the space to live my purpose and surrounded me with love on this journey. I am deeply grateful. Thank you.

www.uuannapolis.org

INVOCATION

Spirit of Life, God of many names, source of all that is sacred and true, we come to this moment with open hearts and minds. As we embark on this journey through words, reflections, and stories, we ask for your presence to guide us, inspire us, and hold us in the embrace of your wisdom.

We honor the power of transformation that is constantly unfolding within us and around us. May this book be a vessel of insight, a catalyst for change, and a source of hope. As we turn each page, let us remember the beauty of our interconnectedness, the courage it takes to grow, and the strength we find in community.

Bless these words, that they may uplift and challenge us. Bless the reader, that they may find the inspiration to be the best version of themselves. And bless all who seek truth, justice, and love, that we may walk this path together with grace and compassion.

May the spirit of renewal and possibility flow through every chapter, reminding us that we are capable of greatness and called to live with purpose. May this book be a testament to the power of faith, hope, and love in all its forms.

In the spirit of all that is holy and good, we dedicate these words to the ongoing work of creating a more just and loving world. May it be so. Amen.

MY BEST STUFF:

21st Century Sermons for the Dawning New Age of Faith, Hope, and Love

FOREWORD

Reverend John T. Crestwell, Jr. has been a transformative leader and a dynamic presence in the Unitarian Universalist community for 25 years. As the Senior Minister and Executive at the Unitarian Universalist Church of Annapolis (UUCA), John has guided his congregation of 440 with a vision of inclusivity, justice, and spiritual growth. His work extends beyond the pulpit, making an impact in the wider community and drawing national attention during critical moments. He is known for his down-to-earth personality, positive outlook, humor, and deep understanding of human nature.

Rev. John's journey into ministry began with his desire to explore faith in a way that embraced questions and inclusivity. Raised amidst America's complexities of race and identity, John found Unitarian Universalism to be a welcoming home that aligned with his values of equity and compassionate action. After earning a BA in Mass Media Arts from Hampton University and a Master's in Theology from Wesley Theological Seminary, he set out to make faith relevant and accessible to all. His first ministry at Davies Memorial Unitarian Universalist Congregation transformed it into one of the most racially diverse UU congregations in the country, highlighting his commitment to breaking down barriers and building bridges among people of all backgrounds.

John's leadership at UUCA has been marked by innovation and a deep commitment to justice. He co-founded AWAKE Ministries, a groundbreaking initiative that redefined worship and community engagement by integrating contemporary worship, music, life coaching, and service. AWAKE Ministries from 2013 to 2019 was not just a program but a movement within the church, expanding the emotional, racial, and intercultural competencies of all involved, demonstrating John's belief that faith communities should be at the forefront of social and cultural transformation.

Rev. John's influence extends far beyond the walls of his church. He serves on the Board of Directors of Annapolis Pride, serves as Lead Chaplain for the Wellness House cancer community, offering ongoing support to individuals and families navigating cancer, participates in the Anne Arundel County Executive's Interfaith Advisory Council, and works with the Anne Arundel Connecting Together (ACT) Strategy Team, an interfaith-based community action group. His involvement in these organizations exemplifies his belief that faith is not just a private practice but a public commitment to justice and community well-being.

One of the most pivotal moments of John's ministry came in 2018 during the tragic Capital Gazette shooting, which claimed the lives of five newspaper employees, including Wendi Winters, a longtime member of UUCA. Winters, remembered as a courageous individual who confronted the shooter, was honored by John through a community memorial service at Maryland Hall. John's leadership during this time of grief and his advocacy for the community drew national attention, highlighting his role as a compassionate leader in times of crisis.

Rev. John is also known for his dynamic singing, which adds a powerful, soulful element to his worship services. His music enriches his sermons, making his messages not only intellectually engaging but also emotionally resonant, reflecting his belief in the healing and connective power of art. His sermons uniquely blend ancient wisdom, science, religious history, philosophy, sociology, psychology, current events, and practical lived experiences to offer a holistic and accessible approach to spirituality.

His latest book, *MY BEST STUFF: 21st Century Sermons for the Dawning New Age of Faith, Hope, and Love,* is a collection of many of his impactful sermons, carefully curated to reflect the pressing questions and spiritual yearnings of our time. Each sermon is a journey—a conversation with the reader that explores topics as diverse as forgiveness, toxic masculinity, the power of mindfulness, and the nature of God.

Rev. John Crestwell's sermons are born out of struggle, resilience, and a relentless pursuit of truth. They are the product of a man who has walked the difficult road of faith—questioning, doubting, and ultimately embracing a spirituality that is both expansive and inclusive. John doesn't just preach; he lives his faith in the real world, wrestling with the same questions we all do: How do we find hope in a fractured world? How do we stay true to our values when everything around us seems to be falling apart? How do we live authentically in a culture that often demands conformity?

In *MY BEST STUFF,* you will find a roadmap for navigating the spiritual and moral challenges of our time. John weaves together themes of justice, love, and personal growth in a way that feels both urgent and timeless. He draws on the wisdom of ancient and modern spiritual traditions offering insights that are both profound and practical. Whether you are a seasoned seeker or someone just beginning to explore the deeper questions of life, this book has something for you.

Reading this book is more than just an intellectual exercise; it is a spiritual experience. It is an opportunity to connect with a kindred spirit who is committed to the work of building a more just, loving, and spiritually grounded world. So, as you turn the pages, let yourself be drawn into the conversation. Let John's words inspire you, challenge you, and, most importantly, remind you of the power and potential that lies within each of us. This is not just a book of sermons—it is a guide for living a life of faith, hope, and love in the 21st century.

John Crestwell's voice is one that our world desperately needs. It is a voice of compassion, courage, and clarity—a voice that reminds us that we are all connected, that our actions matter, and that, no matter the circumstances, we have the power to shape our own lives and the world around us. His sermons are a call to rise above the noise of everyday life and to engage deeply with the questions that truly matter.

Outside of his professional life, John is devoted to his family. He is married to Joan (Joni) Crestwell and together they have a blended family of five adult children. John's deep personal connections and commitment to his loved-ones inspire his work, making him not just a leader, but a relatable and compassionate figure who understands the everyday struggles and triumphs of people.

As you turn these pages, you are joining a journey led by a minister who does not shy away from the hard questions but embraces them, knowing that it is in our deepest inquiries that we find our truest selves. John Crestwell's voice —compassionate, challenging, and always inspiring—urges us all to live more fully, love more fiercely, and transform our world together.

Rev. Dr. Fredric J. Muir
Minister Emeritus, UU Church of Annapolis

INTRODUCTION: CALLING FORTH THE DAWNING OF A NEW AGE

We stand at the threshold of a great awakening–some say at the dawning of the Age of Aquarius—a time not yet fully realized but rising on the horizon, calling us toward a new way of being. Though the Age itself is still forthcoming, beginning around 2160, its promise is already whispering to us, inviting us to step forward with courage and vision. Like John the Baptist calling forth Jesus of Nazareth, I am here, another John, calling you to recognize that we are at the precipice of a new age—not an age that centers a single savior, but one where humanity itself rises to its collective greatness.

The sermons in *MY BEST STUFF: 21st Century Sermons for the Dawning New Age of Faith, Hope, and Love* are written for this dawning new age. They are messages that resonate with the ancient yet timeless truths that have always been with and within us, waiting to be recognized and applied. This new age is not about following the old hierarchies of power and authority. It is about each of us realizing that we are co-creators of a future where every voice matters, every soul counts, and our collective strength becomes our salvation.

The Age of Aquarius calls us to be our own saviors, to manifest a world where love, equity, and justice are not mere ideals but lived realities. It challenges us to move beyond the constraints of the past—beyond fear, division, and scarcity—and to step into a mindset of abundance, interconnectedness, and shared purpose. The sermons in this book are more than reflections; they are a call to action, a roadmap for living in alignment with the values that will define this new era.

We are on the cusp of a transformation—a collective shift that will redefine what it means to be human. My role is not to bring about this new age alone but to call it forth, to prepare the way, and to remind us all that the power to create this future lies within us. The Age of Aquarius is not about waiting for a savior but becoming saviors ourselves, each in our own way, as we manifest the world we know is possible. Together, we are the architects of a new spiritual landscape, a new way of being. Welcome to the call.

Rev. John

Section 1: Personal Growth and Self-Awareness

1. **Authenticity—Freedom—Pain–Pleasure** (Self-Actualization)
   Exploring the meaning of living authentically and the challenges that come with it, from pain and suffering to self-awareness and freedom.
2. **Conquering Fear** (Courage)
   Understanding fear, its impact on our lives, and

how to rise above it through spiritual practice and courage.

3. **Happiness: A Journey** (Inner Joy)
Discovering the true sources of inner joy and how to cultivate lasting happiness.

4. **Becoming Nobody** (Self-Identity)
Reflections on personal transformation, the process of unbecoming, and finding purpose through interconnectedness.

5. **Blink: Improving How We Judge Others** (Discernment)
Insights on rapid cognition, biases, and the importance of blending intuition with informed knowledge.

6. **Lemons to Lemonade** (Resilience)
Turning setbacks into opportunities for growth and learning how to find strength in adversity.

7. **Forgive 70x7** (Forgiveness)
The spiritual and emotional power of forgiveness and its role in personal and collective healing.

8. **Care-Full and Care-Less** (Mindfulness)
Balancing caring for others and self-care.

9. **Wordsmithing** (Mindful Speech)
The power of language to shape thought, influence others, and create change.

Section 2: Spirituality and Inner Wisdom

10. **The Alchemist** (Transformation)
A journey into self-transformation.

11. **Bruce Lee and Jiddu Krishnamurti: Choiceless Awareness** (Mindfulness)
Integrating philosophy and martial arts wisdom to live fully in the present moment.

12. **Hindu Trinity** (Enlightenment)
Exploring the power of the number 3.

13. **Water Metaphors** (Rebirth)
Using the symbolism of water to understand transformation, renewal, and the flow of life.

14. **The Seven Spiritual Laws** (Universal Laws)
Unpacking key spiritual principles that open new pathways of power and discovery.

15. **Law of Surrender** (Acceptance)
Embracing life's challenges through the spiritual practice of surrender and acceptance.

16. **Be Invictus** (Perseverance)
Lessons in resilience and overcoming obstacles with an undefeated spirit.

17. **Heaven & The Afterlife** (Spiritual Beliefs)
Reflections on spiritual beliefs about the afterlife, heaven, and the nature of existence beyond death.

Section 3: Faith, Religion, and Spiritual Reflections

18. **Does God Exist?** (Existential Inquiry)
A deep dive into existential questions about the existence of God and the nature of the divine.

19. **The Aquarian Gospel, Eschatology, and the New Age** (Awakening)
Exploring the metaphysical aspects of the awakened self

through the lens of the Aquarian Gospel of Jesus.

20. **Samhain and the Origins of Religion: Paganism, Magic, Spells, and Harry Potter** (Religious History)
Tracing the roots of spiritual practices and their impact on modern religion.

21. **Easter: The True Meaning of Resurrection** (Rebirth)
Reinterpreting the resurrection story as a symbol of personal and collective rebirth.

22. **Pagan Holidays: Hanukkah, Solstice, Yule, Christmas** (Religious Observances)
Understanding the interconnectedness of various religious observances and their shared themes.

23. **"Insha Allah": God's Will? Bless You?** (Divine Will)
Reflections on divine will, surrender, and the human quest for understanding.

Section 4: Unitarian Universalism

24. **Tipping Point** (Shifting the Paradigm)
Identifying critical moments that drive movements and societal transformation.

25. **Decolonizing Our Spirituality** (Cultural Renewal)
Examining the decolonization of spiritual practices and creating inclusive spaces for all.

26. **New American Transcendentalism** (21st Century UU)
Bridging past and present to create a new understanding

of transcendentalism in Unitarian Universalism.

27. **Heretics Faith: Prayer, Meditation, Contemplation** (Spiritual Practice)
Embracing spiritual practices in a modern, inclusive context.

28. **Why I am a Unitarian Universalist** (A Chosen Faith)
Personal reflections on choosing Unitarian Universalism and its impact on spiritual life.

Section 5: Social Justice and Cultural Critique

29. **Chaos or Community: Dr. King, Oppenheimer, and Barbie** (Social Choices)
Examining social choices and their implications through a blend of cultural and historical lenses.

30. **You Throw Like a Girl: Toxic Masculinity** (Gender Issues)
Challenging toxic masculinity and redefining strength beyond traditional gender roles.

31. **Caste and America** (Social Hierarchies)
A critical look at caste systems in America and their impact on society.

32. **Hacking the Brain & Race** (Race and Psychology)
The intersection of race, neuroscience, and the psychological factors that influence perception.

33. **MLK: 90 Years Later** (Civil Rights Reflection)
Reflecting on Martin Luther King Jr.'s legacy and its relevance today.

34. **The Poor People's Campaign Revisited** (Economic Justice)
Revisiting King's vision of economic justice and its

Section 6: Nature, Science, and Philosophy

the function of the left and right brain in spirituality and daily life.

Section 7: Society, Conflict, and Human Behavior

Section 8: Spirituality in Practice

47. **Tattoos From the Heart** (Faith in Action)
What spiritual entrepreneurism looks like in action.
48. **Invitation as Spiritual Practice** (Grounding Your Faith)
How the heart opens for boundless love.
49. **Final Words & Contact Information**

50. **Benediction**

Section 9: Quotes From the Book

Please Quote Me. I Would Be Honored.

SECTION 1: PERSONAL GROWTH AND SELF-AWARENESS

1. Authenticity—Freedom—Pain–Pleasure

T o live authentically means being true to yourself, following your values and passions, and resisting external pressures that conflict with them. Challenges —rejection, criticism, disappointment, and loneliness—are inevitable on this path. There is no authenticity, no freedom, no joy without enduring some pain.

The word "authentic" comes from the Greek "authentikos," meaning original, genuine, and acting on one's authority. To be authentic is to embrace your truest self, guided by a quest for freedom that leads you toward your highest good. Your authentic self is the Imago Dei—the image of God within you, expressed through the good you do. Forces that deny human freedom are dangerous because they oppose our search for truth and meaning, our inherent worth, and the dignity of every person. Perseverance is required to confront these forces, and the struggle often comes with pain that tests your will. You may face your own Friday crucifixion before reaching

Sunday's resurrection. There is always a price to pay for living authentically.

Dr. James Cone once said, "Real theology begins when your back is against the wall." This has been a truth for me. During my second year of theological seminary, I realized that serving as a minister in a traditional Protestant setting would never allow me to be my authentic self. I felt lost, confused, and forsaken. A once confident and self-assured man became depressed, angry, and unsure of his future. I nearly quit, but a still, small voice urged me to trust the process. One day, I stumbled upon a description of a faith tradition that would change my life. Before this transformation, I was driven by ego, judgment, and self-righteousness. Afterward, I became more curious, accepting, and open. It was a long journey, but that's what it takes to live authentically: a willingness to endure pain to find the pleasure of being true to yourself.

The authentic self isn't driven by ego but by quiet strength rooted in humility. Authenticity isn't about self-promotion or proving your worth; it's about embracing who you are without seeking validation. When we live authentically, our actions speak louder than words, and our presence testifies to the truth within us. Humility shines through the authentic soul, showing up as a willingness to listen, learn, and connect deeply. It's a strength that doesn't dominate but invites others to be their true selves. Authenticity paired with humility has a profound impact—it doesn't seek the spotlight, yet it lights the way for others.

Pain and pleasure are intertwined on the path to authenticity. They teach, motivate, and connect us to the cycles of life: creation and destruction, birth and death, gain and loss. Embracing this relationship helps us grow from our struggles and understand our journey.

Our nation, too, is on a quest for authenticity and freedom. Watching the PBS documentary "God in America," I was struck by how our nation, like each of us, grapples with freedom, authenticity, pain, and suffering. We aspire to live out the true meaning of our creed but often resist what accountability requires. There is the price to pay for real reconciliation of past sins. Our national story—from the Revolution to the Civil War and beyond—reflects an ongoing battle over who gets to be authentically free and who decides. From the start, our morals were shaped by contradictory narratives that proclaimed freedom while justifying conquest and colonization. We will not be an authentic people until we confront this truth.

The words "all are created equal" set us on a path of reckoning with our contradictions. Our nation's journey mirrors our personal quests for authenticity and will continue to repeat cycles of harm until we make amends. We are freedom-seekers, yet our pursuit of freedom often comes at the expense of others, leaving a legacy of pain and suffering.

Christian fundamentalism is complicit in this contradictory history, influencing not just our religious landscape but also our social, political, and cultural fabric. From the Puritans' "city on a hill" to the justification of slavery and exclusionary policies, fundamentalist ideology has shaped norms that prioritize conformity over diversity, creating division and discrimination. But we have the power to change our past by choosing narratives that promote authenticity, inclusivity, justice, and love.

Authenticity, freedom, pain, and pleasure are the intertwined threads of our human experience. To live authentically is to embrace the risks and costs of being true to ourselves, knowing that freedom often comes through struggle. But there is a redemptive kind of pain—the kind that pushes us to grow, evolve, and become our truest selves. This pain draws us closer to the Imago Dei within, closer to our highest potential. It is far better than the pain that binds us to old, harmful stories. Our task is to rewrite those narratives—personal and collective—that keep us stuck. Let us have the courage to tell new stories rooted in humility, freedom, and love, and let those stories light the way to a more authentic humanity. In doing so, we reclaim our birthright and help shape a future where every soul can live in its truth.

Amen.

References

1. Etymology of Authenticity - The origin of the word "authentic" from the Greek "authentikos," meaning original, genuine, and acting on one's own authority. *Online Etymology Dictionary, "Authentic."*

2. James Cone - Quote: "Real theology begins when your back is against the wall." *Cone, James H. **The Cross and the Lynching Tree**. Orbis Books, 2011.*

3. Imago Dei Concept - Understanding the concept of Imago Dei, which means the image of God, manifest in human actions and inherent worth. *Cortez, Marc. **"Theological Anthropology: A Guide for the Perplexed."** Bloomsbury, 2010.*

4. Pain and Pleasure Interconnectedness - Exploring how pain and pleasure are intertwined in human experience, guiding us through life's cycles. *Frankl, Viktor E. **"Man's Search for Meaning."** Beacon Press, 1946.*

5. PBS Documentary "God in America" - Reference to America's struggles with freedom, pain, and suffering throughout its history. *PBS. "God in America." American Experience, 2010.*

6. *Balmer, Randall. **Mine Eyes Have Seen the Glory: A Journey into the Evangelical Subculture in America**. Oxford University Press, 1989.*

2. CONQUERING FEAR

I want to ask you a question: What are you afraid of? Are you afraid to die? Do events beyond your control scare you? Are you afraid of getting terminally ill, losing a loved one suddenly or tragically, or perhaps even afraid for your children in a world filled with hatred? Do you fear losing your mental faculties, your job, or being judged or misperceived? Are you afraid for the planet and the future of humanity?

Fear can paralyze our ability to live with joy, appreciation, and love. The Bible mentions fear or being afraid over 1,500 times, acknowledging its real and pervasive presence in our lives. But what exactly is fear? Webster defines fear as "an unpleasant and often strong emotion caused by the anticipation or awareness of danger." We fear things that can harm us or our loved ones. Yet, if we hope to create a more equitable society, we must learn to rise above our fears, especially the fear of those not like us.

While I don't believe we can fully conquer all fears, we can learn to rise above them with courage. Some fears, however, can be entirely conquered through deep spiritual practice—by thinking and talking about the fear, putting it in perspective, and facing it intentionally. Many fears are inherited traumas from our families and society, stemming from repeated experiences of being let down, abused, or having our hearts broken. Fear is tied to our past and current desires, dreams and expectations. The underlying fear is that we won't be able to handle whatever it is we dread or hope. But as FD Roosevelt said, "The only thing we have to fear is fear itself." And as Susan Jeffers says, "feel the fear and do it anyway."

Ultimately, our deepest fears often revolve around our mortality—the end of ourselves and those we love. Overcoming or coping better with our fears requires deep spiritual work and a willingness to ask existential questions: Who am I? What am I? Where am I going? This journey of self-awareness and spiritual contemplation is essential to conquering fear, yet many are unwilling to face their inner demons and shadows. Why? Many are unwilling because it requires a level of vulnerability and honesty that is profoundly uncomfortable. Confronting our deepest fears forces us to acknowledge painful truths about ourselves, our past traumas, and the fragility of life. It disrupts the comfortable narratives we've built around our lives and exposes us to the raw, unfiltered realities we often try to avoid.

Marianne Williamson has a wonderful poem about our deepest fears. She says: *"Our deepest fear is not that we are inadequate. Our deepest fear is that we are powerful beyond measure. It is our light, not our darkness, that most frightens us. We ask ourselves, 'Who am I to be brilliant, gorgeous, talented, fabulous?' Actually, who are you not to be? You are a child of God. Your playing small does not serve the world. There is nothing enlightened about shrinking so that other people won't feel insecure around you. We are all meant to shine, as children do. We were born to make manifest the glory of God that is within us. It's not just in some of us; it's in everyone. And as we let our own light shine, we unconsciously give other people permission to do the same. As we are liberated from our own fear, our presence automatically liberates others."* Amen! This powerful reflection reminds us that our greatest fear isn't rooted in failure or inadequacy but in our own potential. We fear the responsibility of our greatness, the call to live fully into our purpose, and the courage it takes to be unapologetically ourselves.

The journey of self-awareness demands that we strip away the masks we wear—the personas we create to fit in, to feel safe, or to project a sense of control. It means confronting parts of ourselves that we don't like, that we've suppressed, or that we've denied out of shame, guilt, or fear of rejection. It's easier to stay distracted, to keep moving through life without pausing to reflect, because reflection can bring up old wounds that we'd rather keep buried.

One thing I've learned in life is that when you are seeking to grow your soul, you won't break; instead, you'll have breakthroughs. You'll find that most of your fears will disappear.

Popular psychology tells us that an acronym for FEAR is "False Evidence Appearing Real." It's true, and yet it's not. Many things we fear, like flying, are statistically unlikely to harm us. The odds of dying in a plane crash are 1 in 1.2 million, compared to 1 in 107 in a car accident. Yet many people choose to drive instead of fly because of perceived danger.

The real issue isn't just the fear of a particular event but the broader anxiety that stems from the randomness of life. We know deep down that eventually, something will happen to us —that we will die one day. This awareness of life's uncertainty and inevitable end fuels fear which can lead to paranoia, distrust, and conspiracy theories that can easily spiral into violence.

If you are part of a marginalized group or live in a dangerous environment, fear is more than just a feeling; it's a reality shaped by higher risks. Studies show that fear can lead to increased cortisol levels, high blood pressure, and other health issues. Fear is more than psychological—it physically impacts those constantly under threat. That's why our work to create safer and more equitable communities is so vital; it reduces the fears that keep people from thriving.

Fear is a primal response, rooted in survival, but it also reflects our collective spiritual shortcomings. When we don't work to become better versions of ourselves, we fall prey to a lesser, more fearful nature that blames, attacks, and isolates. Embracing others, despite our fears, is key to our survival. Humanity thrives on cooperation, not competition. Competition may create champions, but cooperation builds community.

The opposite of fear is courage—bravery, confidence, audacity, and faith. These words inspire and call us to build beloved communities that transcend fear. My Unitarian Universalist tradition calls me to live boldly and compassionately, expanding my capacity for great things.

I remember a story my mentor, Rev. Fred Muir shared about a snowstorm that never came. Despite the forecast, schools closed, and people stocked up on supplies. The next day's headline read, "Threat of Storm Paralyzes City." It was not the storm but the threat that paralyzed people. Fear spreads faster than bacteria, as we saw during the Washington DC sniper attacks when many of us were afraid to even pump gas. Fear triggers our survival instincts, making us irrational and overly cautious.

Spiritual people do not let fear guide them but faith, hope, and love. We choose not to let fear win, embracing a kind of holy boldness that keeps us focused on unity and love.

It's hard to live fearlessly, especially when fear is cultivated by the media's constant focus on anomalies and sensational stories. Fear is used to control us, and it takes a deliberate effort not to be manipulated.

Since the election of the first Black president in 2008, we've seen fear mongering on the rise—fear of immigrants, LGBTQ rights, progress and more. In 2016, we elected a fear-driven leader whose politics thrive on division and supremacy. At the heart of this fear is the anxiety over the shifting demographics in our country. White culture's dominance feels threatened by the rise of Black, Brown, Asian, and Indigenous voices. Overcoming this fear of perceived loss is crucial if we are to move forward as a society.

Every time you confront your fears and move beyond them, you help heal our world. Faith calls us to be brave truth-tellers, to fight for a shared future where we embrace our common humanity. We are one species, more alike than unalike, and there is room for all of us if we share and care more.

I'm reminded of a poem by Guillaume Apollinaire:

> *"Come to the edge," he said.*
> *"We can't, we're afraid!" they responded.*
> *"Come to the edge," he said.*
> *"We can't, We will fall!" they responded.*
> *"Come to the edge," he said.*
> *And so they came.*
> *And he pushed them.*
> *And they flew."*

Amen.

References

1. Webster's Dictionary - Definition of fear as "an unpleasant and often strong emotion caused by the anticipation or awareness of danger." Merriam-Webster Dictionary, "Fear."
2. Susan Jeffers - Quote: "Feel the fear and do it anyway." Jeffers, Susan. *Feel the Fear and Do It Anyway*, Ballantine Books, 1987.

3. Franklin D. Roosevelt - Quote: "The only thing we have to fear is fear itself."
   Roosevelt, Franklin D. "First Inaugural Address," 1933.

4. Marianne Williamson - Excerpt from the poem "Our Deepest Fear." Williamson, Marianne. *A Return to Love: Reflections on the Principles of 'A Course in Miracles.* HarperOne, 1992.

5. Etymology of Authenticity - The origin of the word "authentic" from the Greek "authentikos."
   Online Etymology Dictionary, "Authentic."

6. **Fear and Health Impact Studies** - Research on cortisol levels and the impact of fear on marginalized groups. McEwen, Bruce S., and Peter J. Gianaros. "Central Role of the Brain in Stress and Adaptation: Links to Socioeconomic Status, Health, and Disease." Annals of the New York Academy of Sciences, 2009.

7. Guillaume Apollinaire. Poem, "Come to the Edge". Translated by James Kirkup.

3. HAPPINESS: A JOURNEY

I had a dream when I was 16-years-old that still sticks with me—vivid, wild, and a little unsettling. I was leading a group of people across this huge, open field. It felt familiar, like my old elementary school playground, but it stretched way beyond what I remembered, almost infinite. I was out front, confident, leading the way, when suddenly this dark, heavy force came at me out of nowhere. The people behind me vanished, swallowed up by this shadow, and I felt totally alone. I was trapped, stuck, and scared. I cried out for help, desperate for something or someone to pull me out.

Then, in an instant, I started to rise—up, up, and up—lifting off the ground like I was weightless. I soared higher and higher until I was surrounded by the most magnificent sunlight, warm and all-encompassing. It was as if the sun itself had reached out to hold me. The fear vanished, replaced by this incredible sense of peace and power. I woke up drenched in sweat, heart racing, tears in my eyes, completely overwhelmed by what just happened.

I couldn't shake the dream for weeks. I kept replaying it in my head, trying to make sense of it. My aunt, with her usual wisdom, told me, "Boy, you're gonna be a preacher one day." And, well, here I am. But for me, that dream was about something deeper. It was a reminder that no matter what forces come at me, no matter how dark things might seem, I'm not alone. I'm held by something greater, something that lifts me when I call out. That's the kind of hope that fuels me.

I've always been a hopeful person, but I'm realistic about my happiness. I have a simple way of measuring it. My formula is based on where I live—in the great state of Maryland, where we get precipitation about 114 days a year. That's about 30% of the time, or roughly three out of every ten days. If I'm happy seven out of ten days, or even five out of seven, then I think I'm doing pretty good.

Pursuing happiness intentionally is relatively new for us as humans. Our founding fathers in the 18th century said we have the right to life, liberty, and the pursuit of happiness. But this is a new idea in the grand scheme of things. Historically, the purpose of life wasn't to be happy; it was to survive— to make it through each day and pass on your genes. There was no time for contemplating joy or fulfillment. Society was agrarian and you had to work from dusk until dawn. But today, we have the gift of time, the privilege to think about what it means to be happy.

Aristotle once said, "Happiness is the meaning and the purpose of life, the whole aim and end of human existence." For him, happiness was tied to discovering one's true, authentic self through action and thought—through actively pursuing virtue. He saw happiness as both a journey and a destination. It's about choosing a life of appreciation and gratitude, even when the moment you're in feels particularly dramatic or difficult.

For me, happiness is "the joy I feel while pursuing my passions or goals." It's both active and still; it's the energy in motion (emotion) and the quiet contentment of a peaceful mind. The Dalai Lama agrees—he says that happiness can only be sustained and developed through training or disciplining the mind.

Martha Beck's book The Joy Diet echoes this by offering a menu of practices that aren't just about fleeting moments of joy but about creating a sustainable lifestyle of happiness. She describes joy not as something you chase, but as something you cultivate through small, deliberate steps. Beck encourages us to embrace daily rituals like gratitude, truth-telling, and even the radical act of "doing nothing" as ways to create a deeper, more resilient sense of joy. She reminds us that joy is less about a destination and more about the practices that make up our daily lives.

Robert Holden, a British psychologist who has written extensively on happiness, shares a powerful story about his own troubled upbringing with an alcoholic father and a clinically depressed mother. For him, those early traumas were the catalysts that drove him to explore what it means to be truly happy. He discovered that happiness isn't about chasing a carrot but finding joy in the everyday moments. He founded the Happiness Project and identified three types of happiness: one tied to material security, one connected to sensory pleasures, and a deeper kind called "joy happiness."

This "joy happiness" is what we can all experience—it's in the moments—the now and later (my favorite candy). It's about finding joy in the journey, not just the destination. Holden says, "Don't chase happiness; follow your joy." Follow your passions, see the holy in the plain, the majestic in the ordinary, and even the magic in the mess. Happiness is always there, standing at the door, knocking. You decide when to let it in.

Some might say, "Easy for you to talk about happiness, Rev. John—you've always been positive." Maybe so, but as Jonathan Haidt, a renowned researcher on happiness, points out, genetics only account for about 50% of our capacity for happiness. The other half is influenced by our environment, circumstances, and the choices we make every day. Even in the most challenging situations, happiness is still within our reach if we choose it.

Take Nelson Mandela, for example. He spent 27 years in prison, most of it in harsh conditions on Robben Island, where he was forced into hard labor and subjected to isolation. Despite the unimaginable hardships, Mandela famously found a way to cultivate inner joy. He read poetry, built relationships with fellow inmates, and remained steadfast in his belief in justice and reconciliation. Even behind bars, he chose not to let bitterness or hatred consume him. His choice to embrace forgiveness and hope transformed not only his life but the entire nation of South Africa. Mandela's story shows us that happiness is not about the absence of hardship but about our inner resilience and the decisions we make in the face of adversity.

I saw a similar spirit when I visited the Philippines. In a place where people often have so little by first-world standards, I witnessed a joy that seemed almost effortless. It was a profound reminder that while the first world is often about having, the third world is more present with happiness. Whether it's Mandela's story of resilience or the everyday joy of those living with far less, happiness remains a choice we make every single day.

Our faith challenges us to find truth and meaning in the world, even in its darkest corners. Ram Dass once said, "That's where God is—in the mess." We must live in two worlds simultaneously, engaging in justice work while finding joy along the way. Balance the negative with the positive, because one negative can outweigh eight positives. This imbalance is why happiness takes work and practice.

When life feels overwhelming, remember that you don't have to do it alone. Seek out community, friends, and support. Happiness isn't a solo mission. It's about connection, gratitude, and recognizing that you're part of something larger than yourself.

So, when the rain falls in your life, remember it's just like the Maryland weather—it's a necessary part of the cycle, and it doesn't last forever. There will always be sunlight after the storm, ready to lift you up when you need it most. Happiness, joy, contentment, and satisfaction are all standing by, waiting for you to open the door. Choose happiness.

Amen.

References

1. *Aristotle on Happiness - The concept of happiness as the purpose of life and a state of activity.*
   Aristotle, Nicomachean Ethics. Hackett Publishing, 1985.
2. **Dalai Lama and Howard Cutler, The Art of Happiness: A Handbook for Living.** *Riverhead Books, 1998.*
3. **Haidt, Jonathan. The Happiness Hypothesis: Finding Modern Truth in Ancient Wisdom.** *Basic Books, 2006.*
4. **Ram Dass on Presence and Love - The concept of finding God and happiness in life's challenges.**
   Dass, Ram. Be Here Now. Lama Foundation, 1971.
5. **The Joy Diet: 10 Daily Practices for a Happier Life.** *Crown, 2003.*
6. **Mandela, Nelson. Long Walk to Freedom: The Autobiography of Nelson Mandela.** *Little, Brown and Company, 1994.*
7. Norman Doidge on Neuroplasticity - The ability of the brain to rewire itself and adapt for happiness. Doidge, Norman. **The Brain That Changes Itself: Stories of Personal Triumph from the Frontiers of Brain Science.** Viking, 2007.

4. BECOMING
NOBODY

My sabbatical began and ended with powerful experiences that reshaped my understanding of self, community, and the divine. It all started in Memphis, Tennessee, where I spent five days revisiting the legacy of Dr. Martin Luther King Jr. On April 4th, 2022, I stood at the Lorraine Motel, now an incredible museum that captures the entire Civil Rights Movement in vivid detail. I spent four hours there, reflecting on the journey that brought me to this sacred place, where King was assassinated.

I've visited many important historical sites from the Civil Rights Movement—Montgomery, Selma, Atlanta—but never Memphis. I felt compelled to go, to close a chapter and honor King's life. On my last day, I visited Mason Temple, where King delivered his final speech, "I've Been to the Mountaintop." This speech holds deep personal significance for me; I performed it in contests during high school, recited it on the radio in college, and even spoke it at a student protest against the Gulf War.

When I arrived, the temple was closed due to COVID-19. I had rented a white box truck, the only vehicle available. I felt ridiculous driving it, like I was posing as a delivery person rather than a tourist on a pilgrimage. Undeterred, I approached the locked doors and rang the bell. A young janitor answered. I told him, "I'm from Maryland, and I would love to see where King gave his last speech. I know you're closed, but it would mean the world to me." He hesitated but then asked, "Is that your truck?" I nodded. He smiled and said, "Well, you look like you're delivering something, so I think I can let you in without any trouble." Divine intervention I thought.

Inside, I stood in the very space where King had spoken, gazing out from the pulpit. I felt his energy, alive and potent, and I was moved to tears. It was a divine moment, made possible by a serendipitous encounter and that ugly white truck— a reminder that sometimes the most mundane things are vehicles of grace.

A few weeks later, my wife and I went to New York City to visit the World Trade Center Museum. It was a profoundly moving experience, but the most memorable part of the trip was a strange synchronicity involving a family. We saw them at breakfast at our hotel, then again that evening at a Broadway show, and again, strangely, in our elevator on the way back to our hotel room. In a city of millions, this felt like a sign. Each encounter felt like a reminder that there are forces beyond our understanding at play, connecting us in mysterious ways.

In quiet moments, I wrestled with my inner shadows. I faced questions about my purpose now that many of my goals had been fulfilled. I revisited the pain of past traumas—my mother's recent death, my father's passing a decade ago, and the cumulative grief of witnessing deaths in the church. I had to confront fears I had buried for years, realizing that not slowing down had been my way of avoiding the discomfort of these unresolved emotions.

Spirit was speaking to me. I needed to unbecome during my sabbatical before I could truly become. To grow as a person and a minister, I had to embrace my humanity, my flaws, and my mortality and embrace the divine presence that moves in mysterious ways. I had to learn to be present with my life and fears and see them not as things to avoid but as teachers guiding me toward becoming my best self. This journey was like Jacob wrestling with the angel, refusing to let go until he received a blessing. My blessing was the revelation that *I am nobody, everybody and who I choose to be each day.* This time of rest taught me again that I am interconnected with all things. I was rebirthing–waking up again.

I realized that true awakening isn't just about rejecting religious dogma or becoming more progressive. It's about surrendering the ego, accepting our interconnectedness, and leading with compassion that gives our lives meaning, vitality and purpose.

The signs like the miracle in Memphis and the encounter with the family reminded me that we are all part of a larger, divine process. Our individual and collective struggles are not in vain; they are part of a cosmic dance of light and shadow. We must trust the process, even when it feels chaotic and uncertain.

We live in an age of narcissism, where everyone is trying to carve out their own little kingdom on social media. The challenge of our time is to overcome this fixation on the self and rediscover our interconnectedness. We are like colliding galaxies, chaotic now but eventually merging into something more beautiful and organized. To connect, we must let go of our sense of separateness and embrace our common humanity.

My sabbatical was a time of unbecoming—of learning to exist without constant affirmation and validation. It was about reconnecting with the truth that we are all single cells in the body of humankind. Our actions, thoughts, and feelings are interconnected, and we must work together to create a society that honors our shared humanity.

I am nobody because I am everybody. I am every person, woman, man, child. I am special but not that special. I am who I choose to be, and I choose to be love in all of its expressions and manifestations. When in doubt, *I can ask for a sign* and wait expectantly for that amazing grace to remind me that I am on the right path. The divine energy is always present, guiding us toward unity, compassion, and a deeper understanding of ourselves and each other.

> *Norman Cousins is correct: "You are a single cell in the body of over [8 billion cells]. The body is humankind. Your needs are individual but they are not unique. You are interlocked with other human beings in the consequences of your actions, thoughts, and feelings. You will work for human unity and human peace; for a moral order in harmony with the order of the universe. Together you share the quest for a society of the whole equal to your needs, a society in which you need not live beneath your moral capacity, and in which justice has a life of its own. You are single cells in a body of over [8 billion cells]. The body is humankind."*

Amen.

References

1. Martin Luther King Jr. and "I've Been to the Mountaintop" - Reference to King's final speech at Mason Temple and his legacy at the Lorraine Motel.
   Branch, Taylor. *"At Canaan's Edge: America in the King Years, 1965-68."* Simon & Schuster, 2006.
2. Jacob Wrestling with the Angel - Biblical reference to Jacob's struggle as a metaphor for personal transformation.
   The Holy Bible, Genesis 32:22-32 (New International Version).
3. Dark Night of the Soul and Personal Transformation - The concept of spiritual struggle and rebirth through personal challenges. *John of the Cross. "Dark Night of the Soul."* Dover Publications, 2003.

4. Norman Cousins Quote - Reference to the quote on interconnectedness and humanity's collective responsibility. Cousins, Norman. *"Human Options: An Autobiographical Notebook."* W. W. Norton & Company, 1981.

5. BLINK: IMPROVING HOW WE JUDGE OTHERS

Our senses—what we see, hear, feel, smell, or touch in a first encounter—shape our immediate perceptions and judgments. This mental process is known as "rapid cognition" or "thin-slicing," concepts explored by Malcolm Gladwell in his seminal book Blink: The Power of Thinking Without Thinking. Our brains are constantly processing millions of thoughts, and how we decide what to focus on is a sophisticated, lightning-fast survival mechanism that has allowed us to adapt and thrive as a species. In seconds, we assess our environment, gauge threats, identify opportunities, and make split decisions. While many of these decisions are beneficial, particularly those that help us navigate our surroundings, others, especially those directed at fellow human beings, can be flawed.

Gladwell argues that our thin-slicing often fails due to biases, misinformation, or lack of experience. However, by integrating spirituality and science—intuition and reason—we can improve our decision-making process. This approach aligns with our Unitarian Universalist tradition, which encourages us to "heed the guidance of reason and science while warning against idolatries of the mind and spirit." This sermon is dedicated to exploring that wisdom.

Our brains are incredible; they fire millions of signals, making judgments in an instant. We see art and think, "That's beautiful," or "That's objectifying." We look at someone and think, "He's tall; I bet he played basketball," or "They look dangerous." These rapid judgments—often made in a blink—can be both insightful and misguided. We need to approach our judgments with humility, remembering the wise saying, "Judge not, lest ye be judged." This reminder speaks to the karmic consequences of our thoughts and actions—what we put out into the world can cause harm and ultimately it comes back to us. Humility is essential on the path of love.

We rely on our senses, reason, and intelligence to tell us when something feels off, when to proceed with caution, and when to trust. But we also need wisdom to discern the difference between a hasty judgment and a well-considered decision. It takes courage to admit when we don't know something or need help understanding. We should approach each day with the curiosity of a child and the wisdom of an elder—open to learning, yet careful in our actions.

When can we trust our knowledge and experience? There is a difference between opinion and informed knowledge. Everyone has opinions, but how many are backed by informed knowledge and continuous learning? In *Outliers,* Gladwell suggests that it takes 10,000 hours to master a skill. Experts are made, not born. Many people believe they are experts, but true expertise requires deep, sustained practice.

I remember my Methodist minister, Mamie Williams, telling me after my first year of seminary, "John, you've got just enough information to really be dangerous." That cautionary advice has stayed with me. Some of the most troubling people are those with limited knowledge but intense convictions, especially in religion and politics. As Dr. King said, "One tyranny leads to another form of tyranny." This cycle is seen in history, from religious wars to modern-day conflicts. We must be careful not to judge too quickly, as rushing to conclusions has led to countless tragedies.

The less we know about someone's context or experience, the more likely we are to misjudge them. To counter this, we must remain perpetual students—learning, experiencing, and practicing what J. Krishnamurti called "choiceless awareness," the art of observing without judgment. This doesn't mean avoiding action; it means thoughtfully engaging with the world around us, balancing action with reflection.

Psychologist John Gottman, a graduate of MIT, provides a fascinating example of how expertise refines rapid cognition. Through years of study, Gottman developed the ability to predict, with 95 percent accuracy, whether newlyweds would stay married by observing just three minutes of their interactions. His skill wasn't magic—it was the result of countless hours of research and observation. This shows that the more we know, the better our decisions become.

However, two major challenges hinder good analysis: source material and too much information (TMI). What defines credible data? While reputable colleges and researchers often provide reliable information, the landscape today is cluttered with conflicting sources. We must use both wisdom and intuition when evaluating data. Does this information feel right? Is it encouraging courage and hope, or stoking fear and division? We must constantly ask ourselves these questions as we navigate the overwhelming sea of information available today.

Our judgments are influenced by our biases, which we bring into every decision we make, whether reading an article or interacting with someone new. The Implicit Association Test (IAT), discussed in Gladwell's *Blink*, reveals our hidden biases by showing how we associate words and images. Even Gladwell, who is half Jewish and half Black, was surprised to discover his own ingrained stereotypes. These biases are shaped by cultural conditioning that we all must work to overcome.

Improving our rapid cognition requires humility—the courage to admit what we don't know, to recognize our biases, and to challenge our preconceptions. Reinhold Niebuhr's *Serenity Prayer* captures this beautifully: "*God. Grant me the serenity to accept the things I cannot change, courage to change the things I can, and wisdom to know the difference.*" When Gladwell retook the IAT after reading positive stories about Black Americans, his biases diminished significantly. This demonstrates the transformative power of quality associations—real, meaningful interactions that expand our understanding of others.

To treat people fairly and thin-slice effectively, we must engage with others beyond surface-level judgments. This requires ongoing learning, genuine connection, and a willingness to update our understanding continuously. Our ability to build a beloved community depends on being relational beings. It's not just about knowledge—it's about experiencing life together, growing, and transforming through our interactions.

As we navigate this complex world, my litmus test remains: Does this idea, judgment, or action call me to courage and growth, or does it push me toward fear and division? Does it embrace or erase? Is it constructive or merely destructive? Is it universally beneficial, or does it serve only a select few? These questions guide us toward a new, more elastic ethical framework that will shape the future of our faith, our country, and our world.

We are at the beginning of a remarkable new era—one that calls us to be truly free, human, and spiritual beings. Let us explore this journey together, with open hearts and minds, as we learn what it means to connect deeply with one another and the world around us. May it be so.

Amen.

References

1. Malcolm Gladwell and Rapid Cognition - Concepts of rapid cognition and thin-slicing as explored in Blink: The Power of Thinking Without Thinking. Gladwell, Malcolm. **"Blink: The Power of Thinking Without Thinking." Little, Brown and Company, 2005.**

2. 10,000 Hours to Mastery - The idea that it takes 10,000 hours to master a skill, discussed in Gladwell's book Outliers. Gladwell, Malcolm. **"Outliers: The Story of Success."** Little, Brown and Company, 2008.

3. Robin DiAngelo on Opinion vs. Informed Knowledge - Discussions on the difference between opinion and informed knowledge. DiAngelo, Robin. **"White Fragility: Why It's So Hard for White People to Talk About Racism."** Beacon Press, 2018.

4. John Gottman and the Mathematics of Divorce - Gottman's ability to predict marriage outcomes based on rapid analysis of couples' interactions. Gottman, John, and Nan Silver. **"The Seven Principles for Making Marriage Work."** Harmony Books, 1999.

5. J. Krishnamurti and Choiceless Awareness - The practice of observing without judgment, as suggested by Krishnamurti. Krishnamurti, Jiddu. **"Freedom from the Known."** Harper & Row, 1969.

6. Implicit Association Test (IAT) - The IAT's role in revealing hidden biases and how these biases impact judgment, as discussed in Blink.
   Project Implicit. "Implicit Association Test." Harvard University, accessed 2024.

7. Dr. Martin Luther King Jr. on Tyranny - King's caution about the cycle of tyranny and the importance of non-violent approaches. King, Martin Luther Jr. **"Where Do We Go from Here: Chaos or Community?"** Beacon Press, 1967.

8. The Serenity Prayer - The prayer's influence on embracing humility and courage in decision-making.
   Niebuhr, Reinhold. "The Serenity Prayer." Original text, 1930s.

9. Eckhart Tolle on Ego and Awakening - Reflections on ego, surrender, and interconnectedness as part of spiritual growth.
   Tolle, Eckhart. **"A New Earth: Awakening to Your Life's Purpose."** Penguin Group, 2008.
10. Unitarian Universalist Source on Reason and Science - The UU source emphasizing the guidance of reason and science while warning against idolatries of the mind and spirit.
    Unitarian Universalist Association. "Our Unitarian Universalist Principles and Sources."

6. LEMONS TO LEMONADE

A lemon is sour—a wake-up call that jolts your senses the moment it hits your tongue. That first bite is tangy and intense, almost as if the lemon has taken control of your mouth. It's that kind of bite that hurts so good. As the juice slides down, you feel the sharp sting of its bitterness, and you might wonder: Is this good for me, or is it too much? But somehow, despite the intensity, you find yourself wanting more.

Lemons aren't just sour—they're bright yellow, the color of light, happiness, and energy. Yellow radiates optimism, but it also hints at fear and sickness, just like the lemon itself. The peel, if you've ever chewed on it, is dense and conflicted—a strange mix of bitter and tart exactly what you'd expect yet surprising every time.

We're a lot like lemons. We have our own complexities, contradictions, and sharp edges. In cooking, even the lemon's zest—the thin, bright outer layer—can transform a dish, adding depth and unexpected brightness. Those opposing flavors find harmony, creating something greater than the sum of their parts.

We, too, can be like lemons—bringing light and energy when we lead with love, balancing and enhancing the world around us. But just like a lemon, we've got our bitter side. We can be sharp and sour when fear, judgment, or anger takes over. We are a paradox: capable of both sweetness and bitterness, light and shadow. And every day, we get to choose which part of ourselves to bring forward. We are the chefs of our lives, mixing and matching our experiences, crafting the flavor of our days.

Life hands us all kinds of lemons—sweet moments, sour challenges, and everything in between. Right now, with sickness, uncertainty, and loss swirling around us, it's easy to let the bitterness take hold. But we have a choice. We can choose light over darkness, love over fear, and community over chaos. We can take what life gives us and make something beautiful—lemonade.

This is the essence of alchemy, an ancient practice that's not just about turning lead into gold but about transformation on every level. We are all alchemists, taking the raw materials of our lives and transforming them into something meaningful. We mix and match our thoughts, feelings, and actions, shaping our reality. When we add love, kindness, and compassion to the mix, we create something sweet and nourishing. But when we add fear, anger, and blame, the result is bitter and hard to swallow.

Think of making lemonade. You take a lemon, slice it, squeeze out the juice, add water, and stir in some sugar or your favorite sweetener. What was once just a sour fruit becomes a refreshing drink that can lift your spirits. It's all about balance —the right amount of lemon, water, and sweetness coming together. Finding that balance in life is personal—some like their lemonade sweeter, some prefer it tart, and others enjoy it without any sweetener at all. It's not about getting it perfect; it's about what feels right for you.

Finding balance, especially now, is a daily practice. It's about blending the sweet with the sour, the joy with the pain, the light with the dark. And it's not a one-time thing—it's an ongoing process that we have to engage with every day, sometimes every moment. Life will keep handing us lemons, but how we handle them is our choice. When bitterness creeps in, we can reach for sweetness, calm, and connection to balance it out.

Each of us has a unique recipe for handling life's ups and downs. We all have our ways of mixing our emotional ingredients. When life gets tough, do you reach for gratitude? Compassion? A deep breath? Or do you find yourself leaning into anger, fear, or resentment? The choice is always there, and it's a choice we make again and again.

Making lemonade out of lemons is about understanding that balance doesn't mean life is without challenges—it means finding a way to turn those challenges into something nourishing. It's not about avoiding the sour moments but about discovering the sweetness within them. It's about blending the light and energy of the lemon with whatever else you've got on hand to create something that refreshes the spirit.

So, what kind of lemonade are you making today? Are you letting the sourness take over, or are you finding ways to sweeten your mix? Let's take the sour moments and infuse them with our zest for life, our sweetness of spirit, and our capacity for compassion.

Amen.

References

1. *Alchemy and Transformation:* Alchemy, historically seen as a mystical practice, symbolizes the transformation of base materials into something more valuable. The concept of personal transformation is often metaphorically linked to alchemy in literature and spiritual teachings. Principe, Lawrence M. *The Secrets of Alchemy.* University of Chicago Press, 2013.

2. *Positive Psychology and Balance:* The idea of balancing positive and negative emotions to create a fulfilling life is a core principle in positive psychology, often referred to in works on resilience and emotional well-being. Seligman, Martin E.P. *Flourish:* ***A Visionary New Understanding of Happiness and Well-being.*** Free Press, 2011.

3. *Metaphor of Making Lemonade:* The phrase "When life gives you lemons, make lemonade" is a popular adage encouraging optimism and a positive attitude in the face of adversity. While this saying doesn't have a single source, it is widely used in literature and motivational contexts. Carnegie, Dale. ***How to Stop Worrying and Start Living.*** Simon and Schuster, 1948.

7. FORGIVE 70X7

What is forgiveness? The Greater Good Science Center defines it as "a conscious, deliberate decision to release feelings of resentment or vengeance toward a person or group who has harmed you, regardless of whether they deserve your forgiveness." This is not an easy task; forgiveness is complex and layered. I want to explore why choosing forgiveness over bitterness is essential, and how it can liberate us from being trapped in pain.

Kenneth Briggs, in his profound work, "The Power of Forgiveness," captures the raw and often unspoken truth: forgiveness is hard. It's not some easy, surface-level act of letting go. It's a deep, soul-wrenching process that challenges us to confront pain that often runs far deeper than we realize—pain that can be personal, historical, even ancestral. Sometimes, the wounds are so profound that the very idea of forgiveness feels out of reach, as if we're being asked to do the impossible. And yet, despite this daunting challenge, forgiveness remains an essential element of any spiritual path. It is not about excusing the wrong or pretending it never happened; it's about finding a way to release the power it has over us so that we can move forward.

Every major religion—from Christianity to Buddhism, Islam to Hinduism—holds forgiveness as a core tenet because it's necessary for healing and growth. Forgiveness isn't just for the offender; it's for us. It's for our hearts, our communities, and our collective humanity. It's the spiritual salve that allows us to transcend the endless cycles of hurt and retribution, giving us the space to breathe again, to heal, and to reconnect with what is good and holy within us. It helps us to move beyond conflict, allowing us to embody the highest ideals of our faith traditions—grace, mercy, and compassion. Forgiveness calls us back to our better selves, urging us to make peace with the past so that we can live more fully in the present.

The Bible's New Testament provides a powerful illustration of forgiveness through a story that has been retold and reflected upon for centuries. In the Gospel of Matthew, one of Jesus' disciples, Peter, approaches him with a question: "Lord, how many times shall I forgive my brother or sister who sins against me? Up to seven times?" (Matthew 18:21). In the Jewish tradition, forgiving someone seven times was already seen as generous, a symbolic number representing completeness. But Jesus, known for challenging convention, responds with a radical statement: "I tell you, not seven times, but seventy times seven." (Matthew 18:22).

Jesus' response is not about mathematics or counting. He is not suggesting we keep a tally and, at the 491st offense, all bets are off. Rather, the phrase "70 x 7" is a figure of speech, a hyperbole meant to emphasize the boundless nature of forgiveness. It's a call to let go of the mindset that sees forgiveness as a finite resource. Jesus invites us into a more profound understanding that true forgiveness isn't about the other person—it's about us. It's about our liberation from the weight of resentment and the chains of anger.

When we hold on to pain, betrayal, or wrongdoing, we tether ourselves to the perpetrator and the event. It's like carrying around a heavy chain that keeps us anchored to that moment of hurt. Our thoughts, emotions, and even our actions can become influenced by that unresolved bitterness, impacting our ability to live fully in the present. Jesus' teaching is clear:

forgiveness is a spiritual release, an act of reclaiming our power. It allows us to step out of the shadow of the past and into the light of healing.

Science shows that some people are naturally more forgiving, while others struggle. Some hearts have been hardened by life, and that's okay. Forgiveness is hard; it's why grace is needed. It's the acknowledgment that all of us are flawed. We've all been victims and perpetrators in some way. Grace allows us to recognize our shared humanity, even when we fall short.

Forgiveness doesn't mean ignoring or excusing wrongdoing. We are called to stand up against injustices like Charleston, Sandy Hook, and Selma. Yet, we must also understand that grace asks us to pause and see the complexities behind actions —often, those who harm others were harmed themselves. As Marianne Williamson says, "Let redemption win." We hold evil accountable, but we also create space for grace and forgiveness.

Take the contrasting examples of Elie Wiesel and Nelson Mandela. Wiesel, a Holocaust survivor, could never forgive the German government, while Mandela made forgiveness a cornerstone of his leadership. Both responses are valid, but Mandela's path shows us the power of letting go.

I believe we are all born good, but life's challenges can corrupt us. Words like love, peace, generosity, and forgiveness vibrate at a higher level of existence. They call us back to our best selves. Martin Luther King Jr. said, "Forgiveness is not an occasional act; it is a permanent attitude." Thich Nhat Hanh adds that "Forgiveness will not be possible until compassion is born in your heart." Forgiveness, then, is not about forgetting; it's about releasing its power over you.

Forgiveness does not erase memory. Instead, it transforms how we hold those memories. When forgiveness is complete, the hurt no longer controls us. You may remember the wrong, but it no longer triggers anger, pain, or the need for revenge.

The memory loses its sharpness, and the emotional weight lightens.

The benefits of forgiveness are backed by science; studies show it improves our mental and physical health. Forgiveness lowers blood pressure and reduces heart disease risk, but it also frees the spirit. When we forgive, we step into a new reality where grace, mercy, and humility guide us.

As Dr. Robert Enright, a developmental psychologist, points out, "If we don't practice forgiveness, there will be no one left to bring into our community." A culture without forgiveness is destined for destruction. Forgiveness is not weakness; it shows character and strength. It acknowledges our failures while holding space for healing and accountability.

In closing, forgiveness feels like liberation. It's a release, a lightness. It allows us to see the world with new eyes—eyes that recognize our interconnectedness and shared humanity. Imagine a world where we all wear these new glasses, understanding that 'hurt people hurt people'. We would see ourselves in others, knowing that to be renewed, we must let go. Just as nature teaches us through its cycles, we too must release. Forgive—70 x 7. Let go, again and again, until you are free.

Amen.

References

1. **Greater Good Science Center, University of California, Berkeley.** *The Science of Forgiveness.*
   This resource defines forgiveness as "a conscious, deliberate decision to release feelings of resentment or vengeance toward a person or group who has harmed you, regardless of whether they actually deserve your forgiveness." It explores the psychological and emotional benefits of forgiveness.
2. **Briggs, Kenneth.** *The Power of Forgiveness: Forgiving in a World That Does Not Forgive.* Philadelphia: Templeton

Foundation Press, 2005.

Briggs delves into the complexity of forgiveness, discussing its power and importance on a spiritual path. He emphasizes the healing potential of forgiveness for individuals and communities.

3. **The Bible, New Testament.** *Matthew 18:21-22, New International Version (NIV).*

Jesus teaches about forgiveness, urging his followers to forgive "seventy times seven," highlighting the boundless and continual nature of forgiveness in the Christian tradition.

4. **Hanh, Thich Nhat.** *Anger: Wisdom for Cooling the Flames.* New York: Riverhead Books, 2001.

In this book, Thich Nhat Hanh teaches the importance of cultivating compassion as a precursor to forgiveness, stating, "Forgiveness will not be possible until compassion is born in your heart."

5. **Williamson, Marianne.** *A Return to Love: Reflections on the Principles of A Course in Miracles.* New York: HarperCollins, 1992.

Marianne Williamson discusses the power of faith and redemption, quoting, "Believe in good, proclaim it, and stand up for it and hold evil accountable, but let redemption win," emphasizing the role of love and forgiveness in personal and societal healing.

6. **Wiesel, Elie.** *Night.* New York: Hill and Wang, 1960.

Elie Wiesel's autobiographical account of surviving the Holocaust also reflects his refusal to forgive the German government for the atrocities committed, shedding light on the complexities and limits of forgiveness.

7. **Mandela, Nelson.** *Long Walk to Freedom: The Autobiography of Nelson Mandela.* Boston: Little, Brown, and Company, 1994.

In this powerful memoir, Nelson Mandela reflects on his years of imprisonment and his commitment to forgiveness as a leader, even toward those who oppressed him, as part of his vision for reconciliation in South Africa.

8. **Forbes, Rev. Dr. James A.** *Whose Gospel?: A Concise Guide to Progressive Protestantism.* New York: The New Press, 2010.

Rev. Dr. James Forbes discusses grace, forgiveness, and reconciliation, stating, "We have all drawn from the bank of grace. We've all needed to forgive and make amends. We've all been accuser and been accused." His work highlights the shared human experience of seeking forgiveness.

8. CARE-FULL AND CARE-LESS

Fear is one of the most potent forces driving human behavior. Associate Professor Margee Kerr, in her series on The Science of Fear, highlights the Thomas Theorem, which states: "That which is believed to be true carries real consequences." Our perceptions shape our reality, and changing hearts means changing those perceptions. As Sophia Lyon Fahs said, "It matters what we believe." Thoughts become things; beliefs influence actions, and actions have real-world impacts.

We see this clearly in the evolution of policing in America. We must ask: "Who is 'protect and serve' really meant for?" Historically, policing has often protected white communities while disproportionately targeting people of color. This system, driven by fear, has roots in protecting power structures rather than people. We must challenge these subtle acts of exclusion and manipulation that go unchecked.

Fear is often weaponized to control. Powerful entities use fear to keep us on edge, creating trauma and making us constantly vigilant. This fear distracts and drains us, preventing reconciliation and perpetuating America's original sin of slavery.

Fear is seductive. We are naturally drawn to it, as seen when we slow down to look at car accidents. This attraction-repulsion mechanism is exploited by those who use fear to manipulate, like alarm system companies or politicians who exaggerate threats. Not everything that scares us deserves our energy. Sometimes, we must say, "Cancel, cancel, cancel. I'm not taking that in." We must detach from the noise, turn inward, and protect our peace.

Fear's power is in its ability to make us look back, often too long, and lose sight of our path forward. Life is about the balance of attachment and detachment. We care, but we must also care *less* at times for self-care and to maintain our well-being. Harriet Tubman, known as Moses, understood this balance. Guided by faith, nature, and her inner voice, she faced her fears but didn't let them define her. She prepared, strategized, and when the moment was right, she acted and escaped to her freedom while leaving many she cared for behind. But this was necessary, she had to care-less to eventually care-fully. Sometimes we have to hold on and sometimes we have to let go. It takes wisdom to know the difference.

Fear is an enemy that stifles change and perpetuates division. When we fear each other, we become judge and jury, drawing lines that divide. Fear has few redeeming qualities; it creates more fear. Yet, facing fear together during crises like the global pandemic expanded our collective compassion. We saw glimpses of each other's pain and grew more united. Our compassion was evident.

Compassion too is a powerful emotion. Compassion manifests when we suffer with others. As Sharon Salzberg says, "Compassion allows us to use our own pains and the pain of others as a vehicle for connection."

The world is evolving, driven by a need for balance. Gaia, our Earth, is calling us to grow up, to create sustainable systems, and to embrace compassion over fear. The patriarchy must make space for matriarchy; the old ways must adapt to the new. We are all part of this dance of caring *fully* and caring *less,* of pushing forward while knowing when to pull back to take care of ourselves and the communities we serve. Joseph Campbell said, "The purpose of the journey is compassion." We cannot build a beloved community without it. Our world, our faith, and our institutions must evolve. My faith, Unitarian Universalism has been a trailblazing force —supporting abolition, ordaining women, marriage equality, trans rights, environmentalism, human rights, and more. We are leading the fight against systemic racism and all other isms. We must continue to be bold, compassionate, and progressive, embracing both the discomfort of change and the joy of new possibilities.

As we navigate this time, remember to care *fully* and care *less*. Take time to step back, recharge, and then re-engage with renewed compassion and energy. This is how we create a world where justice, equity, and compassion truly lead the way.

Amen.

References

1. Kerr, M. (2020). *The Science of Fear*. [Series]. Thomas Theorem's discussion highlights the power of perception: "That which is believed to be true carries real consequences." Retrieved from [Science of Fear series source, if available].
2. Fahs, S. L. (1952). *It Matters What We Believe*. In **Singing the Living Tradition.** Boston: Unitarian Universalist Association. Fahs's works emphasize the importance of belief and its impact on human actions.
3. Eberhardt, J. L. (2019). **Biased: Uncovering the Hidden Prejudice That Shapes What We See, Think, and Do.** New York: Viking. An exploration of systemic biases in policing and their roots in fear-driven control mechanisms.
4. Alexander, M. (2010). **The New Jim Crow: Mass Incarceration in the Age of Colorblindness**. New York: The New Press. A comprehensive look at the historical and systemic racism in American policing.

5. Salzberg, S. (2011). *Real Happiness: The Power of Meditation.* New York: Workman Publishing. Sharon Salzberg's work on compassion and its power to connect through shared suffering: "Compassion allows us to use our own pains and the pain of others as a vehicle for connection."

6. Tubman, H. (2003). *Harriet Tubman: The Road to Freedom.* Biography by Catherine Clinton. New York: Little, Brown and Company. Insights into Harriet Tubman's courage, strategy, and ability to balance caring and letting go.

7. Campbell, J. (1988). *The Power of Myth.* New York: Anchor Books. Joseph Campbell's quote on the purpose of the journey: "The purpose of the journey is compassion," speaks to the importance of connection and understanding on the spiritual path.

8. Quinn, D. (1992). *Ishmael: An Adventure of the Mind and Spirit*. New York: Bantam Books. An exploration of humanity's relationship with nature, Gaia, and the call for societal transformation.

9. Kimmerer, R. W. (2013). *Braiding Sweetgrass: Indigenous Wisdom, Scientific Knowledge, and the Teachings of Plants.* Minneapolis: Milkweed Editions. Discussion on the importance of balance in nature and the call to evolve sustainably.

9. WORDSMITHING THE POWER OF WORDS

In college, I was a pledge in a fraternity where we learned a poem of unknown origin: "Be careful of the words you say; keep them soft and sweet...for you never know from day to day which ones you'll have to eat." I've never forgotten those words, and though I haven't always heeded them, they have often served me well.

Recently, my family and I have been re-watching the Harry Potter series, and in *Harry Potter and the Deathly Hallows: Part II*, there's a powerful line from Dumbledore: "Words are, in my not-so-humble opinion, our most inexhaustible source of magic. Capable of both inflicting injury and remedying it." J.K. Rowling's words capture the essence of my message to you.

Words have power; they "spell" things into existence. When we think of "spelling," we think of the simple act of arranging letters to form words, but it goes deeper. To spell is to cast a spell — a magical process of communication that can inspire, heal, or harm. In religious contexts, incantations or ritual recitations of words are used to call upon the forces of nature or the divine. Similarly, every Sunday, we use words, songs, and prayers to call upon the spirit of love and justice, expressing our hopes for humanity.

The magic of words lies in their ability to shift perspective, change hearts, and inspire action. Words create energy in motion—emotion—that moves us. They connect us in our highest moments and help us navigate our lowest. The movies often portray magic as otherworldly, but true magic is in how we use our words and actions to bring love, healing, and resilience to our communities.

As we evolved, humans developed letters and words as symbols to convey meaning. In some cultures, the shape of a letter or character reflects what it describes—much like the Chinese character for "house," which resembles its meaning. Words, sounds, and vibrations carry energy that affects us deeply, connecting us to one another and to the world.

Scripture tells us, "The power of life and death is in the tongue," and one of the teachings on the Eightfold Path in Buddhism urges practitioners to practice "right speech"—to do no harm with their words. Our voices, too, are musical instruments, capable of great beauty and great harm. In some cultures, prayer and speech are melodic, as seen in Islamic prayers and the rhythmic preaching of African American "hoopers" who deliver sermons with a musical cadence.

I once conducted an experiment comparing the tonal resonance of Martin Luther King Jr. and Adolf Hitler. King's voice and words were harmonious, filled with love and hope, while Hitler's were sharp, dissonant, and filled with hate. Words have power; they reflect the essence of the speaker. "Be careful of the words you say…"

Science is beginning to catch up to what spiritual traditions have long understood about the power of words. Dr. Masaru Emoto's experiments with water have shown that words and sounds can influence the structure of water molecules, creating either beautiful geometric shapes or distorted forms, depending on the nature of the words used. While his research is controversial, the idea that words can shape reality is a powerful reminder that we are, on average, 60% water. The words we use matter.

This is why we must become effective wordsmiths, carefully choosing language that builds up rather than tears down. We have the power to shape our reality through our words. Think about how toxic relationships or harmful words feel to you— they can be like poison. But words can also be a balm, lifting us up, inspiring us, and drawing us closer to our best selves.

We are called to use words that uplift and empower, that call us to courage and remind us of our inherent worth and dignity. Words that challenge us to grow, evolve, and embrace each other as part of a beloved community.

Here are a few words you can adopt in your vocabulary that embody humanity's sacred values:

- Love (the spirit of our church)
- Vulnerability (courage to share and show up)
- Non-violence (do no harm; "ahimsa")
- Mutuality (collaboration instead of competition)
- Mindfulness (reflection, meditation, prayer)
- Accountability (shared responsibility)
- Forgiveness (apologizing and letting go)
- Reconciliation (coming back to the table; resilience)
- Trust (faith in self and others)
- Authenticity (being your truest self)
- Gratitude (thankfulness and appreciation)
- Meaningful Contribution (creating something meaningful together)
- Compassion (empathetic connection with suffering)
- Principled Action (living our values)
- Anti-racism (liberation for all souls)

These are a few words that help build beloved community

—words that bridge divides, foster inclusion, and call us to courage. May we use our words wisely, as instruments of peace and justice, as incantations that cast a spell of love upon our world.

In the name of all that is holy, righteous, and good, I leave these words. May it be so, and Amen.

References

1. **J.K. Rowling, *Harry Potter and the Deathly Hallows*.** New York: Arthur A. Levine Books, 2007.
   The quote "Words are, in my not-so-humble opinion, our most inexhaustible source of magic. Capable of both inflicting injury and remedying it" is spoken by Dumbledore in the movie adaptation.
2. **Proverbs 18:21, The Bible (New International Version).**
   "The power of life and death is in the tongue," a scripture often cited to emphasize the impact of our words.
3. **Buddhism, The Eightfold Path: Right Speech.**
   Teachings on the Eightfold Path that emphasize right speech, including avoiding harmful words and using speech to build understanding and compassion.
4. **Emoto, M. (2004). *The Hidden Messages in Water*. New York: Atria Books.**
   Dr. Masaru Emoto's research on how words and sounds affect the molecular structure of water, illustrating the impact of positive and negative speech on physical forms.
5. **Pennebaker, J. W. (2011). *The Secret Life of Pronouns: What Our Words Say About Us*. New York: Bloomsbury Press.**
   A study on how language reveals our personality, emotions, and connections with others, supporting the concept that words can shape our reality.
6. **Linguistics and Language Evolution (various sources).**
   Background on the development of language, the symbolism of letters, and the cultural significance of characters in communication.
7. **Bohm, D. (1996). *On Dialogue*. New York: Routledge.**
   A look into how dialogue and language shape our collective consciousness and reality, supporting the idea of words as a medium of connection and transformation.

8. **Islamic Prayer and Chant Traditions (various sources).**
    A reflection on how different cultures, such as Islamic traditions, use melodic speech and prayer as a form of connection and spiritual practice.

9. **Stevenson, L. (2021).** *The Healing Power of Words: The Role of Language in Mental and Emotional Health.* Explores how words and language can influence mental and emotional well-being, reinforcing the sermon's emphasis on using words for healing and connection.

10. **Unitarian Universalist Association (UUA).** *Principles and Purposes.*
    Outlines the UU values, including the power of covenanting and the importance of words that embody shared principles of love, justice, and interconnectedness.

SECTION 2:
SPIRITUALITY AND
INNER WISDOM

10. THE ALCHEMIST

We are pilgrims progressing, as the Unitarian Rev. James Freeman Clarke put it, "Onward and upward forever." Similarly, James Russell Lowell, the son of a Unitarian minister, once said, "The new theology will be the continuity of human development in all worlds, or the progress of humankind onward and upward forever." These words capture the essence of our liberal faith—an unwavering belief in the potential for growth, change, and the continuous betterment of the human spirit.

For centuries, liberal theology has been rooted in optimism and hope. It rejects the notion of eternal damnation, embracing instead the idea of universal salvation—that we are all on a journey, each of us finding our way home. To me, this means that all roads lead to God. No matter how we judge them, every path we take, whether individually or collectively, moves us toward a better version of ourselves. Even when it seems like progress is slow or setbacks occur, I hold firm to the belief that humanity is destined to become better, kinder, and wiser. The journey is never linear, but it is inexorable.

This belief, however, is put to the test when it comes to people I disagree with or even those who frustrate and anger me. It's hard to reconcile the idea that they, too, are on their own journey toward growth and transformation, that they, too, are evolving toward their best selves. But wisdom teaches that we rarely know the full story of our own lives, let alone anyone else's. So, I remind myself to extend the grace I need in my own life to others as well.

I want to share two stories today that illustrate this journey of growth: *The Alchemist* by Paulo Coelho and the parable of *The Prodigal Son* from the *Book of Luke* in the *Bible*. Both stories offer profound insights into what it means to live life as a pilgrimage—a sacred, transformative journey filled with trials, lessons, and moments of profound realization. They remind us that the journey itself is what shapes us and that every step, every detour, has meaning.

The parable of *The Prodigal Son* is a story of a father and his two sons. The older son is loyal and dutiful, doing everything that is expected of him. The younger son, however, is impulsive and reckless, demanding his inheritance while his father is still alive. After receiving his inheritance, he sets off on a journey to a distant land, squandering his wealth on a life of indulgence. When famine strikes, he finds himself destitute, reduced to feeding pigs and longing to eat their slop.

At his lowest point, he decides to return home, humbled and seeking his father's forgiveness. When his father sees him approaching, he runs to him with open arms, overwhelmed with joy. He orders a celebration, saying, "My son was lost but now is found! He was dead but is alive again!" The older son, however, is resentful, unable to understand why his father would welcome back someone who had been so reckless and ungrateful. His father gently reminds him that while the older son has always been by his side, the return of the lost son is an occasion for joy, not judgment.

This story is about the unconditional and abundant love that waits for all of us, regardless of our mistakes or missteps. It reminds us that each person's journey is unique and that what may seem like a failure or a loss is often an essential step toward growth. The younger son needed to leave home, to struggle and lose, in order to appreciate what he had and to find his way back to himself. Sometimes, being lost is the only way to truly be found.

This theme of pilgrimage and personal discovery is also at the heart of *The Alchemist*. In Coelho's story, Santiago, a young shepherd, dreams of a treasure buried near the pyramids in Egypt. Inspired by his dreams and driven by a desire for more than his simple life as a shepherd, he sets out on an adventure to fulfill his "Personal Legend," a term Coelho uses to describe one's life purpose. Santiago's journey is filled with trials, setbacks, and moments of doubt. He is robbed, tempted to give up, and faced with seemingly insurmountable challenges. But with each obstacle, he learns something new—about the world, about himself, and about the nature of true treasure.

Along the way, Santiago meets a series of mentors who guide him, including a king, a crystal merchant, and ultimately, the Alchemist, a mysterious figure who teaches him about the interconnectedness of all things. The Alchemist shows Santiago that the journey itself is the real treasure, that the wisdom gained along the way is far more valuable than any material wealth. Santiago learns that his purpose is not just about reaching the pyramids but about embracing every moment of the journey—the highs and the lows, the successes and the failures.

In the end, Santiago discovers that the treasure he sought was, in fact, buried back home where he started. This alchemical journey was never about the gold; it was about the transformation that occurred within him (he was becoming golden–enlightened–awakened) as he pursued his dream. Santiago's story, like that of the Prodigal Son, reminds us that life is not about the destination but about the courage to follow our hearts, the resilience to keep going in the face of adversity, and the willingness to learn from every experience.

Both stories speak to the core belief that each of us is on a pilgrimage of becoming. We will face trials, we will make mistakes, and we will often feel lost. These experiences are not detours; they are essential parts of our path. The journey refines us, challenges us, and ultimately, brings us closer to our truest selves.

Life, like alchemy, is about transformation. It's about turning the lead of our everyday experiences into the gold of wisdom, compassion, and understanding. It's about realizing that we are all connected, that we are all part of something greater, and that every step we take—no matter how uncertain—moves us onward and upward forever.

So, embrace your pilgrimage. Be bold and compassionate. Trust that even in moments of struggle, you are being guided toward your highest good. Remember that the treasure you seek is not something you will find outside of yourself; it is something you will discover within. You are the Alchemist of your own life. You have the power to transform, to create, and to find the gold that has always been there, waiting for you to uncover it.

Amen.

References

1. **Clarke, J. F. (1886). *Ten Great Religions: An Essay in Comparative Theology*. Boston: Houghton, Mifflin & Co.** James Freeman Clarke's quote, "Onward and upward forever," reflects the Unitarian belief in human progress and evolution.
2. **Lowell, J. R. (1907). *The Function of the Poet and Other Essays*. Boston: Houghton, Mifflin & Co.** James Russell Lowell's thoughts on the continuity of human development and progress resonate with liberal theology's emphasis on growth.
3. **Coelho, P. (1988). *The Alchemist*. New York: HarperOne.** Paulo Coelho's *The Alchemist* is the primary source for Santiago's journey, highlighting themes of personal legend, the pursuit of dreams, and the interconnectedness of all things.

4. **Campbell, J. (2008).** *The Hero with a Thousand Faces.* **Novato, CA: New World Library.**
   Joseph Campbell's work on the Hero's Journey framework explains the stages of departure, initiation, and return, relevant to both the Prodigal Son and Santiago's stories.

5. **The Holy Bible, New International Version. (1984). Book of Luke, Chapter 15:11-32.**
   The parable of the Prodigal Son, illustrating themes of grace, unconditional love, and the transformative journey of coming home.

6. **Armstrong, K. (2005).** *A Short History of Myth.* **New York: Canongate Books.**
   Karen Armstrong's exploration of myth provides context for understanding the archetypal journeys in religious and literary texts.

7. **Cousineau, P. (1990).** *The Hero's Journey: Joseph Campbell on His Life and Work.* **Novato, CA: New World Library.**
   A deeper dive into Campbell's influence on storytelling, myth, and understanding of life as a pilgrimage.

8. **Thurman, H. (1981).** *The Inward Journey.* **Richmond, IN: Friends United Press.**
   Howard Thurman's reflections on the inward journey align with themes of self-discovery, spiritual growth, and embracing one's personal legend.

9. **Emerson, R. W. (1841).** *Self-Reliance.* **Essays: First Series.**
   Emerson's philosophy on individuality and trusting one's path connects to Santiago's journey and the theme of finding treasure within.

10. **Tolle, E. (1999).** *The Power of Now: A Guide to Spiritual Enlightenment.* **Vancouver: Namaste Publishing.**
    Tolle's focus on presence and living in the moment parallels the lessons Santiago learns about being fully engaged in his pilgrimage.

11. **Unitarian Universalist Association (UUA). (n.d.).** *Principles and Sources.*
    The principles of Unitarian Universalism emphasize the inherent worth and dignity of every person, the interdependent web of all existence, and a free and responsible search for truth and meaning.

12. **Kornfield, J. (2008).** *The Wise Heart: A Guide to the Universal Teachings of Buddhist Psychology.* **New York:**

Bantam Books.

Kornfield's exploration of universal spiritual lessons reflects the journey inward and the importance of self-compassion.

11. CHOICELESS AWARENESS

I n the mid to late 1970s in my neighborhood, and likely in many communities across America, young boys measured toughness by who was the strongest, who could out-wrestle the other guy. We all pretended to be Muhammad Ali. When Kung-Fu Action Theater debuted on UHF channel 20 (remember when we had just a handful of VHF channels like ABC, NBC, CBS, and a few UHF channels that required turning the dial and adjusting the antenna?), my friends and I were glued to the fuzzy screen every Saturday at noon. We watched Asian men engage in mesmerizing, dance-like fighting that captivated our young minds.

Like so many kids, I was enthralled. After the movie ended, I'd head outside with my friends, and we would mimic the moves we'd just seen, play-fighting, kicking, punching, and adding our own sound effects. It was pure fun.

Around the same time, the world lost a legend. In 1973, Bruce Lee, born Jun Fan in Hong Kong in 1940, died suddenly at the age of 32. As a child, I didn't fully grasp his impact, but I knew he was extraordinary. Bruce Lee created his own martial art, introduced Chinese Kung Fu to Americans—despite resistance from some Chinese Americans—and founded schools in San Francisco and Oakland. He embraced radical inclusion, welcoming students of all races and genders, and even broke societal norms by marrying a white woman he met in college. He was more than a martial artist; he was a trailblazer.

Watching him, I was inspired. Bruce Lee was everything I wanted to be—strong, confident, original, and charismatic. He was only 5'8" and 140 pounds, but he exuded power, balance, and agility. After starring in just four movies, he became a global superstar before his sudden death. It was as if his boundless energy could no longer be contained within his small, muscular frame.

Behind every person is a philosophy that drives them, and Bruce Lee was no exception. For him, this drive was partly fueled by his desire to prove his worth—not just to his parents but to the world. He was determined to show that Chinese Americans and all Chinese people were equal to others. He drew inspiration from his people's history, a story marked by occupation, separation, and struggle. This determination and aliveness, the way he seemed so awake while others remained stuck, intrigues me now more than ever.

To understand Bruce Lee's mind, you must explore his influences. Taoism, moral philosophy, and particularly the teachings of Jiddu Krishnamurti deeply shaped his understanding of life. Krishnamurti, born in 1895 in South India, was groomed from a young age to be a world teacher— a messianic figure for his time. But when it came time for him to take on this role, he walked away, choosing instead a life of writing, lecturing, and meditation. His teachings on non-judgment, true freedom, and choiceless awareness resonated with Lee in the 1970s.

Krishnamurti once said, "Truth is a pathless land, and you cannot approach it by any path whatsoever, by any religion, by any sect." For him, truth and freedom were found within, away from judgment and expectation. It was an inner knowing that we are connected to all things seen and unseen. He believed that when we sit in awareness without condemnation, we experience unity, oneness, or what some might call the Kingdom of God.

Someone once asked me what I think heaven is like. I said, "Imagine taking in a smell without labeling it as good or bad. Picture watching nature with a cup of coffee in the morning, fully present. Think of stepping into a perfectly decorated room that feels just right, with no words, just awareness. Think of watching a baby sleep. In those moments, you are in eternity, saved, safe. You are no longer the 'I'; you are just pure awareness. That is heaven."

There is no action in this space, only pure watching. But most of us are thrust back into the world of judgment soon enough. We critique the smells, label the sights, and return to the ego's constant narration. But when we practice pure awareness, we are no one. We are unity, the zero point. It is here that healing occurs, insights emerge, and we connect with the all-encompassing force of existence.

This practice is about resetting our brains, stepping away from the endless cycle of judgment and expectation, and finding moments of stillness. In those moments, we are more than our identities, our labels, and our fears. We are participants in something greater.

Bruce Lee, like many of us, had to learn this the hard way. After a severe back injury from over-training, he was bedridden for months. During that time, he rediscovered his passion for reading, including Krishnamurti's works. It was then, lying flat on his back, that he realized he was more than just a martial artist, an actor, or a cultural icon. He was pure awareness. This realization shifted his perspective and ultimately his approach to life.

Imagine that the universe, God, or whatever you believe in, is participating with you and you with it. That when you suspend judgment, let go of expectations, and simply become aware, you are in communion with the divine. You are whole, fearless, and free.

Krishnamurti once wrote, "Awareness is a state in which there is no condemnation, no justification or identification, and therefore there is understanding; in that state of passive, alert awareness there is neither the experiencer nor the experienced... As we understand the near, we shall find the distance between the near and the far is not. There is no distance—the beginning and the end are one."

As busy humans, we often rush to speak, to act, to challenge injustice. But we cannot always be on the front lines. Even the most dedicated soldier needs time to rest, to convalesce. We are many things—advocates, seekers, changemakers—but we are also called to be places of respite, balance, and transcendence. Practicing awareness, stopping to simply stare at life, can help us put everything into perspective.

Friends, as we navigate these tumultuous times, remember to find moments to step back and suspend judgment. Let it all go, even if just for a moment. Before and after the struggles, find your place of stillness. Be aware of when you need to step off the front lines and seek the peace that cannot be touched by fear or despair.

Bruce Lee discovered that surrendering the ego allowed him to transcend his own limitations. When he embraced choiceless awareness, he became a legend—not just for his physical prowess but for the profound way he understood life. His journey reminds us that we, too, are more than our titles, our accomplishments, or our failures. We are pure awareness. And in this space we are our own healing, transformation, and freedom.

Take away the titles and identifications—who are you? As you watch yourself age, as roles shift and identities fade, who are you now? Bruce Lee, drawing from Krishnamurti, offers us this wisdom: "Empty your cup so that it may be filled; become devoid to gain totality... Reality is apparent when one ceases to compare. There is 'what is' only when there is no comparison at all; and to live with what is, is to be peaceful." May it be so. Amen.

References

1. **Lee, B. (1975). *Tao of Jeet Kune Do*. Santa Clarita, CA: Ohara Publications.**
   Bruce Lee's writings on martial arts, philosophy, and life, including his famous sayings like "No way as the way; no limitation as limitation," reflect his belief in transcending rigid structures and embracing fluidity in both combat and life.
2. **Krishnamurti, J. (1954). *The First and Last Freedom*. New York: Harper & Brothers.**
   Jiddu Krishnamurti's teachings on choiceless awareness, non-judgment, and the importance of understanding oneself beyond societal labels and expectations.
3. **Krishnamurti, J. (1985). *Awakening of Intelligence*. San Francisco, CA: HarperSanFrancisco.**
   Krishnamurti's exploration of consciousness, inner freedom, and the rejection of organized paths to truth, which heavily influenced Bruce Lee's philosophy.
4. **Lee, S. (2018). *Bruce Lee: A Life*. New York: Simon & Schuster.**
   A comprehensive biography of Bruce Lee by Matthew Polly that details Lee's life, his philosophies, and his influences, including his relationship with Krishnamurti's teachings.
5. **Campbell, J. (2008). *The Hero with a Thousand Faces*. Novato, CA: New World Library.**
   Campbell's examination of the hero's journey and the universal quest for self-realization, relevant to Bruce Lee's and Krishnamurti's own journeys.
6. **Tzu, L. (1944). *Tao Te Ching*. Translated by Gia-Fu Feng and Jane English. New York: Vintage Books.**
   The foundational text of Taoism, which influenced Bruce Lee's martial arts philosophy and his approach to life, emphasizing balance, flow, and non-resistance.
7. **Chodron, P. (2001). *The Wisdom of No Escape*. Boston, MA:**

Shambhala Publications.

Pema Chodron's reflections on awareness, meditation, and embracing the present moment without judgment align with the principles of choiceless awareness and non-attachment.

8. **Byrom, T. (1976).** *The Dhammapada: The Sayings of the Buddha.* **New York: Bell Tower.**

This ancient Buddhist text discusses awareness, mindfulness, and the practice of living without attachment, similar to the themes embraced by Krishnamurti and Lee.

9. **Hanh, T. N. (1975).** *The Miracle of Mindfulness: An Introduction to the Practice of Meditation.* **Boston, MA: Beacon Press.**

Thich Nhat Hanh's guide on mindfulness and awareness echoes the choiceless awareness philosophy, emphasizing the healing power of being fully present.

12. THE HINDU TRINITY: THE NUMBER 3

Scientists tell us that life, as we understand it, is 3D. Hinduism says that we have three dimensions that shape our reality. The first dimension is creation: we create, copulate, procreate, construct, and craft. The second dimension is preservation: we nurture, savor, and protect that which is created. The third dimension is loss: destruction, dissolution, decay, death, and rebirth. And then the cycle begins anew.

As we navigate loss and trauma, I've come to realize that we must make mental and spiritual peace with this 3D reality. We must accept it and learn to dance with its highs and lows, understanding that "to everything there is a season." This acceptance doesn't mean we tolerate injustices or do nothing in the face of adversity, but it does mean that we maintain perspective while fighting for justice and peace, so we don't lose our minds or our spiritual capacity for love.

The number 3 captures this triad of reality. It's a mysterious number, appearing throughout history, religion, and even in our everyday lives. I often see 3, 33, or 333, and for me, it feels like a sign or an affirmation. Numbers, letters, and sounds hold power. As a mystic, I see deep significance in these symbols.

They say death comes in threes; there are three little pigs, three bears, and the classic trio of mind, body, and spirit.

In the Bible, the number 3 appears over 450 times: three wise men, the three synoptic gospels, Jesus crucified at the third hour and rising on the third day. He was 33 years old when he died, and the Holy Trinity represents God as three in one—God the Father, God the Son, and God the Holy Spirit. In science, we see three laws of motion from Isaac Newton and the subatomic particles—protons, neutrons, and electrons—that make up atoms. The list goes on.

The great mystic and mathematician Pythagoras believed the universe was created through geometry, often through combinations of three-sided triangles, and through sound or vibration, like the Hindu sound of "OM." He saw 3 as the number of completion, perfection, and enlightenment. For Pythagoras and many ancient cultures, the triangle was sacred —a symbol of creation, preservation, and dissolution.

Philosopher Georg Hegel also saw progress through the lens of three: thesis, antithesis, and synthesis—a cycle of conflict and resolution that drives the world forward. In our own lives, we experience this cycle constantly. What are you creating, preserving, and letting go of? Where are you in your own 3D process?

In Christian theology, the Holy Trinity reflects this: God is unity (1), Jesus is the meeting of flesh and spirit (2), and the Holy Spirit is the completion and power of God and Jesus (3). This understanding combines mathematics and spirituality, creating deep meaning and profound wisdom.

The Star of David in Judaism, with its interlocking triangles, also reflects this cycle: one triangle pointing up, one pointing down, symbolizing "as above, so below." It's a representation of divine balance and unity—the above and the below, heaven and earth, interconnected and complete. This corresponds with the scripture "Thy kingdom come they will be done on earth as it is in heaven." It is a powerful symbol, indeed.

The number 33 holds special significance in many traditions. It's the highest level in Freemasonry and symbolizes enlightenment and mastery. In our congregation, our address, 333 Dubois Road, serves as a reminder of our high spiritual calling. We are marked for greatness. Our congregation's founders may have been mystics!

In Hinduism, the number 3 is also central. The Hindu Trimurti comprises Brahma (creation), Vishnu (preservation), and Shiva (destruction). These three forces maintain balance in the universe. For Shaivites, Shiva alone represents all three aspects, embodying the cycle of creation, love, and loss.

Shiva's image, often depicted dancing within a circle of flames, symbolizes the cosmic dance of life and death. The trident in Shiva's hand represents will, activity, and knowledge—the full cycle of existence. Under Shiva's feet lies a misshapen figure representing the illusion of the material world. Shiva teaches us the ultimate knowledge: that everything we cling to will one day dissolve.

Accepting this 3D cycle of creation, preservation, and dissolution is key to inner peace. Life's challenges—losses, endings, and transitions—are part of a broader process that propels us forward. When we learn to dance with life's cycles, to flow with the rhythms of creation and loss, we find our place in the great cosmic dance.

Our world is fraught with conflict and suffering. From wars to personal losses, it's easy to feel overwhelmed by the destructive forces at play. But even amid these trials, the dance of life continues. Wisdom reminds us that we must stay balanced and keep our perspective. Even when the world feels chaotic, we can look to the natural cycles around us—the falling leaves, the rising sun, the ebb and flow of the tides—

to remind us that creation, love, and dissolution are always in motion.

The dance of Shiva, the power of 3, calls us to radical acceptance of life in all its forms. It reminds us to keep creating, to keep loving, and to keep letting go. To live, laugh, and love without fear, knowing that every ending makes way for a new beginning.

Life will break our hearts. It will test us. But as we learn to dance with the 3s, to move with the joy, love, and sorrow, we find that life is not just something we endure—it's something we can dance with. As Ric Masten wrote:

Let it be a dance we do.
May I have this dance with you?
Through the good times and the bad times, too,
let it be a dance.

Learn to follow, learn to lead,
feel the rhythm, fill the need
to reap the harvest, plant the seed.
Let it be a dance.

Morning star comes out at night,
without the dark there is no light.
If nothing's wrong, then nothing's right.
Let it be a dance.

Let the sun shine, let it rain;
share the laughter, bear the pain,
and round and round we go again.

May we embrace the dance of creation, love, and loss. May we accept each step, each phase, and each change as part of the beautiful, mysterious 3D reality of our lives.

Amen.

References

1. **The Holy Bible, New International Version.**
   References to the significance of the number 3, including the three wise men, the crucifixion and resurrection timelines, and the Holy Trinity.
2. **Bhagavad Gita. (1986). Translated by Eknath Easwaran. Tomales, CA: Nilgiri Press.**
   This foundational Hindu scripture explores concepts related to the Trimurti—Brahma (Creation), Vishnu (Preservation), and Shiva (Destruction)—and the cyclical nature of life.
3. **Tzu, L. (1944).** *Tao Te Ching.* **Translated by Gia-Fu Feng and Jane English. New York: Vintage Books.**
   The Taoist text, which deeply influenced philosophical thought, emphasizes the importance of balance, the yin and yang, and the natural cycles of creation, preservation, and dissolution.
4. **Hegel, G. W. F. (1837).** *The Phenomenology of Spirit.* **Oxford: Clarendon Press.**
   Hegel's dialectical process of thesis, antithesis, and synthesis describes the way that progress and understanding unfold through a triadic structure.
5. **Ouspensky, P. D. (1949).** *In Search of the Miraculous: Fragments of an Unknown Teaching.* **New York: Harcourt, Brace & Company.**
   Discusses mystical traditions, numerology, and the significance of numbers in spiritual and religious contexts, echoing ideas about the mystical power of 3.
6. **Pythagoras and the Pythagorean School (Various texts and interpretations).**
   Studies of Pythagoras's belief that the universe was created through geometry and sound, and the sacredness of the triangle and the number 3.
7. **Campbell, J. (2008).** *The Hero with a Thousand Faces.* **Novato, CA: New World Library.**
   Joseph Campbell's exploration of mythological patterns, including triadic cycles and the importance of balance in spiritual and personal growth.
8. **Coogan, M. D., Ed. (2010).** *The New Oxford Annotated Bible with Apocrypha: New Revised Standard Version.* **Oxford University Press.**

Provides context for the biblical references to the number 3, its recurrence, and its theological symbolism.

9. **Watts, A. (1975).** *Tao: The Watercourse Way.* **New York: Pantheon Books.**
Discusses the Taoist concept of balance and the cyclic nature of existence, which parallels the teachings of the number 3 in other spiritual traditions.

10. **Zimmer, H. (1946).** *Myths and Symbols in Indian Art and Civilization.* **Princeton, NJ: Princeton University Press.**
Explores Hindu iconography, including the symbolism of Shiva and the Trimurti, and the cultural significance of triadic concepts in Hindu belief.

11. **Jung, C. G. (1968).** *Man and His Symbols.* **New York: Dell.**
Discusses the power of symbols, including numbers, in shaping the collective unconscious and the role of archetypes like the trinity in human understanding.

12. **Wilber, K. (2000).** *Integral Psychology: Consciousness, Spirit, Psychology, Therapy.* **Boston: Shambhala Publications.**
Explores the three dimensions of reality as levels of consciousness, aligning with the ideas of creation, preservation, and dissolution found in spiritual traditions.

13. **Ric Masten, "Let It Be a Dance." (1971).**
Lyrics from Ric Masten's song that align with the themes of life's cyclical nature, joy, sorrow, and acceptance.

13. WATER METAPHORS

Water sustains, nourishes, and connects us. Sixty percent of what makes us human is water. It flows through us, binds us, and without it, we would not be here. We are water. Like our bodies, Water covers 70% of our planet. We come from the sacred amniotic fluid, where we twirl, spin, and grow for nine months before entering the physical world. Land itself emerges from water, mirroring the same life-giving process. Think about that for a moment: the miracle of emergence.

It is no surprise, then, that John Newton, the infamous slave trader, found the God of his understanding on the water. His transformation is a story of grace that has been told and retold —a testament to the power of water to change lives. Imagine him in the dark of night, deep in the Atlantic, with no land in sight. A storm raged around him, water above and below. Afraid, he took refuge below deck, surrounded by his crew and enslaved Africans, and he prayed. We don't know what words he spoke, but we do know that when the storm subsided and the sun broke through, he was a transformed man. He quit the slave trade and became a preacher, giving us the hymn "Amazing Grace." This story is more than just a dramatic conversion; it is a testimony to water's power to take and give life, to cleanse and renew.

Water has been a symbol of transformation from ancient

times to modern storytelling in Hollywood. Any time you see a character in a movie stepping into the rain, jumping into a pool, or wading in water, they are about to be reborn into a new character with a new outlook. Like John Newton, they are having a death and resurrection experience. The Bible tells us that Jesus, after being baptized, heard a voice from the heavens: "This is my son with whom I am well pleased." That moment of transformation, coming up out of the water, was a new beginning for Jesus, just as water continues to symbolize new beginnings for us all.

Just before the pandemic, I had an awakening that felt like a baptism of sorts. I came to church feeling renewed and alive, only to find that a back closet in the church had flooded. Our Administrator was visibly upset, but I saw it differently. I said: "This church is undergoing a rebirth!" "We are set for a new beginning." She replied back, "Well, maybe Spirit can also cover the cost of cleaning up this awakening!" We laughed, but the lesson was clear: water, whether in the form of rain, flood, or tears, is a harbinger of change.

When we truly know what we are—that we are nature, we are earth, we are water—we begin to see life differently. We understand our place in the grand web of creation. This is the animistic worldview of our ancestors, who believed that everything is alive and has a spirit. Directors, poets, and artists know this truth and they use water metaphors to help us understand our own journeys of transformation.

One powerful metaphor from my tradition is the hymn "Wade in the Water." Born out of the African American experience, this song is a call to enter the waters of change, to step into the current of transformation, and to trust that God's hand will guide us. "Wade in the water, children, God's gonna trouble the water." It's a reminder that when life's waters become turbulent, it is not to drown us but to lead us toward liberation.

Imagine wading into a river, feeling the cool water against your legs, pushing against the current but finding your footing. The water is troubled—not smooth, not calm—but moving, alive. This is what transformation feels like. It's not always easy, but it's necessary. When the Israelites crossed the Red Sea, they waded through muddy waters toward freedom, leaving the land of bondage behind. On one side was slavery; on the other, the promise of liberation. As the waters closed behind them, they were reborn as a free people.

This is why "Wade in the Water" became an anthem for African Americans. It told of our shared story—a story of survival, struggle, and the relentless pursuit of freedom. It's a song of baptism and rebirth, of going down into the water and coming up transformed.

Water is shallow. It can be still, peaceful, and calm. It can be deep, turbulent, and rough. So too are we. We have moments of peace and stillness, and times when life feels choppy, tossing us about. We wade in those waters, sometimes needing to be rescued, needing the love and support of others to pull us to safety.

When my father would take me out on his fishing boat, he'd remind me to respect the water. "Keep a wide stance," he'd say, "so you can keep your balance." That lesson stays with me today. Respect the water, because it's a part of you. Respect its power, because it mirrors your own.

In closing, I invite you to embrace your water nature. Drink deeply—literally and spiritually. Let the water within you remind you of your resilience and capacity for transformation. And when life's waters are troubled, remember that it is in the wading, in the going deep, that we find new life.

Prayer: Spirit of Life, thank you for water. Thank you for reminding us that we are water, that we have the power to transform, to heal, and to begin again. Help us to create a world where all have access to clean, life-sustaining water. May we wade into the waters of justice and emerge renewed, ready to continue the work of building a better world. Amen.

References

1. **Human Composition and Earth's Surface** - Statistics on water content in the human body and Earth's surface.
National Institutes of Health. "Water in the Human Body." US Geological Survey. "How Much Water Is There on Earth?"
2. **John Newton and "Amazing Grace"** - The transformation of John Newton and his creation of the hymn "Amazing Grace."
Turner, Steve. "Amazing Grace: The Story of America's Most Beloved Song." HarperOne, 2002.
3. **Transformation and Baptism Symbolism** - Symbolism of water in transformation stories and biblical references, including Jesus' baptism.
The Holy Bible, Matthew 3:16-17 (New International Version).
4. **Water as a Symbol in Film and Literature** - The use of water metaphors in modern storytelling and transformation narratives.
Kostelnick, Charles. "Rhetorical Uses of Water in Cinema." Film Studies Journal, 2020.
5. **Animistic Worldview and Water Metaphors** - The animistic perspective of water as alive and part of a greater web of creation.
Harvey, Graham. "Animism: Respecting the Living World." Hurst Publishers, 2005.
6. **"Wade in the Water" Hymn** - The history and significance of the hymn in African American culture and its symbolism of transformation and liberation.
Jones, Arthur C. "Wade in the Water: The Wisdom of the Spirituals." Orbis Books, 1993.
7. **The Red Sea Crossing** - The biblical account of the Israelites crossing the Red Sea, representing transformation and liberation.
The Holy Bible, Exodus 14:21-22 (New International Version).
8. **Symbolism of Troubled Waters in African American History** - Understanding the hymn "Wade in the Water" as an anthem for African Americans' struggle and liberation.
Cone, James H. "The Spirituals and the Blues: An Interpretation." Orbis Books, 1972.

14. THE SEVEN
SPIRITUAL LAWS

R EADING: From The Kybalion: A Study of The Hermetic
Philosophy of Ancient Egypt and Greece, by the Three
Initiates

"The majority of people are carried along like the falling stone, obedient to environment, outside influences, and internal moods and desires, not to speak of the desires and wills of others [perceived] as stronger than themselves; or by heredity, environment, and suggestion, carrying them along without resistance on their part, or the exercise of the Will. Moved like pawns on the checkerboard of life, they play their parts and are laid aside after the game is over. But the Masters, knowing the rules of the game, rise above the plane of material life, and placing themselves in touch with the higher powers of their nature, dominate their own moods, characters, qualities, and polarity, as well as the environment surrounding them, and thus become Movers in the game, instead of Pawns—Causes instead of Effects. The Masters do not escape the Causation of the higher planes, but fall in with the higher laws, and thus master circumstances on the lower plane."

Sermon: The Seven Spiritual Laws

I've chosen the topic of "The Seven Spiritual Laws". These beliefs guide my life and worldview. My hope is that you can apply some of this to your life and perspective. I always say, you never eat the entire pie of anybody's ideology—just a slice here and there. But I'm also okay if you eat more than just one slice this morning. Amen.

You see below me, an object—Newton's Cradle. Despite its name, Sir Isaac Newton did not invent this device. An English actor, Simon Prebble, did in 1967. He designed this pendulum to demonstrate the principles of momentum and energy, attributing it to Newton to honor his work in physics.

This pendulum fascinates me. I use it as a reminder of Newton's "Third Law"—'for every action, there is an equal and opposite reaction.' In other words, "you reap what you sow". We know this from experience and intuitively. Energy—action —karma—has a way of balancing things out. We must respect this law of nature and the cosmos.

I keep Newton's Cradle close to me as a reminder that if I get really excited and passionate about something, I'll experience its opposite at some point. It brings me back to balance. When I preach a vigorous sermon and get home, I'm done. The other side of vigor is lethargy, so I must rest and recharge to return to normal. You understand this—this is the way the universe balances itself out. We must expect these highs and lows as part of living.

Studying Newton's Cradle led me to the Seven Hermetic Laws of Ancient Egypt and Greece in *The Kybalion*. These laws or spiritual principles are scientific and nature-based and have been around long before they were codified.

All religion is astrotheological–from the earth and sky. These laws come from our ancestors who experienced the cycles and seasons, the ebbs and flows. They understood, as it is written, "weeping lasts for a night, but joy comes in the morning". They knew something bigger was at play—something awe-filled, not awful but full of awe. Over time, great minds codified these ideas using alchemy, metaphysics, astronomy, and nature to understand this grand mystery of consciousness.

They started with the notion that all living organisms exist within the mind of what they called "The All." Emerson called it the Oversoul.

LAW ONE is the Principle of Mentalism: *"The All is Mind; the Universe is Mental."* That is, God, Spirit of Life, The Tao, Brahma—THE ALL—exists as MIND. We are expressions of this collective consciousness. All creatures, all plants, everything is an expression of this mentalism. This Mind is beyond names and forms, like the Tao Te Ching says: "The Tao that can be told is not the eternal Tao." It is inside you and outside of you; we are all caught in its web of thought and creative action.

Mentalism reminds us that everything begins with thought. Our entire reality is shaped by our minds—how we perceive the world, how we interpret events, and how we choose to respond to life's challenges. Think about it: when we change our mindset, the world around us seems to change. That's the power of this law. When you realize that your thoughts shape your experiences, you become empowered to create the life you want. It's no longer about external circumstances controlling your reality, but about your inner world manifesting your outer one. We are co-creators with the universe.

The Second Law is the Law of Correspondence: *"As above, so below; as below, so above."* There is a correlation between all things. To understand the cosmos, understand the cycles in your own life. To understand others, understand yourself. Dr. King said, "What affects one directly affects all indirectly." This is the Law of Correspondence.

This law teaches us that everything is interconnected. Just

as the planets and stars follow rhythms and cycles, so too do we. When we observe the natural world, we gain insight into our personal lives. The cycles of the moon, the changing seasons, the rise and fall of the ocean tides—all mirror the inner workings of our emotional and spiritual lives. If you're feeling disconnected, spend time in nature and watch how its cycles reflect your own. You'll realize that just like the seasons, your life has times of growth, harvest, rest, and renewal. Correspondence reminds us to look both within and outside to find meaning and understanding.

The Third Law is the Law of Vibration: *"Nothing rests; everything moves; everything vibrates."* Our galaxy is moving, the sun travels around the Milky Way, and the planet moves around the sun. Everything is in constant motion. Heraclitus said, "Change alone is unchanging." I say, master change to master life.

Vibration tells us that everything is in a state of constant motion, even if we can't see it. Your thoughts, emotions, and even your body are vibrating at different frequencies. When you're in a positive state of mind, your vibration is high, and you attract positive experiences. When you're in a negative state, your vibration is low, and you tend to attract more negativity. This law encourages us to become aware of our energetic state. If you want to change your life, you have to change your vibration—raise it by cultivating love, joy, gratitude, and peace.

The Fourth Law is the Law of Polarity: *"Everything has its pair of opposites; like and unlike are the same in nature, but different in degree."* This law speaks to the dual nature of existence. It tells us that all things, all experiences, have their opposites, and though they seem entirely different, they are actually the same thing expressed in different degrees. For example, hot and cold are not fundamentally different; they are just varying levels of temperature.

When applied to politics, the extremes of the far-left and the far-right may seem like opposites, but in their behavior, they often mirror each other. The far-left refers to extreme liberalism, often focusing on drastic and immediate changes in social, economic, and political structures. The far-right refers to extreme conservatism, which is often associated with a desire to maintain traditional structures, sometimes aggressively resisting change.

Despite their opposing ideologies, the behaviors found on both extremes are strikingly similar. On the far-left, you might find rigid dogmatism, where anyone outside their beliefs is condemned or excluded. On the far-right, you often see the same level of rigidity, where dissenting opinions are met with hostility. Both sides may resort to authoritarian tactics —whether through silencing opposing voices, controlling narratives, or, in some cases, justifying violence in the name of their cause.

This is where Newton's Cradle comes in. As we've discussed, the law of cause and effect applies here—what you put out into the universe comes back to you. The energy of extremism on one side inevitably pulls extremism from the other. Just like in Newton's Cradle, when you push the pendulum far to the right, it swings equally far to the left. These polarities feed off each other, creating cycles of division and hostility.

This is why I reference Buddha's teaching of the Middle Way. Buddha understood that the extremes of life lead to suffering. The Middle Way is about balance—understanding that both sides have merit, but living on the extremes creates imbalance, both personally and socially. It's about finding the center, the equilibrium, where we can recognize that we are all interconnected and that wisdom comes from considering all perspectives, not just clinging to one side.

We see this played out in our current political climate. The polarization in our country is pulling people further apart, causing us to forget that we are all part of the same collective. We have forgotten that we must work together for the greater good. The more extreme our rhetoric and actions become, the more we invite the same from the other side, perpetuating an endless cycle of conflict. The key to breaking that cycle is to find balance—to recognize the shared humanity in each other and seek common ground.

The Fifth Law is the Law of Rhythm: *"Everything flows, out and in; everything has its tides; all things rise and fall."* There is a rhythm to life. The ebb and flow of the ocean, the seasons, the in and out of breath—it's all connected. Appreciate everything; flow like water.

Rhythm is about the cycles of life. Think about your own life— how often have you felt like things were going great, only for them to take a turn? Or perhaps you've experienced hardship, and then, like the dawn after a long night, things began to improve. That's the rhythm of the universe. Everything is in constant motion, flowing in and out, rising and falling. The law of rhythm reminds us to embrace the ebb and flow. When times are tough, know that they won't last forever. When times are good, appreciate them fully because they are part of a cycle. Understanding rhythm allows you to stay centered through life's highs and lows, knowing that everything has its season.

The Sixth Law is the Law of Cause and Effect: *"Every cause has its effect; every effect has its cause."* This law reminds us that nothing happens by chance. Everything is interconnected, part of the web of life.

Cause and effect is perhaps one of the most practical laws to apply to daily life. Every action you take sets into motion a chain of events, whether you realize it or not. This law invites us to take responsibility for our lives. If you want to see a change in your life, you must become the cause of that change.

Stop waiting for things to happen to you—make things happen. Every thought, word, and action you put into the world creates a ripple effect that comes back to you. This law isn't about punishment or reward, it's about understanding that we are active participants in the unfolding of our own lives.

The final law is the Law of Gender: *"There is masculine and feminine energy in all things."* This dual nature exists in everything. When we bring these energies into harmony, we find balance.

Gender, in this context, is about balance between the masculine and feminine energies that exist in all of us. It's not about gender in the biological sense, but rather the energies that shape how we act and react. Masculine energy is active, assertive, and analytical, while feminine energy is receptive, intuitive, and nurturing. Both are necessary. Too much masculine energy can lead to aggression and burnout; too much feminine energy can lead to passivity and stagnation. The goal is to find harmony between these energies within ourselves, allowing us to be both assertive and nurturing, both active and reflective.

So, these are the seven laws. Contemplate them and see how they speak to your life. For me, it is clear that much of humanity does not live by spiritual principles—if we did, we'd have a very different world.

Friends, keep the faith, and remember that the seven spiritual laws will guide us to the best version of ourselves. Let these principles be like manna from heaven, healing your soul.

I hope you liked my pie served in seven slices. How many did you eat? Are you full?

May the spirit of love and life be with you now and always.

Amen.

References:

1. *The Kybalion: A Study of The Hermetic Philosophy of Ancient Egypt and Greece* by the Three Initiates. This book is the primary source for the Seven Hermetic Laws. It outlines the principles of Mentalism, Correspondence, Vibration, Polarity, Rhythm, Cause and Effect, and Gender. It offers insight into ancient teachings that influence modern spiritual thought.

2. *Newton's Third Law of Motion.* Newton's Third Law of Motion, stating "For every action, there is an equal and opposite reaction," directly connects with the concept of cause and effect. This foundational law of physics can be found in any standard physics textbook or reputable source.
Source: *Newton, Isaac. Mathematical Principles of Natural Philosophy.* (1687).

3. **Tao Te Ching by Laozi.** The references to the Tao, the nameless and formless aspect of the divine, echo the Kybalion's principle of Mentalism and the broader concept of "The All." The Tao Te Ching is an essential text that discusses the ineffable nature of existence. Source: Laozi. *Tao Te Ching.* (circa 6th century BCE).

4. **Ralph Waldo Emerson's** Concept of the Oversoul. Emerson's idea of the Oversoul is similar to the Hermetic concept of "The All" or the collective consciousness, which you refer to in the sermon. This idea is discussed in his essays. Source: Emerson, Ralph Waldo. *Essays: First Series.* (1841).

5. **"The Arc of the Moral Universe"** Quote by Theodore Parker. This quote speaks to the larger context of justice and moral law, aligning with the Hermetic principles of cause and effect and the pursuit of balance.
Source: Parker, Theodore. *Sermons of Theism, Atheism, and the Popular Theology.* (1853).

6. **Heraclitus' Philosophy of Change.** Heraclitus' statement "Change alone is unchanging" aligns with the Hermetic Law of Vibration and the understanding that nothing is permanent except change.
Source: Heraclitus. *Fragments* translated and compiled in *The Presocratic Philosophers.*

7. **Buddhist Middle Way.** The principle of the Middle Way connects with the Law of Polarity, highlighting balance and avoiding extremes, found throughout Buddhist teachings.
   Source: ***The Dhammapada, Teachings of the Buddha***.

15. LAW OF SURRENDER

"Be like water, making its way through cracks. Adjust to the object. If nothing stays rigid, outward things will disclose themselves." —Bruce Lee

Growing up, I spent many Saturday afternoons glued to martial arts movies on Channel 20. I loved everything about them—the way the fighters moved, the sound effects (pop! boom! poof!), the dubbed-over English that never quite matched the actors' mouths. I was captivated by the ancient settings, the rivalries, the costumes, and especially those acrobatic fight scenes. My friends and I would rush outside to act out what we'd seen on TV, living out those epic battles in our imaginations.

This fascination led me to study various martial arts over the years: Wing Chun, Aikido, Hapkido, and boxing. Each discipline taught me something unique, but it was Bruce Lee's art—Jeet Kune Do, "the way of the intercepting fist"—that really shaped me. Bruce burst onto the scene in the late 60s and early 70s with his lightning-fast moves, revolutionizing action movies forever. Almost every fight scene today bears his influence, and though his life was tragically short—he died at 33—his legacy is timeless.

Bruce Lee was more than a martial artist; he was a philosopher, and his teachings deeply resonated with me. I grew up in a tough community, where knowing how to protect yourself was crucial. Bruce Lee became my role model, my hero, and my first teacher—or at least that's how I like to think of it. Through him, I discovered the spiritual side of martial arts: the discipline, the surrender, and the presence that each move requires. The true martial artist doesn't seek to fight; they seek to resolve. They understand that their greatest weapon is not their fists but their self-control.

Bruce Lee introduced me to Taoism and the concept of Yin and Yang—the interplay of soft and hard forces in the universe. Taoism is all about letting go, finding harmony in simplicity, and flowing with life rather than fighting against it. There's a term in Taoism, *Wu Wei*—"avoid the unnecessary, flow like water, keep it simple, be effortless." It's about engaging with life without forcing it, like a master who effortlessly moves out of the way of a young, aggressive student.

The Yin-Yang symbol beautifully illustrates this philosophy: two halves—one dark, one light—intertwined, each containing a dot of the other. It's a reminder that within every joy, there is sorrow; within every loss, there is hope. Taoism doesn't see life as a battle of good versus evil. Instead, it's about finding balance in the inevitable tensions we experience.

I often say, "If we could blend the democracy of the West with the spiritual wisdom of the East, what a world we'd create!" These ancient lessons teach us that while we can't control everything, we can control our reactions, our attitudes, and our responses to life's challenges. Being like water means rolling with life's punches, like Ali's famous "rope-a-dope"—adjusting and readjusting without exhausting yourself.

I remember sparring with my martial arts instructor on a scorching day years ago. I was eager to prove myself, moving with all the energy I had. But after just a few minutes, I was gasping for air, exhausted and aching. My instructor stood there, barely sweating, and said, "John, you're done. You lost." I was stunned—I had controlled the match! But he pointed out that I'd overexerted myself, using my energy against myself instead of flowing with his.

See, you can work with life or against it. You can be in the flow or out of it. It's your choice. Life has a way of teaching us the same lessons over and over until we learn. And if we're wise, we pay attention, finding peace in rolling with the tides rather than resisting them.

Taoism teaches that when you're rigid, you're working against the natural flow of the universe. Good and bad are not enemies; they are part of the same whole. Peace comes when we embrace the dance of life, knowing that joy and sorrow, gain and loss, are all temporary. You don't have to fight against yourself. You don't have to prove anything. You are enough.

People shy away from the idea of surrender. It sounds like giving up, but real surrender is about letting go of control and trusting the flow. In our culture, we often hear, "No pain, no gain," but the Tao teaches us to let go, to be generous, to move with life rather than force it.

Think of the end of the Civil War when General Robert E. Lee surrendered to General Ulysses Grant. It wasn't a loss of dignity; it was an honorable release from a burden too heavy to bear any longer. Lee's surrender allowed him to move forward, to let go of the past, and find peace in a new beginning. When we let go of what burdens us, we free ourselves physically, mentally, and spiritually.

The Law of Surrender teaches us that there's a time for everything: a time to hold on and a time to let go. If we listen closely, life whispers when it's time to move on or change course. Ignore it, and the whispers turn to shouts. Ignore it longer, and the burdens grow. But surrendering to that still, small voice allows us to adjust, to flow, and to find peace.

This brings us back to expectations. It's good to have them—they keep us moving forward—but we also have to let go of the outcomes. Life is unpredictable. Job said it best: "The Lord giveth and taketh away; blessed be the name of the Lord." Life gives and takes away but thank you life for your many lessons! It's the journey that matters, not the destination. Focus on how you live the process, not on controlling the results.

Oprah Winfrey has a classic story of when she surrendered. She was auditioning for the role of Sofia in *The Color Purple*, a role she desperately wanted but didn't feel she would get. After the audition, she tried to push, plead, and even pray her way into the part, but nothing seemed to work. Frustrated and feeling powerless, she finally decided to let go. Oprah went out for a run, singing "I Surrender All" at the top of her lungs, releasing her need to control the outcome. Not long after, she received the call that changed her life—she got the role. Oprah often says that it was in that moment of true surrender, when she let go of trying to force things, that everything fell into place. This story is a powerful reminder that sometimes, when we step back and release our grip, we make room for life to unfold in ways we couldn't have planned.

When we surrender our need to control outcomes, we adjust to the object presented, just as Bruce Lee taught. We live in the present moment, flowing like water, and embracing each experience as it comes.

I never knew that my love of martial arts movies would lead me to deeper self-understanding. What started as fun turned into a journey of spiritual growth. Life teaches us that everything is connected, and each moment, each challenge, is part of a larger experience.

So, be patient. Hold things lightly. Know when it's time to let go. As Bruce Lee said, "There is nothing more submissive than water, yet nothing, absolutely nothing on earth can surpass it."

Amen.

References:

1. Oprah Winfrey's Story of Surrender. Oprah has recounted her experience of surrendering during the audition process for *The Color Purple* in various interviews and on her platforms.
   Source: Winfrey, Oprah. *Super Soul Sunday*, OWN Network.

2. Bruce Lee and Martial Arts Philosophy. Bruce Lee's philosophy of "being like water" and his influence on martial arts are widely recognized and documented in his writings and interviews.
   Source: Lee, Bruce. **Tao of Jeet Kune Do**. Ohara Publications, 1975.
   Source: Little, John. **Bruce Lee: Artist of Life**. Tuttle Publishing, 2001.

3. Taoism and Wu Wei. The concept of Wu Wei and the principles of Yin and Yang are foundational elements of Taoism, discussed in classic Taoist texts.
   Source: Laozi. **Tao Te Ching**. Translated by Stephen Mitchell, Harper & Row, 1988.
   Source: Watts, Alan. **Tao: The Watercourse Way**. Pantheon Books, 1975.

4. Jeet Kune Do and Bruce Lee's Teachings. Bruce Lee's development of Jeet Kune Do and its underlying philosophy of adaptation and fluidity.
   Source: Lee, Bruce. **Striking Thoughts: Bruce Lee's Wisdom for Daily Living**. Tuttle Publishing, 2000.

5. The Surrender of Robert E. Lee to Ulysses S. Grant. The historic surrender at Appomattox Court House, which marked the end of the Civil War, is a well-documented event.
   Source: Catton, Bruce. **A Stillness at Appomattox**. Doubleday & Company, 1953.
   Source: McPherson, James M. **Battle Cry of Freedom: The Civil War Era**. Oxford University Press, 1988.

6. Surrender and Letting Go in Spiritual Practices. The idea

of surrender in spiritual traditions, including Taoism and other Eastern philosophies, emphasizes letting go of control and embracing flow.

16. BE INVICTUS

William Ernest Henley is the author of the poem Invictus. He was an English poet in the late 19th century and wrote this poem when he was about 26 years old. At the age of 12, he developed tuberculosis of the bone, and his left leg had to be amputated below the knee. He endured many agonizing surgeries and faced the possibility of losing his right leg too—but it was saved. So, you see, he wrote this poem, Invictus, as someone deeply familiar with physical adversity. His ailments shaped his words—words that speak of resilience and facing fear with courage.

This poem was Nelson Mandela's favorite; he recited it aloud in prison on many days, drawing strength from its message. It's a favorite of mine too. I first encountered it when I pledged to a music fraternity in college. It stuck with me as a reminder to persevere in the face of darkness and despair.

Darkness—whether literal or metaphorical—can be unsettling. Some people sleep with nightlights. I am always exploring new ways to enhance my well-being. One day I tried float therapy. It's a form of sensory deprivation where you float in a dark chamber, completely surrounded by silence and stillness. I'll admit, it was the darkest place I'd ever been. You can't see your hands or legs; it's like you're floating in nothingness, just a consciousness in space. It can be disorienting. Although I didn't experience anything transcendent like I'd hoped, I realized that some people fear the darkness because it allows unresolved thoughts and fears to emerge, often making them feel unsafe or anxious.

This feeling of being adrift in the dark is not just physical; it happens when we experience loss or trauma that we can't easily explain. It throws us off balance and can plunge us into what Carl Jung or Eckhart Tolle might call the "dark night of the soul." Tolle describes it as "a collapse of our perceived meaning in life." He likens it to depression, a sense of emptiness where nothing makes sense, and everything seems meaningless. It's painful, but both Tolle and Jung agree that this is an essential part of growing into a healthy human being. It's a stage of spiritual awakening. We may emerge from it with a deeper understanding, more comfortable with ambiguity, randomness, and life's uncertainties.

As we emerge from the dark, we encounter what Jung called the shadow. It's the part of ourselves we often ignore but can no longer overlook. It contains our fears, flaws, and all the things we project onto others. As we begin to work with this shadow, we start to see that what we love or loathe in others is a reflection of what we love or loathe in ourselves. That's where the work begins—not with those "out there" but with ourselves. We learn to forgive and accept ourselves. As Henley writes, "I am the master of my fate, the captain of my soul." In accepting this truth, we stop blaming others and start taking responsibility for our transformation.

The shadow, far from being evil, is a necessary part of our growth. When we look at the Tarot cards, for example, we see that each archetype—the Fool, the Lovers, the High Priestess— has both a light and a shadow side. Both aspects are essential for us to manifest our best selves. The shadow side presents challenges that help us grow, reminding us that life's players —our relationships, experiences—are all part of our journey toward awakening.

This perspective shifts the way we see others and our

relationships. Instead of blaming or judging, we start recognizing that our outward judgments are often reflections of our inner struggles. What if the loss of identity or the end of a relationship isn't a failure, but the shadow awakening you to something new? What if the things we've attached ourselves to, only to have them ripped away, are actually gifts from the universe urging us toward transformation?

Jung believed that much of the world's cruelty and judgment stems from an unwillingness to face the shadow. Instead of reflecting on our inner lives, we project our unresolved pain onto others. The challenge of shadow work is to find those blind spots in our worldview and embrace them. When the shadow teacher arrives, it isn't evil; it's presenting something vital for us to learn.

In times of darkness, we are given the chance to see reality without the distortions of blame or projection. We recognize that all humans, at some point, feel vulnerable, weak, and in need of healing. The shadow allows us to make peace with the entirety of life—the virtue and the vice. It helps us do less harm in our relationships and interactions. I am reminded of a beautiful poem by Suzy Kassem:

> *"You once told me / You wanted to find / Yourself in the world / And I told you to / First apply within, / To discover the world / within you. / You once told me / You wanted to save / The world from all its wars / And I told you to / First save yourself / From the world, / And all the wars / You put yourself through."*

William Ernest Henley's words from *Invictus* are a reminder to face hardship with resilience:

> *"Out of the night that covers me,*
> *Black as the pit from pole to pole,*

I thank whatever gods may be
For my unconquerable soul."

Life will bring its dark moments, its shadow teachers, but I give thanks when they arrive. I am *Invictus*—unconquerable. I will not give up on myself, even when I feel lost.

"In the fell clutch of circumstance
I have not winced nor cried aloud.
Under the bludgeonings of chance
My head is bloody, but unbowed."

Life is hard. I may cry, it may hurt, but I am strong enough to endure. I will overcome and love will prevail in me.

"Beyond this place of wrath and tears
Looms but the Horror of the shade,
And yet the menace of the years
Finds and shall find me unafraid."

Even in the darkest moments, I know that I am closer to the light. I will live with courage and faith.

"It matters not how strait the gate,
How charged with punishments the scroll,
I am the master of my fate,
I am the captain of my soul."

I am responsible for my life. I will not let the judgments of others, or my own projections, dictate my reality. I am the master of my fate. I am the captain of my soul.

Be *Invictus*. Amen.

References:

1. William Ernest Henley and "Invictus." Information on Henley's life, his experiences with illness, and the creation of "Invictus" can be found in biographies and literary analyses of his work.
   Source: Cheney, John V. **William Ernest Henley: A Memoir**. Scribner's, 1905.
2. Nelson Mandela's Connection to "Invictus." Mandela often referenced "Invictus" as a source of inspiration during his imprisonment, and it is widely documented in his biographies and interviews.
   Source: Mandela, Nelson. **Long Walk to Freedom: The Autobiography of Nelson Mandela**. Little, Brown and Company, 1994.
   Source: Stengel, Richard. **Mandela's Way: Lessons on Life, Love, and Courage**. Crown Publishing, 2009.
3. Eckhart Tolle on the Dark Night of the Soul. Tolle discusses the concept of the dark night of the soul in his teachings, linking it to spiritual growth and awakening.
   Source: Tolle, Eckhart. **The Power of Now: A Guide to Spiritual Enlightenment**. Namaste Publishing, 1997.
4. Carl Jung on Shadow Work. Jung introduced the idea of the shadow as a critical part of personal development, emphasizing the importance of integrating our hidden or denied aspects.
   Source: Jung, Carl G. **The Archetypes and The Collective Unconscious**. Princeton University Press, 1959.
   Source: Jung, Carl G. **Psychology and Religion: West and East**. Princeton University Press, 1969.
5. The Concept of the "Dark Night of the Soul." This concept has roots in both psychological and spiritual traditions, often tied to moments of existential crisis and personal transformation.
   Source: John of the Cross, St. **Dark Night of the Soul**. Dover Publications, 2003.
   Source: May, Gerald G. **The Dark Night of the Soul: A Psychiatrist Explores the Connection Between Darkness and Spiritual Growth**. HarperOne, 2004.
6. The Tarot and Archetypes. The Tarot's major arcana and the dualities within each archetype reflect Jungian

psychology's exploration of light and shadow.

Source: Nichols, Sallie. **Jung and Tarot: An Archetypal Journey**. Weiser Books, 1980.

Source: Pollack, Rachel. **Seventy-Eight Degrees of Wisdom: A Tarot Journey to Self-Awareness**. Weiser Books, 1980.

17. HEAVEN & THE AFTERLIFE

I've chosen a field of study and a profession that often has me thinking about death and what, if anything, comes after. I believe our fear of death and our need to survive are among the most powerful driving forces in the world. Because of this, I've been fascinated—maybe even obsessed—with death and what happens when we die.

I know some of you believe that nothing happens when we die. You think we're just dead—lights out, nothing more. I get it. It feels harsh to me, but I've been open to that possibility, even though my own experiences have led me to believe otherwise. So, I'm inviting you skeptics to just listen with curiosity this morning. Let's wonder together.

A few months ago, Time Magazine released a special edition called *Heaven and the Afterlife: What Awaits Us?* The magazine dives into what different religions say about the afterlife and what science has to say. They found that about 72% of humans believe in some kind of life after death. What that looks like varies widely depending on beliefs. Many describe heaven in human terms: a place where you're with family and friends, living in peace and harmony. But when pressed on the details, most can't really say what you *do* there. It's like you're just hanging out. And to me, honestly, that sounds like it might get a little boring!

Some see heaven as a literal place "up there" or an invisible realm. Others say it's a state of being where you exist as pure joy or consciousness. Whatever it is, humans have this deep-seated desire to believe that we are not just extinguished at death—that we go on in some form.

This is the heartbeat of Christianity, isn't it? Jesus rises from the dead, and in that resurrection, Christians find hope—victory over death, a promise that death is not the end. That's a powerful message, especially for those who have suffered, been oppressed, and forgotten by life. Very clever writers knew that death had a hold on us, and they wrote stories that could loosen that grip.

But let's go back further. Imagine the first person who ever died —those early humans must have been stunned. They had to come up with something to make sense of it, so they created stories about an afterlife. They buried their dead with clothes, charms, and symbols to carry with them. Some cultures even killed entire families when a leader died so they could all cross over together.

So where does this idea of an afterlife come from? Are we just making it up? I think, yes, we've made up some of it, but there's something deeper at play, something rooted in our DNA, in our souls. I wouldn't have said that when I first became a Unitarian Universalist—I would've dismissed it as a human construct to ease the pain of life. But as I've gotten older, I've become less skeptical. I've changed. And I'm grateful to be in a religion that allows me to change, grow, and explore.

I've had some experiences that have shaken my skepticism. I've seen too many synchronicities and strange occurrences that have convinced me that, yes, something of us continues. Energy doesn't die; it just changes form. And we, my friends, are energy.

One of the first stories that changed my thinking came from

my ex-wife over 25 years ago. Her mother died of breast cancer at 53 years of age in Philadelphia. About a year later, Sharon and her sister participated in a breast cancer awareness run in D.C. After the race, Sharon was cooling down and took off her race number. As she did, she stepped on another number that someone had discarded. She picked it up, and it read, "In honor of Lena Maloney." That was her mother's name. Her mom, who died 200 miles away. What are the odds of that? To Sharon, it felt like a sign—a whisper from her mom saying, "I'm still here."

Then in 2012, after a series of funerals and losses in our church community, I decided to take a couple of weeks off. I was feeling depleted, so I dove into reading about the afterlife. One book that really grabbed me was by Dr. Michael Newton, an atheist therapist turned believer in the afterlife. Newton discovered that under hypnosis, his patients described not only past lives but also what he called "life between lives." He documented thousands of these sessions, where people consistently described similar experiences after death: being surrounded by loved ones, feeling a sense of healing and understanding, and existing as energy, not as bodies.

I remember reading those books and thinking, "This is wild." It was so out there—so Sci-Fi—that I had to put the book down sometimes to laugh, sometimes to cry, and sometimes to just let it sink in. But it resonated with me, especially when I was grappling with so much loss. It felt like exactly what I needed to hear at the time.

That led me to study Near-Death Experiences (NDEs), and I found the work of Dr. Raymond Moody, who coined the term NDE in 1975. His work led to the creation of the Division of Perceptual Studies at the University of Virginia, which sounds like something straight out of a sci-fi movie, right? But there it is, part of the School of Medicine, investigating what happens when people have these profound experiences near death.

So, when I step back and think about all of this—not just our world but the entire cosmos, with stars being born, galaxies expanding, and the universe endlessly stretching out—I am filled with awe. It reminds me of our hymn: "What wondrous love is this, oh my soul." I don't have all the answers, but I know in my soul that love wins. And if there is a God, that God is love.

That's why our Universalist ancestors could say boldly that God doesn't make junk. If there's a God, that God doesn't condemn what God creates. All roads lead to love. That's universalism in its truest sense—that all of us, from the pauper to the pope, are destined for love. It's all good, even when it feels bad. It's all God (or add an extra "O"—it's all good!).

I often wonder if maybe we get what we desire most after we die. A few weeks before my mother passed, I was taking her to the ER, and she kept saying, "John, do you hear that choir singing?" I didn't hear anything, but my mom loved singing in the choir—she didn't like solos, but she loved the choir. And I like to think that she's up there now, singing her heart out.

I think that maybe our souls know what we most deeply desire, and that's what we go toward when we die. People who've had NDEs often describe meeting loved ones, traveling to distant galaxies, or deciding to come back to Earth after a period of rest. Those who caused great harm in life, like Hitler, needed major rehabilitation before reincarnating to learn again. But mostly, it was all good—everyone finding what their soul needed most.

We are all part of something greater, something eternal. As our UU ancestor, Rev. William Ellery Channing, wrote in his most popular sermon, *The Future Life*:

> "We must not think of Heaven as a stationary community. I think of it as a world of stupendous plans and efforts for its own improvement. I think

of it as a society passing through successive stages of development, virtue, knowledge, power—by the energy of its own members... There the work of education, which began here, goes on without end... Heaven, in truth, is a glorious reality."

Channing's vision reminds us that the afterlife is not a static place but a continuation of the journey we begin here—a journey of growth, connection, and becoming. It's a reminder that our learning never stops, our love never ceases, and our souls never stand still.

We are bound to this cosmic rhythm, to this divine dance of expansion and transformation, forever connected to each other and to the universe itself. And whatever comes next, I believe it is filled with that same spirit of love, endless growth, and infinite possibilities that Channing so eloquently described.

So let us live fully and love fiercely, knowing that we are part of a story that goes on beyond our understanding. Heaven is not just a place; it is a promise—an unfolding journey where our spirits continue to evolve, endlessly and beautifully.

Amen.

References:

1. Time Magazine on Heaven and the Afterlife. This special edition explores what various religions and scientific perspectives say about the afterlife, providing insight into global beliefs on life after death.
   Source: *Time Magazine Special Edition: Heaven and the Afterlife.* Time Inc., 2023.
2. Dr. Michael Newton's Work on Life Between Lives. Newton's research on life between lives and past life regression provides a comprehensive look into what happens after death, based on thousands of patient testimonies.

Source: Newton, Michael. **Journey of Souls: Case Studies of Life Between Lives**. Llewellyn Publications, 1994.

Source: Newton, Michael. **Destiny of Souls: New Case Studies of Life Between Lives**. Llewellyn Publications, 2000.

3. Near-Death Experiences and Raymond Moody's Research. Dr. Raymond Moody is a pioneer in the study of Near-Death Experiences (NDEs), and his work led to the creation of the Division of Perceptual Studies at the University of Virginia.

   Source: Moody, Raymond. **Life After Life: The Investigation of a Phenomenon—Survival of Bodily Death**. HarperOne, 1975.

   Source: Moody, Raymond. **The Light Beyond**. Bantam Books, 1988.

4. Rev. William Ellery Channing's Sermon on the Afterlife. Channing's sermon *The Future Life* reflects early Unitarian Universalist thoughts on life after death and spiritual development beyond this world.

   Source: Channing, William Ellery. **The Future Life**. American Unitarian Association, 1834.

5. Carl Jung on Shadow Work and Personal Development. Jung's exploration of the shadow self highlights the importance of integrating hidden aspects of our psyche as part of personal and spiritual growth.

SECTION 3:
FAITH, RELIGION, AND SPIRITUAL REFLECTIONS

18. DOES GOD EXIST?

Today, we're diving into a topic that has stirred humanity's deepest questions, sparked endless debates, and inspired countless acts of love and service: GOD. Now, let's be clear—I'm not talking about the old man in the sky, casting lightning bolts, or checking off a list of rights and wrongs like Santa Clause. No, I'm talking about something far deeper, broader, and more profound. For me, GOD isn't a being out there; GOD is energy. GOD is the ALL. The Tao. Brahma. The divine spark that runs through everything. GOD is that force that moves in us, through us, and connects us. Add an "O" to "God," and you get "good"—and that's what GOD is: the highest big G Good, the ultimate source, the essence of all that is, was, and ever will be.

GOD is energy. The breath you just took, the sunlight touching your skin, the feeling of love when you hold a child—all of that is GOD. GOD is not confined to a church, mosque, or temple. GOD isn't even confined to a name. GOD is beyond our words, beyond our limited human understanding. This is why so many traditions use different names: The Taoists call it the Tao, the Way that cannot be named but is the source of all life. In Hinduism, it's Brahma, the creative force that births the universe into being. Science calls it the Big Bang, that miraculous moment when all matter, all energy, and all possibilities exploded into existence. These are just different ways of trying to touch the ineffable, to grasp that something greater that moves all things. But whatever name you give it, it's pointing to the same sacred truth: GOD is in everything, and we are all connected to and come from this divine source.

When I say GOD is energy, I mean that GOD is the life force that flows through all creation. It's the pulse that beats in your heart, the gravity that holds the planets in orbit, and the inspiration that sparks your creativity. GOD is the Ground of Being, the substance from which everything emerges and to which everything returns. And in this grand, cosmic dance, we are all participants—each of us a unique expression of that divine energy. We're not separate from GOD; we are a part of GOD, intertwined with this great, unfolding story of the universe.

For me, GOD is not about fear or punishment. It's not about rules and restrictions designed to keep you in line. GOD is about love, connection, and living your highest good. It's about aligning yourself with that deep, centered part of you that knows what is right, true, and just. GOD is that still, small voice inside you that nudges you toward compassion when it's easier to judge, that pulls you toward courage when fear has you paralyzed, that whispers peace when chaos reigns around you.

We often think of spiritual practices as ways to connect with GOD—prayer, meditation, yoga, singing. But GOD isn't waiting for you to show up in a particular place or do a particular thing. GOD is always here, always present, always inviting us to recognize that divine spark within ourselves and others. It's like tuning into a frequency that's already broadcasting; we just need to dial in. When you feel joy, when you act with kindness, when you forgive, when you create something beautiful, you are tapping into that frequency. You are aligning with GOD.

Think about those moments when you've felt most alive, most connected, most whole. Maybe it was watching a sunset, listening to a powerful piece of music, or holding the hand of someone you love. Those moments aren't just coincidences or fleeting emotions—they are sacred. They are glimpses of the divine, reminders that GOD is not distant but right here, woven into the fabric of our everyday lives. Those moments are the universe's way of saying, "I am here. I am with you. You are part of something greater."

Living in alignment with GOD means striving to bring your highest self to each moment. It means making choices that reflect your deepest values, even when it's difficult, even when it goes against the grain. It's about choosing love over fear, unity over division, and compassion over indifference. It's about being present, paying attention, and showing up fully as the person you were created to be. That's where we find GOD—not in some far-off heaven, but right here in the messy, beautiful, sacred now.

We often get caught up in thinking that GOD is something outside of us, something we have to search for or earn. But what if GOD is as close as your next breath? What if GOD is the love that flows through your relationships, the passion that drives your work, the hope that keeps you moving forward? What if, instead of looking up or looking out, you simply looked within? Because that's where GOD is. GOD is in you, and GOD is in me. GOD is in the spaces between us, calling us to be more, to love more, to give more.

It's easy to get caught up in the noise of life, to be overwhelmed by the demands and distractions that pull us away from our center. But GOD is always calling us back, inviting us to return to that place of stillness, that place of truth. It's not about perfection; it's about presence. It's not about having all the answers; it's about asking the right questions. It's about being willing to sit with the mystery, to trust in the process, and to know that, no matter what, you are held by something greater.

And here's the beautiful part: When we align with GOD, when we commit to living our highest good, we don't just change ourselves; we change the world. Because when you operate from that place of divine connection, it shows up in everything you do. It shows up in how you treat others, how you handle challenges, and how you live your life. You become a conduit for that divine energy, and through you, GOD's love and light are made manifest in the world.

I invite you to see GOD in a new way. Not as some distant deity watching from afar, but as the very energy of life itself. The breath in your lungs, the beat in your heart, the spark in your soul. GOD is here, now, in every moment, inviting us to live fully, love deeply, and strive always toward our highest good. GOD is not a destination; GOD is the journey—the constant unfolding of love, grace, and infinite possibility.

May we live each day aware of this divine presence. May we find the courage to align with our highest selves and trust that, in doing so, we are aligning with GOD. And may we remember that, no matter where we are on our path, we are never alone. We are always connected to the source, always held by that great, mysterious force that is, at its heart, nothing less than pure, boundless, unconditional love.

Amen.

References:

1. **The Tao Te Ching** by Laozi – This ancient text explores the Tao, a concept similar to your description of GOD as the underlying energy and essence of all things. The Tao represents the ultimate source and the Way of life, aligning closely with your perspective on the divine.
2. **The Upanishads** – These sacred Hindu texts delve into the concept of Brahman, the ultimate reality and divine essence that permeates everything. The idea of Brahman resonates with your view of GOD as the Ground of Being and the source of all creation.
3. **A New Earth: Awakening to Your Life's Purpose** by Eckhart Tolle – Tolle speaks of GOD as presence, awareness, and the underlying consciousness in all life. His work

emphasizes living in alignment with this divine energy, much like your call to live from our highest good.

4. **The Power of Now: A Guide to Spiritual Enlightenment** by Eckhart Tolle – Tolle's exploration of living in the present moment as a way of connecting with the divine aligns with your perspective that GOD is always here and now, within us and around us.

5. **The Hidden Gospel: Decoding the Spiritual Message of the Aramaic Jesus** by Neil Douglas-Klotz – This book reinterprets Jesus's teachings in a way that emphasizes connection, oneness, and the divine energy present in all things, similar to your description of GOD.

6. **God Is Not One: The Eight Rival Religions That Run the World—and Why Their Differences Matter** by Stephen Prothero – Prothero's examination of different religious understandings of GOD highlights the universal search for the divine across cultures, aligning with your idea of GOD as the ALL.

7. **The Book of Joy: Lasting Happiness in a Changing World** by Dalai Lama, Desmond Tutu, and Douglas Carlton Abrams – This book highlights the interconnectedness of all beings and the importance of living from a place of compassion and love, aligning with your view of GOD as the highest good.

8. **Quantum Theology: Spiritual Implications of the New Physics** by Diarmuid O'Murchu – O'Murchu explores how the concepts of modern physics intersect with spirituality, especially the idea of a connected, divine energy that underlies all existence.

19. THE AQUARIAN GOSPEL, ESCHATOLOGY, AND THE NEW AGE

Reading: *The Aquarian Gospel of Jesus*, written by Levi H. Dowling, 1907

"In silent meditation, Jesus sat beside a flowing spring. It was a holy day, and many people of the servant caste were near the place. And Jesus saw the hard, drawn lines of toil on every brow, in every hand. There was no look of joy in any face. Not one of all the group could think of anything but toil. And Jesus spoke to one and said, 'Why are you all so sad?' The man replied: 'We scarcely know the meaning of that word. We toil to live and hope for nothing else but toil, and bless the day when we can cease our toil and lay us down to rest in Buddha's city of the dead.' And Jesus' heart was stirred with pity and with love for these poor toilers, and he said: 'Toil should not make a person sad; people should be happiest when they toil. When hope and love are back of toil, then all of life is filled with joy and peace, and this is heaven. Do you not know that such a heaven is for you?'

The man replied: 'Of heaven we have heard; but then it is so far away, and we must live so many lives before we reach that place!' And Jesus said, 'My brother, man, your thoughts are wrong; your heaven is not far away; and it is not a place of metes and bounds, it's not a county to be reached; it is a state of mind. God never made a heaven for humans; he never made a hell; we are creators and we make our own heaven or hell. Now cease to seek for heaven in the sky; just open up the windows of your hearts, and, like a flood of light, a heaven will come and bring a boundless joy; then toil will be no cruel task.'"

"All this time I was finding myself, and I didn't know I was lost," says Aloe Blacc. The world waits for sages and saviors, but we forget to see ourselves as the harbingers of hope and peace. We look outside of ourselves when we think about peace, assuming it's something someone else will deliver. We do our part, vote our conscience, elect leaders who reflect our values. But what is the goal? Inner peace? World peace? A Beloved Community?

As Unitarian Universalists, our principles guide us: justice, equity, and a world community with peace, liberty, and justice for all. We're striving for a day when love prevails. But what if that day is today? What if there's no grand beginning or end?

Our shared yearning for safety, freedom, and a better world is ancient, embedded in our DNA. We might call it heaven or paradise, but at its core, it's a universal longing. This longing gives birth to eschatology—a theological term that means "the last word." It's about God's final say in human history, often tied to the idea of the Second Coming of Christ, where good triumphs over evil in an ultimate reckoning. Revelation 21 paints a vision of a new heaven and earth, part of what scholars call "apocalyptic literature." These ancient texts, full of cryptic imagery, were debated fiercely before making it into the Bible. The Book of Revelation, filled with death and destruction, wasn't included until the 200s of the common era. Even today, its influence persists—billboards remind us that "the end is coming."

The literalist reading of these texts has caused harm, fostering division and a culture of judgment. "We're right, you're wrong. We're saved, you're doomed." This blaming mentality, inherited from fundamentalist interpretations of Christianity, pits us against each other. History repeats itself because humans are cyclical beings; the struggles of the past mirror the conflicts of today.

Whether Christian, Humanist, or Buddhist, we all wrestle with the end—our end. And that uncertainty has led us to some rather creative guessing on how it will all go down. Those in power aren't immune; they manipulate these narratives, projecting their fears and hopes onto us. Institutional Christianity has often preached that the end is nigh, urging us to straighten up if we want to escape hellfire. The dominant narrative says we're powerless, sinful, and helpless without God. But there's another story—a secondary story.

This secondary story, often sidelined, is what we now call "New Age" teachings. But there's nothing new about them; they're ancient, rooted in the esoteric wisdom of Hinduism, Zoroastrianism, Judaism, and more. Dowling's *Aquarian Gospel* caught my attention because it offers a different view—a nuanced take on how Jesus became wise, learning from sages across the world. Dowling believed that one day, this mystical narrative would become primary. I agree.

New Age philosophies encompass all that traditional Christian dogma rejects: astrology, metaphysics, reiki, psychic readings, symbolic interpretations of sacred texts, and more. These teachings are making a comeback, even infiltrating mainstream churches. The old story of sin and salvation is making room for a new, or rather ancient, understanding of interconnectedness and inner power.

In contrast to the primary story, which tells us we are powerless, New Age teachings say: You are divine. You are a small "g" god in human form. Everything is God, and all are anointed. This narrative views sacred texts as symbolic guides to self-understanding, layered with astrological meaning. The Bible's stories of fish, for instance, align with the Age of Pisces —a time of empire-building that we are now leaving behind as we dawn toward the Age of Aquarius.

The Age of Aquarius, heralded by hippie anthems in the '60s, is said to be a time of truth-telling, higher consciousness, and global interconnectedness. This resonates deeply with our UU principles. It's a vision of a world where heaven is not a distant place but a present possibility, created within us.

In the Gnostic Gospel of Thomas, Jesus says, "The end will be where the beginning is." The circle of life is real, and we see it everywhere—in nature, in the turning of the seasons, in the patterns of our lives. Science tells us energy never dies; it transforms. We are part of that transformation. We are the circle.

We can lean into this knowing, trusting the cycles of life. We are the creators of our own heavens and hells, shaping our reality with every thought, every choice, every breath. The primary story may tell us we're unworthy, but the secondary story—the one that whispers in the quiet moments—reminds us that heaven is not a distant place but a state of mind we cultivate. Let's balance the stories, paying attention to the signs, the patterns, and the wisdom that speaks to our deepest selves. As Mary Oliver wrote, "It's the beginning of devotion." Every ending is just the start of something new, a call to begin again. Dowling captures it best:

"The man toiling in the soil replied, 'Of heaven we have heard, but then it is so far away.' And Jesus said, 'Your heaven is not far away; it is a state of mind. God never made a heaven or hell; we create them. Stop seeking heaven in the sky; open your heart, and heaven will come like a flood of light.'"

My friends, stop searching outside yourself. Open the windows of your heart and let that light pour in. Be the light that turns toil into joy, the light that makes the ordinary sacred. This is our power. This is our calling. Heaven is here, within us, waiting to be realized. Amen.

References:

1. **The Aquarian Gospel of Jesus the Christ** by Levi H. Dowling – A channeled work that presents an alternative narrative of Jesus' life, emphasizing mystical teachings and esoteric wisdom from various ancient cultures.
2. **The Gospel of Thomas** (part of the Nag Hammadi library) – A Gnostic text that contains sayings attributed to Jesus, offering a more mystical and symbolic interpretation of his teachings, often emphasizing inner wisdom and the interconnectedness of life.
3. **The Sacred and the Profane: The Nature of Religion** by Mircea Eliade – This book explores the sacred and cyclical nature of religious beliefs, rituals, and the human experience, connecting to the themes of cycles and patterns you discuss.
4. **The Varieties of Religious Experience** by William James – A classic work on the psychology of religion that delves into mystical experiences, spiritual awakening, and the subjective nature of divine encounters, resonating with New Age and esoteric themes.
5. **The Hero with a Thousand Faces** by Joseph Campbell – This book explores the universal patterns of myths, including those found in religious texts, which align with your discussion on cyclical human nature and eschatological themes.

20. SAMHAIN AND THE ORIGINS OF RELIGION: WICCA, PAGANISM, MAGIC, SPELLS, AND HARRY POTTER

Throughout history, Wicca, Paganism, magic, spells, and even pop culture phenomena like Harry Potter have been viewed by orthodox religion as anti-Christian, even labeled as the work of the Devil. Hollywood hasn't helped with its horror movies and portrayals of witches and wizards that vilify what magic truly is. At its core, magic is about intention—using thoughts, words, and phrases to manifest desires. While there can be a darker side, most magic aims to do good, to heal, and to make the world better. Here's a fun fact: the Druids used the wood of the holly tree to make their wands, which makes the name "Hollywood" quite fitting.

Nature-based religions are widely misunderstood, often shrouded in fear and misinterpretation. But their origins are rooted in healing, community, and providing meaning through rituals—just like all religions. Paganism is no different. From the persecution of the Celts to the Salem Witch Trials, traditional religion has been antagonistic toward earth-based practices. Yet, many of these so-called "pagan" rituals and beliefs can be traced back to the same nature worship found in the origins of major world religions. Early humans revered the earth, the stars, the sun, the moon, and the five visible planets, crafting rituals and symbols that persist in religions today. It's all there if you dig deep enough into religious history, spanning continents from India to Europe, from Africa to the Americas.

I love exploring the origins of things. Whether it's the history of coffee, cheese, or the beginnings of an industry, I find joy in tracing roots. But what fascinates me most are the origins of religion. When you peel back the layers of time, you find that early humans—long before the rise of agriculture and empires—were nomadic, tribal, and deeply spiritual. Their spirituality was astrological, oriented by the stars, while their theology was grounded in the earth. Life was understood through the cycles of the seasons, the tides, and the celestial bodies above.

Early humans created rituals around the four elements—earth, air, fire, and water—which they saw as magical forces of life. The dirt where things grow, the invisible air we breathe, the warming and transformative power of fire, and the life-sustaining gift of water —all were sacred. The four directions—North, South, East, and West—formed the ancient symbol of the cross, later popularized in Christianity. From these elements and directions sprang the rituals we still observe in religious practice: communion, baptism, blessings, chants, healings, and more. All of these rituals can be traced back to pagan religious practices. To me, all religion is fundamentally *astro-theological*—of the stars and the earth. When we approach sacred texts with this perspective, it becomes clear how much we share across our diverse faith traditions.

But what does "pagan" really mean? It simply means "not of the orthodoxy" or "not of the accepted tradition." The term is related to pre-Christian tribal religions, often dismissed as primitive or outdated. Paganism reflects earth-based spirituality that predates institutional religions. Even in the Old Testament, paganism is misunderstood and misapplied. Consider the ancient Israelites, who were influenced by Sumerian and Egyptian astrology as early as 6000 BCE. They revered the astrological ages of Taurus (the Bull) and Aries (the Ram or Lamb), interpreting the movement of the planets as divine signs. The Moses story marks a shift from this type of worship to monotheism. In the New Testament, we see the symbols of the Virgin Mary (linked to the constellation Virgo, an ancient moon goddess) and Jesus, the Lamb of God, ushering in the Age of Pisces.

Astrological symbolism permeates religious texts. When Jesus says, "I will make you fishers of men," he's referencing Pisces. Before Islam, Mecca was a hub of 360 gods—note the symbolic completeness of 360 degrees. The crescent moon on the flag of Islam hints at ancient moon worship, while the counterclockwise walk around the Kaaba is a practice rooted in pre-Islamic pagan rituals.

These insights reveal a universal truth: the roots of religion are shared. No one path is superior. Understanding our collective spiritual heritage helps us see beyond dogma to the common human yearning for connection and meaning.

Ken Burns' documentary on the buffalo, narrated by Peter Coyote, shows us how the Lakota's Sun Dance ritual celebrated the buffalo hunt, demonstrating the deep connection between the earliest Americans and the earth. This story repeats itself around the world— earth-based spirituality is our shared legacy.

We are all moving toward Spirit, God, the Cosmos, or whatever we call the divine, from different paths, but with one shared longing— for home, for understanding, for community. We all use stories and rituals to make sense of suffering, death, and life. Paganism, when practiced responsibly, teaches balance, moderation, forgiveness, and love—values that lead to wholeness.

As we enter the time of Samhain (pronounced Sow-an), Halloween, or All Saints' Day, remember that these celebrations are rooted in ancient traditions of honoring the dead. Samhain, a Gaelic festival marking the end of the harvest and the thinning of the veil between the living and the dead, reminds us of our own mortality and the importance of remembering those who have passed.

Over 109 billion people have lived and died on this planet, compared to the 8 billion alive today. Death has always been an ever-present reality, even more so for the ancients who lived shorter lives. So, it makes sense that they created rituals to honor and remember. It's a practice that reminds us to cherish our time and our loved ones, to reflect on our lives, and to connect with something greater than ourselves.

Religion, at its core, is not so mysterious when you dive deeper. It's about aligning our hearts and minds with something bigger, about recognizing the sublime in the visible and invisible forces of the universe—gravity, wind, the sun and moon, the divine mystery. This is what many call God, and it's worthy of our reverence.

As you reflect on this message, think about the invisible powers that shape our lives, and take a moment to honor those who have gone before us. Let the falling leaves of this season remind you of our connection to the ancient rhythms of life. This is my prayer for you and for all of us.

May it be so.

Amen.

References:

1. **The Triumph of the Moon: A History of Modern Pagan Witchcraft** by Ronald Hutton – This book provides a comprehensive history of modern Paganism and Wicca, exploring their ancient roots and how they have been shaped over time, including connections to traditional religious practices.
2. **The Golden Bough: A Study in Magic and Religion** by James Frazer – A classic work that explores the common elements of magic, religion, and myth across different cultures, highlighting the shared origins of many religious rituals.
3. **Drawing Down the Moon: Witches, Druids, Goddess-Worshippers, and Other Pagans in America** by Margot Adler – A deep dive into contemporary Paganism in America, exploring its roots, rituals, and the way it has been perceived by mainstream society.
4. **The Book of Symbols: Reflections on Archetypal Images** by the Archive for Research in Archetypal Symbolism (ARAS) – This book provides insight into the universal symbols found in religious and spiritual traditions, including those rooted in nature and ancient earth-based practices.
5. **Astrology and the Rising of Kundalini: The Transformative Power of Saturn, Chiron, and Uranus** by Barbara Hand Clow – This book connects astrology

with ancient spiritual practices, discussing the impact of celestial movements on human spirituality, including those seen in early Pagan traditions.

21. EASTER: THE TRUE MEANING OF RESURRECTION

Easter is a time filled with symbols, many of which predate Christianity. The rabbit, a creature long associated with spring and fertility, represents new life, abundance, and nature's relentless renewal. These symbols and traditions actually have pagan roots, celebrating the arrival of spring, the goddess Eostre, and the rebirth of the earth after winter's slumber. Christianity co-opted these ancient celebrations, merging them with the story of Jesus' resurrection to create the holiday we know today. This blending of traditions underscores the deeper message of Easter: the transition from death to life, like winter to spring, and hope blooming after despair.

Christianity's rise to become the largest and most powerful religion in the world is no mystery. If you dive into the 'triple threat' of the Apostle Paul, Emperor Constantine, and the Holy Catholic Church, you'll find all the answers. Today, Christianity boasts over 2 billion followers, representing one-third of the world's population. That's real power!

But you might wonder why I didn't include Jesus in that triad. Well, I think Jesus is the most misunderstood person ever written about. I left traditional Christianity a long time ago because it felt too rigid, too "traditional." But my fascination with Jesus—who he was and what he stands for—has never waned. I watched the National Geographic movie *Killing Jesus*, based on Bill O'Reilly's book, and it was the first time I saw a portrayal of Jesus that resonated with me. I remember thinking, "I could follow this guy!"

In the film, Jesus wasn't depicted as the European figure we've all seen. He looked like the Semitic man he was, spending his life under the hot sun with a complexion and features typical of someone from the Middle East. And let's not forget, Jesus wasn't a Christian—he was a Jew. The movie captured these basic facts, portraying Jesus as a real human being with flaws, doubts, and fears.

This portrayal showed a reluctant Jesus, apprehensive and growing into his role, discovering his power along the way. He wasn't always confident; he sometimes seemed unsure of his gifts but pressed forward anyway. This human Jesus gave hope and spiritual freedom through radical love in action, speaking truth to power and bringing the altar of worship out of the temple and into the streets. He got angry, showed compassion, laughed, cried, and, in the end, sacrificed everything for what he believed.

Now, you should know that Jesus has been so mythologized over the centuries that it's challenging to separate the historical figure from the legend. Some scholars even question whether he existed at all. In fact, in the book *The Jesus Mysteries*, authors Timothy Freke and Peter Gandy explore the idea that the story of Jesus could be a reworking of older pagan myths, suggesting that much of what we know about Jesus may be more symbolic than historical. They argue that the narrative of Jesus shares striking similarities with ancient mystery religions and myths of dying and resurrecting gods, like Osiris, Dionysus, and Mithras. These parallels raise questions about how much of Jesus' story was crafted to fit into a larger, timeless narrative of death and rebirth, intended to convey spiritual truths rather than literal events. This mythologizing doesn't diminish his impact; rather, it speaks to the enduring power of his story to transcend time and culture, offering us profound lessons on love, sacrifice, and transformation.

Beyond the literal story, the resurrection is a powerful metaphor for transformation—a call to die to the old self so the new self can be born. Every day, cells in our bodies die and are renewed; night turns into day; winter gives way to spring. These natural cycles remind us that death is not an end but a passage to new beginnings. Jesus "springs forth from death," embodying the very essence of the season.

The story of Jesus' resurrection teaches us about hope in tomorrow and belief in our ability to be the best version of ourselves. It's about rising above our past, our mistakes, and our old ways of being. To embrace resurrection is to believe that no matter how many times we stumble, we can get back up, renewed and ready to start again. It's a reminder that every setback is a setup for a comeback, that even in our darkest moments, there's always a new dawn waiting to break.

Jesus' story is not just about his life, death, and rising—it's a mirror reflecting our own journeys. It tells us that we, too, have the power to let go of what no longer serves us, to shed old habits, fears, and doubts, and step into a new way of being. It's about the daily resurrection that happens within us when we choose to live with purpose, hope, and love.

So, when we talk about Easter, let's remember it's not just a historical event but a living, breathing call to action. It's a call to die to the old versions of ourselves and embrace the possibility of who we can become. Resurrection is not just Jesus' story—it's our story. It's the story of believing in tomorrow, trusting in the process, and knowing that the best is yet to come.

This is the true meaning of resurrection: the relentless belief that we are made for more, that we are constantly evolving, and that no matter how many times we fall, we can always rise again. May it be so.

Amen.

1. **You Were Made for So Much More** by John Crestwell – This book explores the themes of transformation, personal growth, and embracing the best version of yourself, aligning closely with the message of resurrection as a metaphor for self-renewal and hope in tomorrow.
2. **The Jesus Mysteries: Was the 'Original Jesus' a Pagan God?** by Timothy Freke and Peter Gandy – This book delves into the mythological roots of the Jesus story, examining how ancient myths of dying and rising gods influenced the narrative of Jesus, reinforcing the symbolic nature of resurrection.
3. **Killing Jesus: A History** by Bill O'Reilly and Martin Dugard – This book offers a historical perspective on Jesus' life and death, portraying him as a complex and human figure, which aligns with the sermon's emphasis on the humanity of Jesus and his transformative journey.
4. **The Hero with a Thousand Faces** by Joseph Campbell – Campbell's exploration of the hero's journey parallels the story of Jesus and many other mythological figures, emphasizing themes of death, rebirth, and the quest for transformation that resonates with Easter's deeper meaning.
5. **Resurrection: Myth or Reality?** by John Shelby Spong – This book reinterprets the resurrection story through a modern lens, arguing that resurrection is more than a physical event; it is a profound symbol of hope, personal transformation, and the power to rise above life's challenges.

22. PAGAN HOLIDAYS: HANUKKAH, SOLSTICE, YULE, CHRISTMAS

Hanukkah, Winter Solstice, Yule, and Christmas—all these sacred celebrations are strikingly similar, each shaped by the cultures that created them. They are connected through the practice of religious syncretism—the blending of religious ideas as cultures interact, trade, engage in conflict, and build relationships.

Hanukkah is a minor Jewish celebration. But like most winter holidays, it's part of a long tradition of celebrating nature and the cosmos—particularly the sun, moon, earth, and stars. Ancient cultures across the globe honored their gods through these natural and cosmic cycles, creating rituals and festivals that reflect both their similarities and differences. As I often say, original religions were both earth-based and astrological, involving a cosmic reverence for the stars. Think of the story of the three wise men following the star—it's a narrative that captures humanity's awe at the heavens above.

I can imagine ancient people staring up at the sky, seeing the shimmering stars and planets, and asking, "What wondrous work is this, oh my soul?" The marvels of the cosmos gave them pause, inspiring them to create stories and rituals to explain these extraordinary sights. They weren't distracted by the noise of television, social media, or the latest Netflix series. Instead, their entertainment was rooted in the earth and stars, and from this deep presence came profound insights about the world.

An article on Second Nexus News aligns with this idea, suggesting that Hanukkah's origins may have pagan roots. The author writes, "Many believe that Hanukkah's origins are rooted in pagan celebration. Jews may have been capturing a pagan solstice festival that had won wide support, and in order to make it a day of God's victory over paganism, they modified their own celebration. Even the lighting of candles for Hanukkah fits the context of the surrounding torchlight honors for the sun." The ancient Israelites, like their neighbors, were influenced by the sun-worshiping cultures around them, such as the Egyptians and Greeks, who honored sun gods like Ra and Zeus. Hanukkah, then, can be seen as both a continuation of and a pushback against these traditions.

This brings us to the Winter Solstice. The very word "solstice" reveals its connection to the sun, derived from the Latin "sol" (sun) and "sistere" (to stand still). During the solstices, the sun appears to pause at its farthest points before reversing direction. In the Northern Hemisphere, the winter solstice, around December 21-22, marks the longest night of the year, followed by a gradual return of daylight—a cosmic turning point that ancient people celebrated as a sign of hope and renewal.

Yuletide celebrations in ancient Germany followed similar themes. During December, the Norse people celebrated this shift of light with feasting, drinking, gift-giving, and games, honoring their gods as they prepared for the winter hunt. Today, this tradition has been absorbed into Christmas, a process that began in the 900s as Christianity spread across Europe.

The story of light and darkness is an ancient one. For millennia, humans have revered both the light and the dark. Unfortunately, in our modern world, darkness often gets a bad rap. But to the ancients, darkness was a time of rest and reflection, of stillness and peace. It was a cool, calm place where seeds grew, where ideas were fertilized; where dreams took shape. As we sing the hymn "Dark of Winter," pay attention to the lyrics:

> *"Dark of winter, soft and still,*
> *your quiet calm surrounds me.*
> *Let my thoughts go where they will,*
> *ease my mind profoundly.*
> *And then my soul will sing a song,*
> *a blessed song of love eternal.*
> *Gentle darkness, soft and still,*
> *bring your quiet to me."*

Shelley Jackson Denham's hymn blesses the darkness, inviting us to embrace its gentle, quiet presence. She captures the essence of this season, reminding us that darkness is not something to fear but a sacred space where stillness, rest, and renewal can flourish.

So how does Christmas fit into all this? As the Roman Empire expanded, ancient earth-based practices were absorbed and syncretized into Christian tradition. Even today, our Christmas traditions are echoes of old ways of worshiping the sun (SUN-day); the stars, and the earth. We may not light candles to honor the sun god directly, but we know we need the warmth of the sun's rays, just as the ancients did. The light, whether from the sun or the Son of God, renews us and moves us forward.

Christianity in the Western world continues this ancient symbolism, celebrating Christmas as a festival of light—the light of the sun and the light of love that Jesus, the Son of God, symbolizes. Hanukkah, Yule, Solstice, and Christmas are all about the same thing: sun worship—light returning, life enduring, hope reborn. They remind us to be resilient, to trust that there is enough light to carry us through, that whatever challenges we face will pass in due time.

So as you light your candles, decorate your trees, and sing your songs, remember that these rituals connect us to ancient practices. The lights on your tree are like the stars in the sky, a reminder of the billions of lights that have guided humanity for centuries. When you sing "O Christmas Tree," know that you are part of a tradition that stretches back thousands of years to pagan worship.

The word "pagan" itself is interesting. It means "country dweller," referring to those who practiced traditional religions outside the urban centers of early Christianity. As Christianity spread, pagans were often the last to convert, and the syncretism between their ancient practices and Christian beliefs helped ease the cultural transitions. While I don't blame any particular faith tradition for these changes, it's important to recognize that cultural and religious blending has always been part of our shared history.

My point is this: no single culture or religion owns this time of year. If anyone does, it's the sun, the moon, the earth, and the cosmos. Our ancestors understood this truth deeply.

As we reflect on these blended traditions, let us see the beauty in their diversity. Hanukkah, Yule, Solstice, Christmas —they all carry the same ancient message of light, love, rest, and renewal. Despite our modern distractions, we are still connected to these stories, still bound to the sun, the moon, the stars, and the earth. We are all part of something much larger, something sacred and majestic.

Take time to pause, reflect, and connect with the cycles of nature. Light your candles, sing your songs, and let this ancient wisdom remind you of your place in the great cosmic dance.

Amen.

References

1. **The Winter Solstice: The Sacred Traditions of Christmas, Hanukkah, and the New Year** by John Matthews – This book explores the historical and spiritual significance of the winter solstice and how it has influenced various traditions, including Christmas, Hanukkah, and other celebrations of light.
2. **The Stations of the Sun: A History of the Ritual Year in Britain** by Ronald Hutton – This comprehensive work delves into the seasonal festivals of Britain, including Yule, and explores how these ancient traditions were absorbed into modern religious practices like Christmas.
3. **Pagan Christmas: The Plants, Spirits, and Rituals at the Origins of Yuletide** by Christian Rätsch and Claudia Müller-Ebeling – This book provides an in-depth look at the pagan roots of many Christmas traditions, examining how elements like the Yule tree, gift-giving, and the celebration of light have ancient origins.
4. **The Golden Bough: A Study in Magic and Religion** by James Frazer – A classic study of myth and ritual, Frazer's work explores the common threads between ancient pagan traditions and modern religious practices, shedding light on the syncretism between different cultures' celebrations of light and rebirth.
5. **Dark of Winter** (Hymn) by Shelley Jackson Denham – This hymn, found in *Singing the Living Tradition* (Unitarian Universalist hymnbook), is an evocative piece that honors the quiet and reflective nature of winter's darkness, highlighting its spiritual and emotional significance.

23. "INSHA ALLAH": GOD'S WILL? BLESS YOU?

Our beliefs drive our thoughts, words, and actions. Today's world is struggling, in part, because too many extreme views threaten our present and future. These beliefs, often fear-based, build walls instead of bridges.

One major harm in the world today comes from fundamentalist religious views. Fundamentalism takes a literal approach to interpreting religious scriptures—whether Christian, Muslim, Jewish, or Buddhist. These scriptures can be interpreted in many ways, which is fine until someone decides their way is the only right way. If that person has power, they can impose their beliefs on others, often leading to harm. The remedy is to deepen our understanding, to discern what is true and what serves us well.

Years ago, I had a Muslim friend who often said "Insha Allah," meaning "God's will." This phrase is an Arabic expression translating to "if Allah wills." In Islam, it reflects the belief that everything happens according to God's divine will. This concept of surrender to God's will—accepting whatever outcome unfolds, whether yes, no, or not right now—shapes the life of a Muslim. It's a phrase used to cultivate humility, reverence, and selflessness. Not "I" but "Thou." Not 'Me' but 'Thee' that's the idea here.

There's something refreshing about this kind of humility, especially in a world filled with self-proclaimed experts and social media gurus. But there's also a darker side. Fundamentalists can misuse this belief to justify harmful actions, such as the suppression of women, holy wars, or hatred of non-Muslims. They claim these actions are God's will, making it difficult to question or challenge.

Christianity has its own complexities around God's will. The idea that God has a specific plan for each person is ingrained, often inherited from fundamentalist Judaism's strict obedience to divine command. For some, this belief becomes a dangerous justification for violence or exclusion. For centuries, people have acted in God's name, believing they were fulfilling divine will—sometimes with devastating consequences.

The phrase "God's will" reflects the belief in a divine plan guiding the universe, a comforting yet often misused concept. Who really knows what God's will is? When I told my friend that, "brother. Yes, no, or not right now," is the answer to everything related to God's will, it gave him pause, and then we both laughed out loud because he knew I'd stumped him. That's because life is uncertain and outcomes aren't always in our control. That uncertainty can be terrifying or freeing, depending on how you look at it.

In our faith tradition, I don't ask you to leave your brain at the door. We value questioning, thinking critically, and holding space for uncertainty. And this brings us to the phrase "Bless you." You've probably heard it said after a sneeze, but have you ever wondered why? Folklore says that sneezing could expel the spirit from the body, leaving a person vulnerable to evil forces or illness. Saying "bless you" was meant to protect and restore the spirit.

Today, "bless you" is often a casual expression of goodwill. It's a desire for positive outcomes, an expression of care, and a way to invoke divine favor. But when I once blessed someone in the church, they asked, "If you're blessing me, does that mean others are cursed?" The question startled me, but I understood it. The idea of blessings has often been intertwined with the notion of some being chosen and others not.

Blessing someone means wishing them well, asking for positivity, protection, and the best possible outcomes. It's not about exclusion but about extending goodwill and encouragement. It's about showing appreciation and support in a world that often needs more of both.

But what do we do with the phrase "Insha Allah" or "God's will" from this perspective? Maybe we can reframe it, refresh it, or make it meaningful for us. We live in a world with big problems, some solvable, some not. We can't control everything, and sometimes, letting go is the only option. "Letting go" means accepting that some things are beyond our control and embracing the flow of life. It's a way of surrendering to something bigger than ourselves.

This is, in some ways, saying "Insha Allah" or "not my will, but thy will be done." It's about acknowledging our limitations, our fragility, and the vastness of existence that is beyond our understanding. It's a surrender to the unknown, an acceptance that there's more at play than we can see or comprehend.

When we look at the vastness of space—the billions of galaxies, stars, and planets—we are reminded of our smallness, our place in a grand, mysterious cosmos. And sometimes, that is enough. To surrender, to let go, to accept that we are part of something much bigger.

I am a finite being with limitations and more questions than answers. But in my uncertainty, I find a blessing. It is in letting go and surrendering that I find peace. It's okay to believe in something greater, as long as that belief builds bridges, not walls.

So, "God's will" for me becomes "Goodwill." Goodwill toward all, for deep down, we all wrestle with big questions and seek understanding. I bless you in the name of love. I wish you all the good that life can bring. Blessings on this community, goodwill toward all beings.

Insha Allah.

Amen.

1. **You Were Made for So Much More** by John Crestwell – This book explores interfaith themes related to transformation, and embracing uncertainty, aligning with the sermon's message of letting go and trusting in something greater than oneself.
2. **The Quran** – The Quran frequently emphasizes the concept of "Insha Allah" (God's will) throughout its verses, particularly in Surah Al-Kahf (18:23-24), where it advises believers to always remember to say "Insha Allah" when making plans, highlighting the importance of divine will in daily life.
3. **The Bible** – The concept of divine will is deeply embedded in both the Old and New Testaments. For instance, in James 4:13-15, the Bible cautions against making plans without considering God's will, reminding readers to say, "If it is the Lord's will, we will live and do this or that." Jesus says in Luke 22:42 (KJV): *"Father, if thou be willing, remove this cup from me: nevertheless not my will, but thine, be done."*
4. **No God but God: The Origins, Evolution, and Future of Islam** by Reza Aslan – This book provides an accessible exploration of Islamic beliefs, including the concept of "Insha Allah" and the role of divine will in Muslim life, offering context for understanding these phrases.
5. **The Great Transformation: The Beginning of Our Religious Traditions** by Karen Armstrong – Armstrong's work examines the origins of major world religions, including Christianity and Islam, discussing how beliefs about divine will have influenced human history and

actions.

6. **Blessing: The Art and the Practice** by David Spangler –
   This book explores the concept of blessings as acts of
   goodwill, positivity, and spiritual connection, reflecting
   the sermon's theme of offering blessings and reframing
   traditional religious language.

SECTION 4:
UNITARIAN
UNIVERSALISM

24. THE TIPPING POINT

From the book *The Tipping Point* by Malcolm Gladwell:

"At the same time Paul Revere began his famous ride north and west of Boston, another revolutionary, a tanner named William Dawes, set out on the same urgent mission. Dawes took a similar route, carrying the same critical message over just as many miles as Revere. But unlike Revere, Dawes's ride didn't ignite the countryside. The local militia leaders weren't alerted, and few men from key towns like Waltham fought the next day. Historians once assumed Waltham was a pro-British community, but it wasn't. The people simply didn't hear the news in time. If the message alone were enough, Dawes would be as famous as Paul Revere. But he isn't. Why did Revere succeed where Dawes failed?"

Transformation. I love this word—it's powerful, full of possibility and hope. Transformation means change, conversion, renovation, and revolution. It's about becoming something new and better. Positive transformation is our focus today and understanding how we can make it happen. Transformation is a lifelong process. It can happen in seconds, or it can take years, even centuries. Our job is to recognize change, embrace it, engage it, and maximize the possibilities—one step at a time. As it is written, "Step by step, the longest march can be won." And though transformation often happens gradually, there are ways to fulfill our vision faster.

The reading today highlighted Paul Revere's historic ride. Why was Revere's message so effective while William Dawes's wasn't? Why did Revere's cry start a social epidemic that Dawes's did not? Malcolm Gladwell, in *The Tipping Point*, argues that Revere had a unique gift: a rare ability to communicate a message that compelled people to respond with direct action. Revere had the right knowledge, connections, and charisma to push the colonial militia forward in 1775. His cry was the tipping point that helped catalyze America's eventual freedom from Britain. Two men, same message, different results.

Gladwell's book shows how small things, when in the right hands, can make a huge difference. But it's not just about exceptional individuals; it's about the power of connections, the impact of human relationships, and how each of us, like pebbles in a pond, can create ripples that change communities, countries, and even the world.

Gladwell studies how things grow—businesses, movements, and organizations, all driven by people. He found that the most successful entities often share a key quality: what he calls the "stickiness factor." This stickiness, a combination of a compelling message and substantive content, often determines an organization's long-term success.

Think of it this way: you go shopping and see a "Buy one, get three free" deal on toilet paper. You're drawn in by the message and think you've scored a bargain. But when you try it, you find out the product is terrible. Will you buy it again? Absolutely not. No matter how enticing the message, if the product doesn't deliver, it's not going to stick. Your compelling message must also have compelling substance behind it. It's not just about grabbing attention; it's about delivering on the promise. The message might pull people in, but it's the quality of the experience, the integrity of the product, or the depth of the engagement that keeps them coming back. Without that real, meaningful connection, even the most attractive offer will eventually fall flat. It's the combination of a strong message and a solid foundation that creates lasting impact, whether in marketing, relationships, or our spiritual communities.

For a message to reach the few who will impact the many, it must not only grab attention but also offer something truly meaningful. It has to resonate deeply, compelling people to talk about it, integrate it into their lives, and share it with others. That's the essence of the stickiness factor: the message and the moment coming together in a powerful way.

Unitarian Universalism has some of the best slogans out there: "Different People. Different Beliefs. One Faith." "Home of the Free Spirit." "Answering the call of Love." These are catchy, inclusive, and compelling. But we need more than a good message. We need to embody the substance of our principles in everything we do.

We have a message so powerful that it was once labeled the "most dangerous faith in America" by a leader of another denomination. Why? Because our arms are open. Our doors are wide open, metaphorically speaking, and if our message ever truly caught on, it could change the world! But we haven't reached that tipping point yet.

The challenge is to live up to our ideals in tangible ways. We can't be the faith that says "all are welcome" while remaining largely homogeneous in a rapidly changing, multicultural world. We can't be the faith that welcomes diverse beliefs but struggles with differences in worship practices.

We need to understand what Gladwell calls the "Power of Context." A fascinating study at Princeton University explored how context can significantly influence our actions, even when our intentions are aligned with compassionate values. The researchers chose seminary students—individuals presumably inclined toward kindness and service—to participate in an experiment that revolved around the parable of the Good Samaritan. After a lesson on the importance of helping others, the students were asked to head to another building for a meeting. However, there was a twist: some students were told they were running late and needed to hurry, while others were told they had ample time to get there.

On their way, each student encountered a person lying on the ground, visibly in need of help. The results were telling: the students who believed they were pressed for time often hurried past the individual without stopping, their minds focused on their next task rather than the immediate need before them. In contrast, those who felt they had time to spare were far more likely to pause and offer assistance. The study revealed a profound truth: the context we find ourselves in—the pressure we feel, the urgency of our schedules—can dramatically alter our behavior, sometimes even overriding our moral compass.

This experiment shows that small things like feeling rushed can have a powerful impact on our decisions and actions. It's not just about what values we hold; it's also about how we navigate the moment-to-moment realities of our lives. The lesson is clear: context matters, often more than we realize, shaping our choices in ways that can either bring us closer to our ideals or pull us away from them.

Therefore, what people see, hear, and experience when they walk through our doors matters. It's not enough to have mission statements that say the right things. Our actions, our interactions, our worship, and our teachings need to reflect our message fully. Living our faith means embodying our principles in our thoughts, words, and deeds. It's about the little things that create a big impact.

For our faith to transform into a fully intergenerational, multicultural community, we need a conscious, deliberate, and loving effort. We must engage in personal transformation —doing our own inventory on our own biases, preferences and prejudices and ask, "how can I be more open?" By doing the small things–the small "t" transformations, we set the stage for the BIG "T" Transformations that can reshape ourselves and our congregations into true reflections of the Beloved Community.

Who knows—you might be the pebble that creates the ripple leading Unitarian Universalism into a new era.

To close, I want to share one more thought from Gladwell's second book, *Blink*:

> *"When it comes to understanding ourselves and our world, we often pay too much attention to grand themes and too little to fleeting moments... But what if we examined our own decision-making? The little things... could change the way wars are fought, the products on our shelves, the kinds of movies that get made. And if we combined all those little changes, we would end up with a different and better world."*

May it be so. Amen.

References

1. *The Tipping Point and Paul Revere's Ride* explores the comparison between Paul Revere and William Dawes and analyzes their differing impacts during the Revolutionary War. (**Gladwell, Malcolm. *The Tipping Point: How Little Things Can Make a Big Difference.* Little, Brown and

Company, 2000.)

2. The Stickiness Factor discusses the concept of compelling messages combined with substance to create a lasting impact. (Gladwell, Malcolm. *The Tipping Point: How Little Things Can Make a Big Difference.* Little, Brown and Company, 2000.)

3. Princeton University Study on Context and the Good Samaritan illustrates how context affects our actions, even among those inclined to act compassionately. (Darley, John M., and Batson, C. Daniel. "From Jerusalem to Jericho: A Study of Situational and Dispositional Variables in Helping Behavior." *Journal of Personality and Social Psychology,* 1973.)

4. The Power of Context focuses on understanding how the environment and situational factors influence behavior. (Gladwell, Malcolm. *The Tipping Point: How Little Things Can Make a Big Difference.* Little, Brown and Company, 2000.)

5. Living Our Faith and Principles highlights the importance of embodying Unitarian Universalist values in actions and interactions, not just in mission statements. (Unitarian Universalist Association. "Our Principles." UUA.org.)

25. DECOLONIZING OUR SPIRITUALITY: A RETURN TO EARTH-CENTERED ROOTS

I want to take you on a journey—a journey that takes us back to the origins of human spirituality and moves us forward toward a more integrated, earth-centered faith. This sermon is about decolonizing our spirituality, about reclaiming the sacred practices and understandings that have been pushed aside by centuries of conquest, colonization, and cultural suppression.

Let's begin with the original human connection—with the earth. Earth-based cultures moved with the rhythms of the natural world. They sang and danced, beat drums, and told stories, all within the traditional frameworks of their communities. These cultures were steeped in the wisdom of hunter-gatherers and agrarian societies. Daniel Quinn, in his seminal work, reminds us that hunter-gatherers were "leavers"—taking only what they needed from the earth. In contrast, agrarian societies became "takers," cultivating and expanding their reach in ways that often exploited the land. Quinn argues that while we need both perspectives, the takers have dominated our relationship with the planet for far too long.

This disconnection from the earth intensified with the rise of the Roman Empire, Christianity, and the spread of Western civilization. The expansion of the Roman Catholic Church, especially in Europe and then to the Americas, further severed humanity's connection with its earth-based roots. The first teachings of Christianity were deeply entwined with nature, blending earth, mind, body, and soul. Yet, as Christianity spread, it supplanted the indigenous spiritualities of those it conquered. Even within Protestantism, the earth-centered elements were largely lost, leaving behind a spirituality disconnected from the natural world.

We often see earth-based practices—like dancing, chanting, and the use of fire and percussion—as "primitive" or superstitious. But these practices are deeply spiritual, full of rich meaning and power. African traditions such as Voodoo and Santeria, often misunderstood and vilified, are beautiful expressions of earth-centered spirituality. When we study them deeply, we discover layers of wisdom, rituals that connect us to the elements of fire, wind, water, and earth. These elements are not just symbolic—they are integral to our understanding of the world. Fire represents action, wind brings change, water symbolizes rebirth, and earth grounds us. We are not separate from these elements; we are part of them. As the ancient teachings say, "Thou art that."

Our modern spiritual traditions, including Christianity, still contain echoes of these earth-based roots. Rituals like lighting candles, kneeling, or invoking blessings are calls to connect with the powers of heaven and earth. The problem is, much of this knowledge has been hidden, reserved for the clergy while the common folk were kept in the dark. The sacred was cloaked in mystery, perpetuating the idea that only a select few could access divine wisdom. But now, you are the priest. You are the keeper of the sacred. Our gatherings are where sacred souls come together, not just as individuals, but as a collective consciousness. Together, we heal and draw strength for the journey ahead.

When we pray, "Thy kingdom come, thy will be done on earth as it is in heaven," we are calling for a reality where heaven and earth are united—where the spiritual and the physical coexist in harmony. This is not some distant, future kingdom; it is a present reality that we can embody here and now. This is earth-based spirituality, woven throughout Christian and Hebrew scriptures and seen in the traditions of our ancestors.

Today, many of us identify with earth-centered spirituality, whether through CUUPS (Covenant of Unitarian Universalist Pagans), Wicca, or other traditions that honor the natural world. These paths remind us that to decolonize our faith, we must move from a Eurocentric to a multicentric perspective, embracing religious syncretism—a blending of different spiritual traditions. Decolonizing our spirituality means going back to go forward. We reclaim our relationship with the earth not only through social justice but also in our worship. We reconnect with the symbolic and literal meanings of the elements, tapping into our full power for healing ourselves and the world.

The future of our faith lies in the past—the ancient, earth-connected practices that have been marginalized and forgotten. In our Unitarian Universalist communities, we must realize that our gatherings are not just meetings but sacred spaces where collective consciousness shapes our values and actions. Our work is to embody this awareness, to connect more intentionally with nature, and to use our senses in worship—whether through meditation, yoga, or simply walking in the woods. As we deepen this connection, we prepare for the emergence of a new green society—one that is decolonized, freeing, and joyous.

In this reimagined spiritual community, I see more movement

for those who are able, more rituals with deep, explained meanings so their full power can be understood. I see a blending of the sacred and the everyday, where hidden teachings become visible and accessible to all. Questions like, "Why do we kneel? Why do we light candles? What do the elements truly mean?" become opportunities for discovery. We stand in circles, honoring sacred geometry. We design our spaces with intention, using feng shui principles to generate more light, energy, and love.

Our work is to reclaim what has been lost—to understand why we do what we do, to find the deeper meanings behind our rituals, and to embrace a spirituality that celebrates our connection to the earth and the cosmos. We are not separate from the elements; we are part of the grand tapestry of existence, woven together in a dance of fire, wind, water, and earth. In this new understanding, the esoteric becomes exoteric, the hidden becomes seen, the unknown becomes known.

As your minister, I hope to walk with you on this journey, growing together in our understanding of what it means to decolonize our spirituality. Let us remember that the kingdom is not some distant hope; it is here, now, in every act of wholeness and connection. Let us reclaim our earth-centered roots and boldly move forward, creating a faith that honors all of creation.

Amen.

References:

1. Daniel Quinn's **Ishmael: An Adventure of the Mind and Spirit** (Bantam Books, 1992) offers a critical exploration of the divide between hunter-gatherer societies, which he describes as "leavers," and agrarian societies, termed "takers." Quinn argues that the latter's domination over the earth has severed our spiritual connection with nature. His insights are foundational for understanding how

our current spiritual disconnection stems from historical shifts in human civilization.

2. Gustavo Gutiérrez's **A Theology of Liberation: History, Politics, and Salvation** (Orbis Books, 1973) emphasizes reclaiming marginalized voices and spiritualities, highlighting how colonization and conquest have suppressed earth-centered spiritual practices. Gutiérrez's work is essential for understanding the intersection of spirituality, social justice, and decolonization.

3. Fikret Berkes' **Sacred Ecology** (Routledge, 2012) examines traditional ecological knowledge among indigenous and local peoples, showing how spirituality and earth-based practices are deeply intertwined. Berkes provides a thorough analysis of how ancient spiritualities are connected to ecological stewardship, making it a valuable resource for reclaiming these traditions.

4. David Tacey's **The Spirituality Revolution: The Emergence of Contemporary Spirituality** (Routledge, 2004) explores the movement away from institutionalized religion towards a spirituality that is more nature-based, embodied, and personal. Tacey's work helps contextualize the modern shift back to earth-centered spiritual practices and rituals.

5. Bell Hooks' **Belonging: A Culture of Place** (Routledge, 2008) reflects on the intersections of place, nature, and spirituality, challenging dominant Western and Eurocentric narratives. hooks invites readers to reconnect with a more inclusive, earth-centered way of being, providing a framework for understanding the spiritual implications of cultural dislocation.

6. Starhawk's **The Earth Path: Grounding Your Spirit in the Rhythms of Nature** (HarperOne, 2004) delves into the practices of modern earth-based spirituality, offering insights into how reconnecting with nature's rhythms can heal and transform our spiritual lives. Starhawk's teachings are especially relevant for understanding the power of ritual and movement in spiritual practice.

7. Malidoma Patrice Somé's **Of Water and the Spirit: Ritual, Magic, and Initiation in the Life of an African Shaman** (Penguin Books, 1994) provides a profound exploration of indigenous African spirituality and rituals, offering a

window into earth-based traditions that were suppressed by colonial powers. Somé's work helps us appreciate the depth and significance of earth-centered spiritual practices and their potential to reconnect us with our ancestral roots.

26. NEW AMERICAN
TRANSCENDENTALISM

The reading today is a poem titled "Reflections and Meditations for Spiritual Awakening" by Steve Taylor. Taylor, a renowned figure in transpersonal psychology, blends modern psychology with spirituality, drawing on the thinking of William James, Carl Jung, and Abraham Maslow. He challenges us to embrace strangeness and awe in our everyday lives:

"Don't let the world become familiar—don't forget the sheer strangeness of being alive. Don't forget the sheer strangeness of being here on the surface of this spinning globe. Don't forget the sheer strangeness of being this body that breathes and blinks and heals and grows—a miracle of precision and complexity. Don't forget the strangeness of seeming to be a ghostly self that lives inside your body, that has attached itself to your form, that seems to stare out from your eyes and can spin webs of logic, create alternate abstract worlds. Don't forget the sheer strangeness of this world of form where matter pulses with consciousness. It's a strangeness even stranger because it's not hostile or indifferent but right and reassuring, somehow warm and welcoming, like a chaos that was always planned, a riddle that makes perfect sense, a cacophony of meaning, full of hidden

harmony."

I want to explore what it means to be a New American Transcendentalist. As Unitarian Universalists, we are part of a transcending faith—a tradition that stretches us to define our understanding of the divine, or even to embrace the absence of it. To transcend means to go beyond, and my goal today is to help you move beyond the limitations that hold you back from unity, peace, and balance. I hope my message encourages you to transcend the dichotomies that divide us and embrace a new understanding, much like our Transcendentalist ancestors who moved beyond traditional Christianity.

We are witnessing a paradigm shift in Western society, a convergence of the linear and nonlinear, of science and spirituality. This shift challenges us to see the world as a unified whole, not as separate parts. We are moving from a world defined by "either/or" thinking—where we separate ourselves by race, class, gender, and more—to a "both/and" reality. Evolution is pushing us forward, and we must choose to adapt and embrace the change or risk being left behind.

This shift involves a move from linear thinking to quantum thinking, where the future is shaped by our perception of the past in the present moment. The term "paradigm shift" was popularized by Thomas Kuhn in his book, *The Structure of Scientific Revolutions,* describing it as a fundamental change in basic concepts and practices within a discipline. A paradigm shift occurs when new ideas challenge established norms, often clashing with what we consider "normal."

Historically, we've seen paradigm shifts with figures like Copernicus and Galileo, whose groundbreaking discoveries forever changed our understanding of the universe. These shifts often meet with fierce resistance, as people cling to established beliefs, but over time, they transform our worldviews and open up new possibilities. This pattern of resistance followed by transformation is evident not just in science, but in how societies evolve.

Even though these changes can be tumultuous, they often lead to progress. As Steven Pinker points out in *The Better Angels of Our Nature*, despite our ongoing struggles and conflicts, humanity has gradually become less violent and more cooperative over time. This long-term trend toward greater peace and reduced violence reminds us that, though paradigm shifts can be uncomfortable, they often pave the way for a better, more enlightened world.

Every paradigm shift requires daring individuals to think outside the box. As Unitarian Universalists, we have consistently positioned ourselves on the front lines of societal change—championing marriage equality, advocating for LGBTQ+ rights, and working tirelessly to dismantle racism. But our journey doesn't stop there. Now, we are being called to go further, to challenge not just the social norms but also the very ways we perceive reality. It's time to embrace a non-dual understanding of existence, where God and truth are not confined to "either/or" but are instead expansive, inclusive, and "both/and." This means moving beyond binary thinking that separates us into categories and embracing the sacredness in the intersections, the complexities, and the blending of opposites. By doing so, we continue our legacy of transformative action, but now with a broader, deeper spiritual awareness that sees unity in diversity and finds the divine in every aspect of life.

This brings me to Sir Isaac Newton, whose contributions to science helped shape our linear thinking. While Newton's scientific method revolutionized our understanding of the world, it also became its own form of dogma, dismissive of anything that could not be empirically proven. Traditional religion made the same error, enforcing dogmatic beliefs that stifled new ideas. Are we, as UUs stuck in our own dogma?

New paradigms are emerging today that integrate science, spirituality, and the unknown. Quantum physics, the double-slit experiment, and the science of complementarity reveal a reality filled with awe and mystery. The world is shifting toward a "both/and" narrative, blending the scientific and the spiritual, the known and the unknown.

Quantum thinking asks us to look beyond linear equations and see the interconnectedness of all things. It's about shifting perspectives and embracing the unknown. A circle reminds us that we are more than just straight lines; we are also curved, diverse, and multifaceted. We are asked to solve for "X," the unknown, embracing the strangeness and awe of existence.

Dorn Swerdlin, speaking at a conference of actuaries, captured this shift beautifully when he said:

> "The first idea is that Newtonian thinking talks about 'either/or.' It is either this or that, whereas the quantum point of view is 'both/and.' Quantum thinking is more multidimensional... A third alternative might have no relationship to the other and can emerge as completely different."

This is process theology in action, where two ideas create a third, something entirely new. As George Hegel's dialectic suggests, tension between opposing ideas creates synthesis—a new reality. We must embrace this multidimensional thinking as we navigate the complexities of our evolving world.

As you consider your personal journey, think beyond traditional boundaries. Dare to do something different, just as our Transcendentalist ancestors did. They saw that God was bigger than any one book, and they dared to explore new spiritual landscapes.

We live in unprecedented times—a 21st century of probability and possibility, of science and spirituality, of you and me. Let us transcend the old paradigms and embrace the new. In the name of transformation I leave these words.

Amen.

References:

1. **The Structure of Scientific Revolutions** by Thomas Kuhn – Kuhn's concept of paradigm shifts provides a foundation for understanding how transformative changes in thought occur across disciplines, including religion and science.
2. **Better Angels of Our Nature: Why Violence Has Declined** by Steven Pinker – Pinker argues that, despite current conflicts, humanity is moving towards a more peaceful and cooperative state, reflecting the positive potential of paradigm shifts.
3. **A New Earth: Awakening to Your Life's Purpose** by Eckhart Tolle – Tolle's work discusses the shift from egoic, dualistic thinking to a more conscious, interconnected perspective, aligning with the idea of embracing a "both/and" reality.
4. **The Tao of Physics: An Exploration of the Parallels Between Modern Physics and Eastern Mysticism** by Fritjof Capra – Capra draws parallels between quantum physics and Eastern spiritual traditions, emphasizing a non-dual understanding of reality.
5. **Religion and Science: Historical and Contemporary Issues** by Ian G. Barbour – Barbour's work provides insight into how scientific advances challenge traditional religious beliefs, supporting the idea of a convergence between science and spirituality.
6. **The Varieties of Religious Experience** by William James – James explores the personal, experiential aspects of religion, contributing to the idea that spirituality can transcend traditional boundaries.
7. **The Essential Writings of Ralph Waldo Emerson** edited by Brooks Atkinson – Emerson's writings, foundational to

Transcendentalism, advocate for an expansive view of God and nature that aligns with your call for a "both/and" understanding of reality.

8. **Reality is Not What It Seems: The Journey to Quantum Gravity** by Carlo Rovelli – Rovelli's exploration of quantum physics challenges conventional notions of space, time, and reality, supporting the shift from linear to quantum thinking.

9. **Integral Spirituality: A Startling New Role for Religion in the Modern and Postmodern World** by Ken Wilber – Wilber integrates science, spirituality, and philosophy, aligning with the concept of transcending dualistic thinking.

10. **Wholeness and the Implicate Order** by David Bohm – Bohm's work on quantum theory and holistic thinking echoes the sermon's call for embracing interconnectedness and seeing reality as a unified whole.

11. **Transpersonal Psychology: Exploring the Farther Reaches of Human Nature** by Abraham Maslow – Maslow's work on human potential and spirituality supports the call for a non-dual understanding of reality that transcends traditional religious boundaries.

12. **Process Theology: A Guide for the Perplexed** by Bruce G. Epperly – Epperly's book on process theology supports the idea of a dynamic, evolving understanding of God that transcends rigid doctrines.

13. **New Thought: A Practical American Spirituality** by C. Alan Anderson and Deborah G. Whitehouse – This book explores the New Thought movement, which shares similarities with Transcendentalism and emphasizes a non-dual, inclusive view of the divine.

27. HERETICS FAITH: PRAYER, MEDITATION, CONTEMPLATION

We, Unitarian Universalists, call ourselves heretics because we are not orthodox–among the accepted traditional protestant faith traditions. I'm left-handed and that's not orthodox either and that's just fine by me. Ours is a living tradition that is non creedal. This place we find ourselves in historically as a chosen faith oftentimes puts us at odds with religious language. For far too long, we've struggled with religious language, often distancing ourselves from it. But we must remember that Unitarian Universalism at its core is a religion. We are both a spiritual and secular faith, an institution grounded in a sacred system of beliefs.

In our evolving journey of consciousness, what are we, UUs, ultimately seeking? I believe we want transcendence—a way of perceiving life that moves beyond the literal and the tribal. We're seeking something deeper–a divine experience of wholeness. Our goal is unity consciousness, not separation. The old ways we ran from often remind us of division. We don't want that and yet we carry our baggage with us and some of those ways have followed here. We too can become trapped by polarization–stuck in dichotomies that split people, places, and ideas. But as a heretical faith—a dynamic, living tradition —Unitarian Universalism must never be stuck. Our spiritual evolution calls us to continually expand beyond limitations. This, at its heart, is what it means to be a religious liberal: to grow, to transcend, and to seek deeper connections that unite rather than divide.

As Rev. Dr. Fredric Muir writes in his book *Heretics Faith:*

> *Vocabulary for Religious Liberals, "...like the word heretic, liberal has a special meaning for UUs: its root means 'to be generous and open.' As religious liberals, we seek deeper and wider understanding, greater tolerance, broader definition, more inclusive language; we want to stretch our minds and souls, pushing the limits of thought and spirit, redefining the boundaries of tradition and orthodoxy." Today, that's exactly what I wish to do—seek deeper understanding, broader definitions, and more inclusive language to stretch our minds.*

Which takes me to the religious traditions of prayer, meditation, and contemplation. For me, these are fundamentally the same spiritual practice. While their subtle differences can be explored, they all aim for the same outcomes: oneness, tranquility, centeredness, community, unity, healing, and love. We need time for prayer, meditation, and contemplation to calm our mind and bodies when the storms of life rage. In the eye of even the most powerful storm, there is stillness. That stillness is the zero point, the calm center. It's like gazing at a mandala, where the focus is always drawn to the center. Mysticism offers a similar teaching, as seen in the 231 gates of initiation: focusing on the center leads you to your true self, the place where you recognize that you are as Teilhard de Chardin says, "made by love for love."

Prayer, meditation, contemplation, stillness, and silence are all pathways that lead us to love. Whether in quiet or in moments filled with noise, we naturally turn to these practices as part of our human experience. In times of happiness or sorrow, joy or solitude, courage or fear, we instinctively turn inward, seeking connection and solace within ourselves.

Now, let's explore the subtleties. Traditional prayer, as we've learned in church, is often formulaic and different from meditation or contemplation. Prayer can be communal, such as those offered at special occasions, dinners, blessings, or community events, with the intent of bringing people together and consecrating a specific space. These prayers typically follow a pattern with elements like praise or thanksgiving, repentance or confession, intercession for others, blessings, and an ending.

Rev. Fred Muir, quoting Greta Crosby, wrote that there are four types of prayers: conflict, sorrow, peace, and joy. These prayers, though rooted in tradition, follow ancient formulas. This pattern has been used by cultures as diverse as the Nubians, Egyptians, and Hindus. Why does it persist? Because it works!

When I "pray" publicly, I use this basic formula. Here are three short examples:

1. **Christian Prayer:**
   God, our Father, we thank you for this day. We praise your holy name. We are grateful for the life you've given us. Forgive us where we have sinned and fallen short of your glory. We pray for the sick and those in pain, asking that you heal them physically and spiritually through the power of your Holy Spirit. Bless us, let your will be done and your kingdom come. In the name of Jesus Christ, our Lord, Amen.
2. **Earth-Based Tradition Prayer:**

Spirit of Life, we give thanks for this day. We give thanks for the earth, sea, and sky. We are grateful for the life and love we have. May we be reminded of where we have missed the mark. We ask for healing energies to be with us and those in need. We pray for the sick and those in pain, hoping for their swift recovery. May we find inner and outer peace in our quest for beloved community. Blessings on this community. In the name of all that is holy, Amen.

3. **Unitarian Universalist Prayer:**
We give thanks for this day, for life, love, and health. We are grateful for what we have. Let us strive to do our best every day and not be too hard on ourselves. We remember those who are sick and in pain, sending healing thoughts for their speedy recovery. May we be reminded of our highest aspirations in our quest for beloved community. Blessings on this community. May it be so.

Though distinct, these prayers all follow the same pattern —a pattern refined through thousands of years of experimentation. But as I said, these types of prayers differ from meditation and contemplation, which are less formulaic and more aligned with personal spiritual practice.

Rev. Muir writes, *"Prayer is an opportunity in conflict, sorrow, peace, or joy to see life in a larger way, to see life as a vision, living in connection instead of separation, gaining a sense of being tied to something other than what we can see and feel in our immediate circle of people and things."* Prayer, in this sense, is a gateway to deeper understanding—a way to look beneath the surface to the greater wisdom that lies beneath. It is a place to take our burdens and sorrows, to find joy and comfort.

Non-formulaic prayer, unlike traditional structured prayer, closely resembles meditation and contemplation, guiding us into a deeper, more intimate spiritual space. It's not about reciting words but about quieting the mind and turning inward. This distinction reminds me of passages from the New Testament, where it says, "Jesus went to the Garden of Gethsemane to pray," or when he is described as praying for long periods. These stories, often read literally, are deeply allegorical and point to a different practice. Jesus was not engaging in repeated, spoken prayers for hours—he was meditating. Like the Buddha and other spiritual teachers, he was engaging in a profound inward journey, seeking stillness and inner connection rather than simply following a formula.

To pray traditionally means to call on, beseech, or petition—to ask for guidance, help, or strength. But prayer can also mean to invoke, tapping into the spirit or inner power within us. When Jesus went to pray, he wasn't merely speaking words; he was meditating, drawing on his inner strength. His story of temptation in the desert is similar to the biblical narrative of Jacob wrestling with the angel—a powerful metaphor for the inner battles we all face. We wrestle with our thoughts, fears, and doubts, but through meditation and prayer, we find release and transformation. After overcoming his struggle, Jesus began his ministry, and Jacob, after his night of wrestling, was reborn with a new name—Israel. Both stories are about facing internal conflict and emerging renewed and ready for the next chapter.

We all sit with our thoughts, searching for release or answers. Just as our bodies heal when we rest—going to sleep in pain and waking up feeling refreshed—prayer, contemplation, and meditation provide a similar kind of healing for our minds and spirits. These practices allow us to move beyond mere words, helping us reframe religious language and uncover the deeper wisdom that lies within us.

Every practice has levels or stages of development. With meditation and stillness, it's about going deeper into the mind until we experience detachment from pain and constraint.

Each level of letting go brings new awareness. The great sages tapped into these deeper levels of consciousness, connecting the conscious with the superconscious. They had intentional spiritual practices, sitting in silence until the inner turmoil passed.

For those who practice regularly, you understand the calm within the storm—the zero-point where healing and insight naturally arise. This is the theta brain state, a place of deep relaxation and calm where we release control and allow life to flow. It's why sleep and rest are essential for creativity, healing, and managing anxiety.

Some believe these states of consciousness give us access to the collective unconscious, the hive mind where all thoughts and possibilities exist. It's in moments of stillness that inventors, writers, and creators often find their greatest inspiration. The answers, the questions, the breakthroughs, the "peace that surpasses understanding"—they're all waiting in this quiet space.

The ancients understood this, and our modern, secular culture is beginning to rediscover it. When we meditate, contemplate, or simply pause, we connect with our best selves. Without intentional practice, we risk becoming reactive, tossed about by the randomness of life. A consistent spiritual practice helps us remain calm amidst chaos, guiding us back to a place of peace, clarity, and power.

Rev. Muir wisely said, *"Life can be a prayer; but only if you maintain a sense of awareness of what's going on. If you blindly walk through your days...without giving them any thought, context or grounding...then there won't be any sense of prayer to life."* When you see life as a prayer, every moment becomes an opportunity to connect deeply, to live beyond randomness, and to find calm perspective.

My prayer for you today is that this peace, this tranquility, this calm be yours today. May it be so.

Amen.

References:

1. **Heretics Faith: Vocabulary for Religious Liberals** by Fred Muir – Muir's work provides a foundational understanding of the liberal religious approach, emphasizing openness, deeper understanding, and the redefining of traditional religious boundaries.
2. **The Varieties of Religious Experience** by William James – James explores the personal nature of religious and spiritual experiences, aligning with the sermon's emphasis on meditation, prayer, and contemplation as pathways to inner transformation.
3. **The Power of Now: A Guide to Spiritual Enlightenment** by Eckhart Tolle – Tolle's teachings on presence, stillness, and the meditative state underscore the transformative power of going inward, resonating with your emphasis on meditation as a way to connect deeply with oneself.
4. **Man and His Symbols** by Carl Jung – Jung's exploration of the collective unconscious supports the idea of tapping into a shared well of thoughts and inspiration through deep meditative and contemplative states.
5. **The Bible, New Testament** – The references to Jesus praying in the Garden of Gethsemane and his time in the desert are used allegorically in the sermon to illustrate deeper spiritual practices, aligning with themes of meditation and internal struggle.
6. **Wholeness and the Implicate Order** by David Bohm – Bohm's work on holistic thinking and the interconnectedness of all things supports the sermon's emphasis on non-duality and the unity found through contemplative practices.
7. **The Essential Writings of Ralph Waldo Emerson** edited by Brooks Atkinson – Emerson's emphasis on self-reliance, inner wisdom, and the connection between the individual and the divine echoes the call for deeper, non-formulaic spiritual practices.
8. **Siddhartha** by Hermann Hesse – Hesse's novel illustrates the journey of meditation and self-discovery, reflecting the

transformative power of going inward and finding peace amid life's challenges.

9. **The Tao of Physics: An Exploration of the Parallels Between Modern Physics and Eastern Mysticism** by Fritjof Capra – Capra's exploration of the convergence between modern science and ancient spiritual wisdom supports the sermon's themes of unity and transcending dichotomies.

10. **The Book of Secrets: Unlocking the Hidden Dimensions of Your Life** by Deepak Chopra – Chopra's work explores the deeper dimensions of meditation and consciousness, aligning with your emphasis on spiritual practices that lead to inner calm and healing.

28. WHY I AM A UNITARIAN UNIVERSALIST

I wrote these words in my book The Charge of the Chalice:

It was summer 2001. I was a recent theological school graduate and had just finished writing the last few pages of my first book when I read something that rocked my world! I had been analyzing various religions in America over the last few months, using Leo Rosten's Religions of America, a religious almanac, and had gone through at least two dozen faiths, not finding one that met my theological, psychological, or sociological needs. I was near the end of the book when I saw the heading: Unitarian Universalism. "What in the hell is that?" I thought. I began perusing the chapter. What I read changed my life. In fact, it "rocked my world"! I read a summary on Unitarian Universalism — its history, principles, and legacy, and could not believe such a religion existed! As I read the words, tears came down my face. This was manna from heaven, and I ate every word. I examined the few pages over and over until my soul was full.

I read about a religion that did not believe in a specific creed but upheld the worth and dignity of all human beings. I read about a religion that recognized the many truths in life and honored each religion's unique but similar message. I read about a faith that respected Buddhists, Humanists, Taoists, Agnostics, Christians, Muslims, and Atheists alike. I read about a phenomenal faith that asked its adherents to freely find their spiritual path and celebrate the journey. A religion that honored differences. A belief system that almost exactly matched mine. I said to myself, in that wonderful moment, "I'm going to be a Unitarian Universalist minister!"

I never wanted to be a minister. I wanted to be a sportscaster. There was no special event that brought me to ministry. I didn't have an Apostle Paul-like experience with a bright light or a voice from heaven calling me. Instead, there were many signals and events over the course of ten years that led me to accept my call. Like some Native American cultures where the community calls its Shaman to serve as healer and teacher, my community of friends, family, and associates called me to ministry. Yet, even with all the affirmations, at the time I learned about Unitarian Universalism, I was a "Motherless Child," a man with a theological degree, $40,000 of post-graduate educational debt, and no place to minister. I was wandering through a philosophical wilderness—a lonely place.

I was frequently depressed as I contemplated the meaning of life. I had left the United Methodist Church months before over theological issues and had long since dropped out of their path to ministry. I am truly thankful for the writings of Joseph Campbell, Daniel Quinn, John Shelby Spong, Timothy Freke, and others whose books saved my life! They showed me I wasn't alone in having what I thought were "radical" religious ideas. I had gone from being a religious fundamentalist to a religious, liberal free thinker. I went from condemning my first girlfriend's dad to Hell to not believing in a literal Hell at all.

But I needed a place to live out my new beliefs. I was a church person. Grew up in the church. Where would I go? Davies Memorial UUC. It happened. It finally happened! I "was lost but now I was found." I didn't know I was searching for Unitarian Universalism, but I was. I found my life's call and my journey through the wilderness was over. I was reborn that day, and that is why the tears flowed. I knew this was what I was searching for. I was going to be a Unitarian Universalist and a UU minister!"

That's how I became a UU and, more importantly, a UU minister. My first congregation was Davies Memorial UU in Camp Springs, Maryland, named after Rev. Dr. A. Powell Davies, a significant figure in Unitarian Universalism. Davies was an early influence on my understanding of what UU, at its best, can be—a place where we say, "An end to all exclusions"—not some souls included, but ALL souls!

Rev. Dr. A. Powell Davies was the longtime minister at All Souls Church in Washington, DC, and helped start many of the area's congregations as "satellite churches." He was immensely popular in his time, a kind of UU rock star. The people at Davies shared how, when they were a young congregation, they would put on their worship service, but when it was time for the sermon, they'd tune into a radio channel that broadcast Dr. Davies' sermons live on Sunday. They would "watch the radio" for 30 minutes, finishing their service after his message. That's what early Unitarian Universalism was like in the Washington DC Metropolitan area in the 1950s.

Religious liberalism was thriving then, matching the 1950s post-World War II optimism—a belief that humanity could defeat evil and prosper. Hitler was dead; Nazism was destroyed. But, as we know, liberalism didn't go deep enough. It failed to fully include Black and Brown people. Rev. Dr. King often spoke of his disappointment with liberalism's over-optimism and its lack of a theological response to the evils of racism.

Dr. Davies preached, "We are a religion that proclaims that humanity is not divided—except by ignorance and prejudice and hate." These were wise and aspirational words, but they also challenged us. Unitarian Universalism, like other institutions, has excluded and been prejudiced. So, we cannot yet claim to be the FREE church where everybody, regardless of race or socioeconomic status, can come to worship in spirit and truth. Not yet.

And that's our work today—to be radically welcoming and to share our message more broadly with those seeking a faith that strives for greatness. We are each called to be stewards of this living tradition, embracing its high ideals and committing to radical acceptance. We are called to welcome the stranger, manifest love in all its forms, and embody our values in all we do.

So why did you come to be a part of this religion? What compelled you to embrace the call of religious freedom? Why has Unitarian Universalism drawn you to this community and this transformative work?

For me, there is a scripture that says it all: "To whom much is given, much is required." This faith saved my life, so I feel called to give back—to offer my time, talent, and treasure because, with "great freedom comes great responsibility." To be part of a tradition that prides itself on religious freedom is a rare gift in a world dominated by fundamentalism. I want to preserve this faith, this church, and this community because it is a vital voice in a world of polarization and division.

This religion has stood by me through raising my children, divorce, cancer, the loss of my parents and more. It's been there during the trials and tribulations I've faced over the years. This faith, and the people I've met along the way, have made me feel cared for, supported, validated, and affirmed.

It's been a long time now but back then I was lost and unsure about where to find a community of people who shared similar understandings. It was lonely. And in that book, *Religions of America*, way in the back under U for Unitarian Universalism (it was alphabetized), I found manna from heaven and immediately knew it was a gift. And I said YES and haven't looked back. Friends, our lives are filled with death experiences—losing things, letting things go, and finding new things. When I lost my religion, I knew I wasn't a traditional, literalist Christian. I knew I was something "divergent." There were many dark nights of the soul back then, but they were precursors to many bright days of transformation. This renewal has occurred over and over in my life—so much so that I trust the process. I believe it conspires for me, teaching me to be more resilient and persevering in my quest to live an authentic life. How has your faith challenged you to live an authentic life?

Friends, endings come. But so do new beginnings. I will keep saying YES because, as Theodore Parker says, there are transients and permanents in life—"change alone is unchanging," said Heraclitus of Ephesus. An easier way to say it is LOVE is permanent. And love comes again for you "in due season if you faint not." That is truly the only message of UUism; that LOVE is the spirit of our church. In all the transient ideas, dogmas, and ideologies, what remains the same is love. I am a UU and will always be a UU as long as LOVE is at the center of what we do. Our central task, then, is to *become better lovers.*

I am a Unitarian Universalist because this faith has changed me. It challenges my assumptions, allows me to let go of fear-based narratives, and calls me to be my best self. I have learned more about life and myself from being a UU, and that matters. I have been able to challenge and change many of my suppositions and presuppositions. I believe it has made me a better human being—a more humane being—and I've come to understand differences and diversity in ways I never imagined. There is no other institutional church like this in America—in the world. If there is, please show it to me, and I'll gladly retract my statement.

I said YES to Unitarian Universalism decades ago (in a very emotional moment), and I am grateful for deciding to make this my chosen faith. I did not choose this faith to do social justice (even though I know that's important). I did not choose UU to save the planet (important work). I chose it because I needed affirmation of my humanity; I needed a beloved community to raise my family and to grow my soul. In the process, I also found a calling.

Friends, as long as we continue to say YES to the call of that Supreme Love, Unitarian Universalism will not only survive but thrive, lighting the way for generations to come.

Amen.

References

1. **John T. Crestwell, Jr., *The Charge of the Chalice: The Davies Memorial Growth & Diversity Story* (2005)** – John's book recounts his personal journey into Unitarian Universalism, capturing the pivotal moment when he discovered the faith and felt called to become a UU

minister.

2. **Leo Rosten,** *Religions of America: Ferment and Faith in an Age of Crisis* **(1975)** – This book introduced you to Unitarian Universalism, providing the initial context for your discovery of the faith and its principles.

3. **A. Powell Davies,** *The Urge to Persecute: Essays on Religion and Society* **(1953)** – Rev. Dr. A. Powell Davies was a key influence on your understanding of Unitarian Universalism, exemplifying the inclusivity and radical acceptance that drew you to the faith.

4. **Martin Luther King, Jr.,** *Why We Can't Wait* **(1964)** – Dr. King's critique of liberalism's failures, particularly in confronting racism, echoes your reflections on the limitations of religious liberalism in the mid-20th century.

5. **Joseph Campbell,** *The Power of Myth* **(1988)** – Campbell's exploration of spirituality and personal transformation mirrors your journey and the significance of finding a faith that aligns with your evolving beliefs.

6. **Theodore Parker,** *Ten Sermons of Religion* **(1853)** – Parker's thoughts on the permanence of love and the inevitability of change align with your message on the enduring spirit of Unitarian Universalism and its commitment to renewal and inclusivity.

SECTION 5: SOCIAL JUSTICE AND CULTURAL CRITIQUE

29. CHAOS OR COMMUNITY: DR. KING, OPPENHEIMER, AND BARBIE

T hank you once again for the time off in July. During my break, I immersed myself in the Civil Rights Movement by reading six books, including all three authored by Dr. Martin Luther King, Jr. His first book, narrating the Montgomery Bus Boycott, is powerful, but it was his last book, Where Do We Go From Here—Chaos or Community?, that I found riveting and incredibly relevant to the social struggles we face today. I also read King: A Life by Jonathan Eig, which I highly recommend. As you can see, I am a big Dr. King fan. He was my height, 5'7. But he was an extraordinary man—brilliant, courageous, and deeply human, with all the foibles and frailties that come with being human.

During my time away, I rested, reflected, and took a break to see the big summer blockbusters: *Oppenheimer* and *Barbie*. I was effectively "Barbenheimer-ed," like many of you. *Barbie*, directed by Greta Gerwig, who was born and raised in a Unitarian Universalist congregation in Sacramento, California, offers a unique perspective that resonates deeply with our UU values. You can clearly see her UU influence throughout the film, as she challenges societal norms and flips traditional paradigms on their heads.

The period between 1945 and 1968, those 23 years, stands out as one of the most profound in human history. It was a time of significant change, driven by technological advances, global revolutions, and movements for social justice that continue to shape our world today. Whether in Africa, Asia, or America, revolution was in the air, presenting moral dilemmas that we are still wrestling with. One theme emerged from both movies and the books I read: the worth and dignity of every person, aligning with our First Principle. Every person matters. Every child born is sacred and has the capacity for greatness, deserving a life free from trauma and abuse—a life where they are respected and treated as fully human and fully divine. Amen?

Yet, human dignity is missing in far too many places in our world. *Oppenheimer* tells the story of J. Robert Oppenheimer, a brilliant theoretical physicist who wanted to make a difference. But when you play with weapons of mass destruction, you cannot control how that power will be wielded. The atomic bombs dropped on Japan in 1945 were a show of force—revenge for Pearl Harbor. The war was already won; Germany had surrendered in May of that year. But we still dropped two bombs in August, killing up to 200,000 people, innocent civilians whose lives were snuffed out in an instant.

Oppenheimer's most famous quote is from the Hindu Upanishad: "Now I am become Death, the destroyer of worlds." Dr. King would say, "The means by which we live cannot outdistance the ends for which we live." The bombs brought a false peace—one rooted in fear and domination, not in justice or reconciliation. The same conditions that led to war continue to manifest today in global conflicts, authoritarianism, and violence. We are left to question whether the end justifies the means.

War is messy, and it often becomes a self-perpetuating cycle of violence. What we did in Japan wasn't necessary, and war itself can be avoided if we address the underlying needs that drive people to violence: the need to survive, to be free, to self-govern, and to have a safe and dignified life. Dr. King warned us, "We have to become a people-oriented society instead of a thing-oriented society." When we treat people as objects, when we prioritize things over human beings, we perpetuate a cycle of abuse that keeps us stuck in conflict.

This pattern extends beyond wars between nations—it's visible in our personal lives, our communities, and our social structures. For every stride toward justice, there is pushback. Dr. King and the Civil Rights Movement demonstrated that while peaceful means may eventually lead to peaceful ends, the journey there is often bloody and fraught with setbacks. But I refuse to believe that violence and division are our destiny. We must commit to applying peaceful means to create peaceful ends.

The movie *Barbie* also speaks to this struggle. Gerwig presents a world where traditional gender roles are upended. In Barbie's world, women lead, and the men—the Kens—take a backseat. It's a playful, yet powerful critique of patriarchy and the ongoing struggle for equality.

Actress America Ferrera's character, Gloria, delivers a monologue that captures the impossible standards women face, highlighting the contradictions and pressures of living in a world that demands perfection while constantly finding fault. She gave a powerful testimony in the film:

> *"It is literally impossible to be a woman. You are so beautiful, and so smart, and it kills me that you don't think you're good enough. Like, we have to always be extraordinary, but somehow we're always doing it*

wrong. You have to be thin, but not too thin. And you can never say you want to be thin, you have to say you want to be healthy, but also, you have to be thin. You have to have money, but you can't ask for money because that's crass. You have to be a boss, but you can't be mean. You have to lead, but you can't squash other people's ideas. You're supposed to love being a mother, but don't talk about your kids all the time. You have to be a career woman, but also always be looking out for other people. You have to answer for men's bad behavior, which is insane, but if you point that out, you're accused of complaining. You're supposed to stay pretty for men, but not so pretty that you tempt them too much or that you threaten other women because you're supposed to be part of the sisterhood. But always stand out and always be grateful. But never forget that the system is rigged, so find a way to acknowledge that but also always be grateful. You have to never get old, never be rude, never show off, never be selfish, never fall down, never fail, never show fear, never get out of line. It's too hard! It's too contradictory, and nobody gives you a medal or says thank you! And it turns out, in fact, that not only are you doing everything wrong, but also, everything is your fault. I'm just so tired of watching myself and every single other woman tie herself into knots so that people will like us. And if all of that is also true for a doll just representing women, then I don't even know."

Her extraordinary words resonated with so many women (and men) and it's clear the film struck a chord. There were even reports of women leaving relationships after watching the movie, feeling empowered to reject second-class treatment in their relationships.. This is the kind of cultural shift we need— a collective awakening toward the worth and dignity of every person.

Today, we are at a crossroads. As Dr. King asked, "Where do we go from here—chaos or community?" Chaos arises when we deny the humanity of others, when we allow fear and hatred to rule. Community is built through collaboration, humility, and the recognition that we are all interconnected. We build community when we embrace diversity, when we teach our children that every person is worthy of love and respect, when we choose to be woke rather than ignorant.

Betsy Jo Angebrant, our beloved Minister of Music Emeritus, wrote a hymn that captures this vision of community:

> *"When all the peoples on this earth know deep inside their precious worth. When every single soul is free, we'll earn the name humanity. The choice to be the best we can begins the day we say, 'I AM.' The unity for which we sigh will never come through hate or lie."*
> *Amen!*

So, let us choose community over chaos. Let us be the voices that call for justice, the hands that build peace, and the hearts that hold space for love. May it be so.

Amen.

References:

1. **King, Martin Luther Jr.** *Where Do We Go from Here: Chaos or Community?* Boston: Beacon Press, 1967. Dr. King's final book, examining the struggles for civil rights and the future of American society.
2. **King, Martin Luther Jr.** *Stride Toward Freedom: The Montgomery Story.* New York: Harper & Row, 1958. A detailed narrative of the Montgomery Bus Boycott, offering insights into the early days of the Civil Rights Movement.
3. **King, Martin Luther Jr.** *Strength to Love.* New York: Harper & Row, 1963. A collection of King's sermons that explore

his philosophy of nonviolence and the moral challenges of the 20th century.

4. **Eig, Jonathan.** *King: A Life.* New York: Farrar, Straus and Giroux, 2023. A comprehensive biography that provides fresh insights into King's life, his struggles, and his legacy.

5. **Welch, Sharon.** *A Feminist Ethic of Risk.* Minneapolis, MN: Fortress Press, 1990. Welch's influential work that rethinks ethics through the lens of feminist theory, emphasizing the need for communal action and social change.

6. **Hanh, Thich Nhat.** *Peace Is Every Step: The Path of Mindfulness in Everyday Life.* New York: Bantam Books, 1991. A spiritual guide emphasizing mindfulness and compassion as tools for personal and societal transformation.

7. **Oppenheimer, J. Robert.** *Science and the Common Understanding.* New York: Simon and Schuster, 1954. A collection of essays by Oppenheimer, reflecting on the impact of science on society and ethics.

8. **Gerwig, Greta.** *Barbie: The Making of the Movie.* New York: Rizzoli, 2023. A behind-the-scenes look at Gerwig's film *Barbie*, exploring her inspirations and vision for challenging societal norms.

9. **Hogue, Mike.** *American Immanence: Democracy for an Uncertain World.* New York: Columbia University Press, 2018. Hogue's exploration of democracy, power, and the ethical challenges of our time.

10. **Parker, Palmer.** *Healing the Heart of Democracy: The Courage to Create a Politics Worthy of the Human Spirit.* San Francisco: Jossey-Bass, 2011. Palmer emphasizes the importance of relational power and the role of individuals in transforming society.

11. **Angebrant, Betsy Jo.** *Hymn 121: We'll Build a Land.* Boston: Unitarian Universalist Association, 1993. This hymn captures a vision of community and shared humanity, aligning with the message of working towards a just and inclusive society.

30. YOU THROW LIKE A GIRL: TOXIC MASCULINITY

Being a man is a privilege in our culture, and almost all cultures across the planet. Recognizing this privilege can be as challenging as understanding racial privilege; it requires a willingness to lower our defenses. First, I want to affirm that being a man is good. Being male, embodying masculine energy, is inherently good. But like all things, there are aspects of masculinity that can become off-balance and harmful, and that's what I'm naming today. I'm calling out the part of manhood, the part of humanity, that has been distorted and misaligned for far too long.

As I see it, many of today's problems stem from unchecked yang energy—the aggressive, dominating force that too often manifests through boys and men, and those who mimic these toxic behaviors. I speak from experience because I, too, have struggled with toxic male behavior. I've said things I regret; I've used my manliness to suppress, control, and dominate. Yet, I know that if I can evolve, anyone can. But being a Black man adds another layer of complexity.

I grew up in a hyper-masculine time, where showing toughness was a survival mechanism. As a Black boy with separated parents, I was taught not to show vulnerability.

In my community, just a decade removed from Black men holding signs declaring "I am a Man!"—we were still unlearning the brutal legacy of chattel slavery. Many of us learned toxic lessons about manhood: "Be tough," "Man up," and "Don't throw like a girl." Men in our neighborhoods, often broken themselves, tried to teach us the rules of male superiority—rules they believed we needed to survive.

I don't blame them; these were misguided attempts to help. Black and Brown men in America reflect the virtues and vices of the dominant culture, and the same is true in reverse. The stereotype that our communities don't take care of their families is a condemnation of a system that has long torn fathers from their homes. The real work lies in unlearning these toxic narratives and rebuilding relationships based on mutuality, reciprocity, and respect, regardless of gender.

Black and Brown men, in particular, grapple with the unique challenge of balancing their masculine energy in the context of a painful history where their families were systematically torn apart—whether through the brutality of slavery, which ripped fathers from homes and families, or through the legacy of colonization, which disrupted traditional family structures and devalued their cultural heritage. This history has often left Black and Brown men without healthy models of masculinity, perpetuating cycles of trauma, dominance, and survival.

Meanwhile, White men must confront the god-like power they have inherited from a history of colonialism, imperialism, and systemic dominance—power that has allowed them to set the standards of "goodness" and "righteousness" in terms of control, conquest, and winning at all costs. This inherited power, often unexamined, reinforces the idea that to be a man means to dominate, succeed, and control. This imbalance between masculine and feminine energies disrupts our ability to nurture, collaborate, and heal. It perpetuates a cycle of harm that affects everyone—fueling violence, inequality, and disconnection. To move forward, men of all backgrounds must acknowledge these destructive legacies, own their part in this imbalance, and actively work to restore harmony with the divine feminine energy that fosters compassion, mutual respect, and true partnership.

Right relationship is about complementarity—harmonizing masculine and feminine energies to create balance. It's about learning to coexist and nurture connections that are based on equality and mutual respect. I didn't understand this as a child. I grew up doing what I was shown—what I thought was expected of me. And while there's no one person to blame, the responsibility lies with all of us. The work begins with examining our own stories and acknowledging where we've been taught that dominance equals strength.

I remember David Reynolds, the neighborhood bully who constantly tested my manhood. He was a tough, older boy who dominated others and made me prove myself time and again. He introduced me to cigarettes, pressured me into grown-up situations, and constantly forced me to show I was "cool" or "manly." David's life was a cliché—a tragic story of a boy with no father figure, a struggling mother, and an inability to channel his masculine energy positively. He was a reflection of a system that teaches boys that manhood is about brutality, dominance, and survival.

David was killed at 16, a victim of the same toxic masculinity that he embodied—a masculinity that taught him to prove his worth through violence, aggression, and control. He was never given the tools to express his pain, vulnerability, or fear; instead, he was conditioned to suppress these emotions, projecting them outward in harmful ways. David's life was a tragic reflection of a system that fails boys by teaching them that to be a man means to be invulnerable, to never show weakness, and to equate respect with intimidation and dominance.

I think of the millions of Davids out there—boys who never learn what it means to be a real man. They are trapped in cycles of aggression, violence, and emotional suppression, lacking role models who demonstrate that strength does not come from control but from connection. These boys are taught to harden their hearts, to mask their emotions, and to engage in a constant battle for validation through force. They are lost in a world that prioritizes power over compassion, and winning over understanding.

So, what is a real man? A real man seeks harmony within himself and with others. He respects those around him and recognizes the inherent worth in every person, regardless of gender, race, or status. A real man does not measure his value by his ability to dominate, but by his capacity to uplift, nurture, and collaborate. He embraces vulnerability as a strength, not a weakness, and he understands that true courage lies in facing his own fears and insecurities, not in masking them with aggression.

A real man listens more than he speaks, builds up rather than tears down, and knows that his power is magnified when shared rather than hoarded. He rejects the toxic scripts handed down through generations and instead chooses a path of empathy, accountability, and love. Real manhood is not about conforming to outdated ideals of masculinity but about redefining those ideals to include gentleness, kindness, and a commitment to being a whole, *humane* being. It's about showing up authentically, leading with heart, and creating a legacy of peace instead of pain.

Don McPherson's book, *You Throw Like a Girl: The Blindspot of Masculinity*, resonates deeply with my own experiences. Like me, McPherson grew up immersed in a culture that promoted toxic ideas of manhood, where phrases like "You throw like a girl" were used to shame and belittle. These messages taught us that to be a man meant to dominate, control, and objectify others. McPherson's transformation began after his football career ended, prompting him to confront the violent and narrow definitions of masculinity that had defined his life. His journey is a powerful exploration of how deeply ingrained toxic masculinity can be—and the ongoing work required to unlearn it and redefine what it means to be a man.

McPherson writes:

> *"Therein lies the insidious hypocrisy of old-school masculinity—we cannot have it both ways; we cannot continue to ask young men to 'suck it up,' 'take it like a man,' or solve problems by going to 'fist city,' but remain oblivious to the carnage that this perspective leaves in its wake. We must seek a pure and authentic understanding of masculinity...engage in honest discourse about what it truly means to be a whole and healthy man."*

Ultimately, transcending toxic masculinity requires going outside the box. Outside the box, men can cry, express fear, ask for help, and lead with their hearts. Outside the box, we strive to be humane beings, letting go of the need to dominate and embracing a life of love and mutual respect.

> *"If every man in the world had his mind set on freedom, if every man in the world dreamed a sweet dream of peace, if every man of every nation, young and old, each generation, held his hands out in the name of love, there would be no more war. If every nation in the world set a true course for freedom, if every nation raised its children in a culture of peace, if all our sons and all our daughters reached in friendship across the waters, refusing to be enemies, there would be no more war."*

May it be so.

Amen.

References:

1. **McPherson, Don.** *You Throw Like a Girl: The Blindspot of Masculinity.* New York: Akashic Books, 2019. McPherson's book addresses toxic masculinity and explores how men can redefine their identities beyond harmful stereotypes.
2. **Hooks, Bell.** *The Will to Change: Men, Masculinity, and Love.* New York: Atria Books, 2004. This book examines how traditional masculinity harms men and offers a vision for healing and embracing a healthier, more loving form of manhood.
3. **Kimmel, Michael.** *Angry White Men: American Masculinity at the End of an Era.* New York: Nation Books, 2013. Kimmel's work explores the cultural forces that shape toxic masculinity and its impact on men and society.
4. **Welch, Sharon.** *A Feminist Ethic of Risk.* Minneapolis, MN: Fortress Press, 1990. Welch's book offers insights into ethical responses to societal power imbalances, emphasizing the need for mutual respect and collaborative relationships.
5. **DiAngelo, Robin.** *White Fragility: Why It's So Hard for White People to Talk About Racism.* Boston: Beacon Press, 2018. DiAngelo's analysis of privilege and power parallels discussions on masculinity by highlighting how unexamined privilege perpetuates harm.
6. **Brown, Brené.** *Daring Greatly: How the Courage to Be Vulnerable Transforms the Way We Live, Love, Parent, and Lead.* New York: Gotham Books, 2012. Brown's exploration of vulnerability challenges traditional views of masculinity, encouraging men to embrace vulnerability as a strength.

31. CASTE AND AMERICA

Readings from **Caste: Origins of Our Discontent** by *Isabel Wilkerson.*

Reading 1: Divine Will

"Before the age of human awareness, according to the ancient Hindu text of India, Manu, the all-knowing, was seated in contemplation when the great men approached him and asked, 'Please, Lord, tell us precisely and in the proper order the Laws of all the social classes as well as of those born in between.' Manu proceeded to tell of a time when the universe as we know it was in a deep sleep, and the One 'who is beyond the range of senses,' brought forth the waters and took birth himself as Brahma, the 'grandfather of all the worlds.' He created the Brahmin, the highest caste, from his mouth, the Kshatriya from his arms, the Vaishya from his thighs, and from his feet, the Shudra, the lowest of the four varnas..."

Reading 2: Divine Will—Book of Genesis

"Noah became a man of the soil. His sons were Shem,

Ham, and Japheth, who would become the progenitors of all humanity... 'Cursed be Canaan! The lowest of slaves will he be to his brothers.' The sons of Shem (Asian humans), Ham (African humans), and Japheth (Caucasian humans) spread across the continents, Shem to the east, Ham to the south, Japheth to the west... The story of Ham's discovery of Noah's nakedness passed through millennia, interpreted by some to justify the enslavement of Black bodies..."

We are all victims of destructive psycho-social programming. These are the stories we've been told, stories that have seeped into our institutions and our minds, and they drive much of the division and discord we see today. The structures we live within are cracked because they are built on immoral foundations—made-up myths, quite frankly. These falsehoods are rooted in superiority, designed to create division—this idea of "us" versus "them." These stories tell us that some people are more valuable than others. But these narratives don't hold up under the scrutiny of love, justice, or truth.

Now, we've all been programmed. All of us. No one escapes the influence of society's harmful messages, especially when it comes to race. That programming pits us against one another, encourages us to see Black and brown bodies as "other," as something to be feared or controlled. That is the great lie we must dismantle. This is THE GREAT WORK of our time: to free ourselves from these mental and physical tyrannies.

Let's dig deeper into the roots of this discontent, and we'll be guided by the remarkable scholarship of Isabel Wilkerson. I can't recommend her book enough. The Hindu story about the creation of the caste system is just one of many that have been used to divide humanity. The social order in India, codified as divine, justified inequality based on birthright for over 3,000 years. That story—the one that assigned people to different roles, from the Brahmin at the top to the Shudra at the bottom —has justified the oppression of millions of people.

But here's the kicker: the story didn't stop with those four castes. What Wilkerson points out, and what's so crucial to remember, is that there were people even lower than the Shudra. There were those outside the system altogether. They were the Dalits—the untouchables—those who did the dirtiest, most dehumanizing work. They were seen as less than human. And let's not ignore the fact that these outcasts were often the darkest-hued people in the culture. The caste system in India was officially outlawed in 1950, but the tradition persists even today, challenged though it may be.

Now let's shift to our own context. In America, we've had a different, but equally toxic narrative. We had the so-called "Curse of Ham." You heard the reading. Noah's son Ham is said to have discovered his father's nakedness, and when Noah woke up and found out, he cursed Ham's son, Canaan, to be "the lowest of slaves." For centuries, this story has been used to justify the enslavement of African people. It was manipulated by the clergy, the merchants, and the ruling class to rationalize the brutal enslavement and subjugation of Black bodies. That's the power of stories—whether they're true or not, people believe them, and they shape the world.

This isn't ancient history. We are still living with the consequences of these narratives. As Wilkerson points out, we have been taught, over and over again, to see black and brown bodies as different, as dangerous, as inferior. And this mindset isn't just about hatred—it's about structure. It's about a caste system. And in this country, that caste system has been intertwined with race from the very beginning.

But let me clarify something. When we talk about caste,

we're talking about more than just racism. Caste is deeper. It's the structure itself, the invisible framework that has propped up inequality for centuries. Wilkerson defines caste as *"the granting or withholding of respect, status, honor, attention, privileges, resources, benefit of the doubt, and human kindness to someone on the basis of their perceived rank or standing in the hierarchy."*

Here's the thing—caste isn't personal. It's not necessarily about hating someone or even consciously thinking they're inferior. Caste is insidious because it's woven into the very fabric of society. It's those unspoken rules we all follow without even realizing it. It's the boundaries we accept as "the way things are." And those boundaries have been in place for so long that they feel natural.

Wilkerson is clear that caste predates the concept of race. It's older than formal racism, and it has survived long after the legal end of state-sponsored racism. Caste is what holds the hierarchy together, even when racism becomes less overt, more deniable.

Now, as a Black man who grew up in Southeast Washington, D.C., I know a thing or two about caste. No matter how far I've come, no matter how much education or success I've attained, I cannot fully escape the caste that society assigned me because of the color of my skin. And that's the thing about caste—it's a permanent marker. It's not something you can work your way out of. You carry it with you.

Wilkerson identifies eight pillars that hold caste together. Each one of them is worth examining in detail. Divine will —religion has often been used to justify caste. Heredity— privileges passed down through generations that people are reluctant to let go of. Mating rules—marrying within your own kind, within your station. Purity versus pollution— white as pure, Black as dirty. Occupational hierarchy—certain jobs deemed unworthy. Dehumanization—the exploitation of those deemed less than human. Terror enforcement—the use of violence to maintain the system. And finally, perceived superiority and inferiority, the natural result of all the other pillars.

But what makes caste different from racism? Wilkerson makes an important distinction here. Racism is about the stereotypes and assumptions attached to race—the social construct of race, as we often say. Caste, on the other hand, is about positioning. It's about ranking people, about keeping them in their place. It's about maintaining the hierarchy at all costs, even when it's not explicitly about race.

You see, caste is the root, and racism is the flower. It's like a play—caste assigns the roles, and racism is the script that tells us how to treat each other based on those roles. In America, these two systems are so deeply intertwined that it's hard to separate them. But if we're going to truly understand and dismantle racism, we've got to go deeper. We've got to understand caste.

So how did we get here? Well, I have a theory. I believe that caste and racism are the natural outgrowths of agrarian societies. As humans moved from tribes to nation-states, the division of labor became necessary. Over time, some people—usually those with the most power—decided that they didn't want to do the hard, menial work. They used their intellect, their cunning, and eventually, their weapons to force others into subservience. And once that system was in place, it became self-perpetuating.

I've seen this dynamic bullying behavior up close. Growing up, I was picked on a lot, and I developed a deep disdain for tyrannical behavior. It's the same story, over and over again—those in power exploit the weak. Look at what's happening with Russia and Ukraine right now. It's yet another example of one nation using force to dominate another. When will we learn that true power lies in love and collaboration, not in violence and control?

For me, caste and racism are about the manipulation of natural systems of collaboration for personal gain. It's about controlling people, places, and things—all for the benefit of a few. To be clear, hierarchical structures aren't evil, but how we treat people within the structure can be. We must continue to dismantle or debug the programs until they become compassionate.

What can we do? We can start by noticing. Noticing is half the battle. Notice the humanity in the people around you, especially those society has placed in lower castes. See them. Acknowledge their struggles. And speak out when you see injustice. When enough of us shift our thinking, the world will begin to change. As Wilkerson reminds us:

> "We are not personally responsible for what people who look like us did centuries ago. But we are responsible for what good or ill we do to people alive with us today. We are, each of us, responsible for every decision we make that hurts or harms another human being. We are responsible for recognizing that what happened in previous generations at the hands of or to people who look like us set the stage for the world we now live in. What has gone before us grants us advantages or burdens through no effort or fault of our own, gains or deficits that others who do not look like us often do not share."

Faith demands that we be the change we wish to see in the world. We can no longer turn a blind eye to the suffering that caste imposes. We can no longer pretend that this system— this toxic hierarchy that diminishes and dehumanizes so many —is someone else's problem. It is our problem. And the time to act is now.

May it be so. Amen.

References:

1. **Wilkerson, Isabel.** *Caste: The Origins of Our Discontents. New York: Random House Publishing Group, 2020. Kindle Edition. Wilkerson's book provides a comprehensive exploration of caste systems across history, including their impact in the United States, India, and Nazi Germany. It serves as the primary source for understanding the modern concept of caste in relation to race, class, and societal hierarchy.*

2. **The Holy Bible, New International Version.** *Genesis 9:18-27. This passage discusses the "Curse of Ham," often cited throughout history as a biblical justification for racial hierarchies, including slavery and segregation. It is essential for understanding how religious texts have been used to perpetuate caste-like systems.*

3. **The Laws of Manu.** *Translated by G. Bühler, Clarendon Press, 1886. These ancient Hindu texts form the basis for the caste system in India, detailing the social hierarchy that places people in rigid categories based on birth. This reference provides a historical perspective on how religious doctrines can create enduring systems of inequality.*

4. **The Holy Bible, New International Version.** *Ephesians 6:5. This verse, "Slaves, obey your earthly masters with respect and fear, and with sincerity of heart, just as you would obey Christ," has been historically used to justify slavery and the subjugation of lower castes, showing the religious reinforcement of caste-like dynamics.*

32. HACKING THE BRAIN & RACE

T o change this world, it's going to take a revolution of the mind and a transformation of the heart. Getting beyond racial prejudice, systemic racism, and cultural biases will take everything we've got. I'm hopeful, but I know it's a hard, long road ahead.

We live in a reality that's been constructed for us—where whiteness is seen as rightness. Think about how many of our systems, especially law enforcement, are rooted in this. The police, as we know them, were originally created by wealthy landowners to protect their interests. In the South, this took the form of slave patrols—groups that enforced the brutal system of slavery, hunting down escaped enslaved people and maintaining racial control. In the North, early police forces were designed to suppress labor strikes and protect property from working-class uprisings. At their core, these institutions were not built to serve all people equally; they were built to maintain social hierarchies. This legacy still shapes how law enforcement operates today. Police are often trained, either directly or indirectly, to see people of color as threats. We see it in video after video, but this is nothing new. It's simply more visible now.

Yet, there is progress. Some police departments in places like

Oakland are leading the way, thanks in part to people like Dr. Jennifer Eberhardt and her research in *Biased*. But the bigger picture is clear: reeducation is necessary—on every level.

Reeducation is about building up white stamina around race. It's about embracing anti-racism as the way, the truth, and the light. If you are white it is your pathway to real freedom.

I want to ask you a question, and I want you to think deeply about it. Close your eyes if it helps. When you picture Jesus Christ, what color is his skin? What race was he? Most Americans, if they're honest, will say Jesus was white. But he wasn't European. He was a brown-skinned, Middle Eastern man. And yet, the image we hold of Jesus is often a white man. What does that say about the world we live in?

Think about it: If Jesus is white, that makes God white too. And if God is white, then whiteness becomes the standard for everything that's good, pure, and holy. Salvation gets tied to whiteness. I'm not exaggerating. This has been the message for centuries. The implications are profound. We've internalized these ideas, whether we're aware of it or not. White equals good. Black equals bad. If you're black, you're pushed to the margins, seen as less than. If you're white, you benefit from a system that elevates you.

This isn't just in America. You can see this all over the world. In Europe, blackness is associated with inferiority. Africa has long been seen as a dark, savage place, while Europe is positioned closer to the heavens. These ideas are deeply embedded in how we think, how we act, and how we structure our societies.

Robin DiAngelo, in her book *Nice Racism*, names this as "the ultimate othering." She says that white supremacy needs blackness to exist. Without black as its opposite, white cannot stand as superior. Racial trauma expert Resmaa Menakem echoes this when he says, "The white body is the supreme

standard by which all bodies' humanity shall be measured."
Think about that. If whiteness is the standard, then everyone
else is measured against that, and everyone else comes up
short.

So how do we begin to dismantle this? We start by recognizing
that our minds have been hacked. We've been programmed
from birth to see the world through this false lens. And
we need to rewire our brains, our thinking, and our hearts.
This is where Unitarian Universalism comes in. As a faith
that believes in freedom, in worth, in dignity—we have a
responsibility to reset the moral compass. But let's be real: even
within Unitarian Universalism, we've got our own reckoning
to do. Our forebears Ralph Waldo Emerson and Henry David
Thoreau, as great as they were, held racist views. We have to
name that. Our faith has to be about action, not just words.

Where do we begin? We begin with the brain. Our biases are
hardwired into us from centuries of conditioning. But here's
the good news: we can change that. Our brains can be rewired.
I encourage you to watch the PBS documentary series *Hacking
Your Mind*. It shows how our biases start early—really early.
In one study at Yale, children were asked to choose a favorite
color—either green or blue. Then they were shown pictures of
characters wearing both colors and asked questions like: "Who
looks mean?" "Who looks happy?" "Who do you trust?" Time
and time again, the children assigned negative traits—like
being mean or untrustworthy—to the characters wearing the
opposite color from the one they had chosen. This showed that
even without race being involved, bias was already present in
their thinking.

Why does this happen? It's a survival instinct. We evolved to
trust those who look like us, to stick with our tribe, because
that's how we survived. Most of the time, we aren't even aware
of these biases—they're operating in our subconscious.

Nobel laureate Daniel Kahneman says that we have two

systems in our brain: fast thinking and slow thinking. Fast thinking is our autopilot; it's what we use when we're doing things we know well, like driving or making quick decisions. Slow thinking is the system we use for deeper analysis. The problem is, fast thinking takes over when we're tired, stressed, or overwhelmed, and that's when our biases kick in. In conversations about race, people often shut down or get defensive because their fast-thinking brain can't handle the discomfort. This is where we see harm, ignorance, and, sometimes, violence.

So how do we change this? We have to strengthen our slow-thinking brain. We do that by educating ourselves, by reading, by attending classes, by talking about race even when it's uncomfortable. This is the work of anti-racism. And I'm asking you today to commit to it. This is what it means to be truly human.

We are living in a time of great change. Two paradigms are colliding: one says we are all equal; the other says we are not. One system is dying, and it's fighting back with all it's got. But another system is emerging, one rooted in the earth, in humanity, in the belief that all souls are worthy.

My message is this: Hack your brain. Commit to reprogramming how you see the world. This is the greatest work you can do—for yourself, for your faith, and for the world.

And here's the good news: you're not alone. With practice, you will get better. And the changes you make will ripple out. Studies show that your behavior impacts up to six degrees of people around you. So, what you do matters. As A. Powell Davies once said, "It matters what you believe." Let's make those beliefs count because this is the work of saving humanity. This is the work for our time. May it be so.

Amen.

References

1. Dr. Jennifer Eberhardt's research is highlighted in her book **Biased: Uncovering the Hidden Prejudice That Shapes What We See, Think, and Do**, which explores implicit bias and its impact on law enforcement and society.
2. Robin DiAngelo's insights on white supremacy and the black/white binary come from her book **Nice Racism: How Progressive White People Perpetuate Racial Harm**, which discusses the nuances of racism, particularly among well-meaning white liberals.
3. Racial trauma expert Resmaa Menakem's thoughts on the white body as the standard of humanity are explored in his book **My Grandmother's Hands: Racialized Trauma and the Pathway to Mending Our Hearts and Bodies**, where he addresses the physical and emotional impact of racism on both black and white bodies.
4. Nobel Prize-winning psychologist Daniel Kahneman's research on fast and slow thinking is detailed in his book **Thinking, Fast and Slow**, where he explains how our brains operate on two systems and how biases are part of our fast-thinking brain.
5. The PBS documentary series *Hacking Your Mind* examines how biases form and operate in our subconscious, including studies from Yale University on children's innate biases.
6. Rev. A. Powell Davies' famous quote, "It matters what you believe," is a reflection of his broader theological work in **The Faith of an Uncertain People**, where he explored the impact of belief on behavior.

33. MLK: 90 YEARS LATER

To understand where the world is today, we have to look back at what it was. This morning, I want to take us back to 1968, into the mind of Rev. Dr. Martin Luther King Jr. Near the end of his life, just days before his assassination on April 4th, Dr. King delivered a powerful sermon on March 31, 1968, at the Washington Cathedral in DC. His message that day named the same ills that plague us now—racism, poverty, and war. These three forces stand in the way of the Beloved Community, and King's sermon, "Remaining Awake Through a Great Revolution," still resonates today.

America was in the midst of a paradigm shift then, moving from an overtly exclusive, "whites only" mindset to a more inclusive approach to co-existence. Yet the struggle remains. It is the legacy of our 1619 original sin when the first enslaved Africans arrived in this land. Dr. King's message from 1968 is still relevant for us today. He said:

"I am sure that most of you have read that arresting little story from the pen of Washington Irving entitled 'Rip Van Winkle.' The one thing that we usually remember about the story is that Rip Van Winkle slept

twenty years. But there is another point in that little story that is almost completely overlooked. It was the sign in the inn, from which Rip went up in the mountain for his long sleep. When Rip Van Winkle went up into the mountain, the sign had a picture of King George the Third of England. When he came down twenty years later, the sign had a picture of George Washington, the first president of the United States. When Rip Van Winkle looked up at the picture of George Washington, he was amazed—he was completely lost. He knew not who he was.

And this reveals to us that the most striking thing about the story of Rip Van Winkle is not merely that Rip slept twenty years, but that he slept through a revolution. While he was peacefully snoring up in the mountain, a revolution was taking place that would change the course of history—and Rip knew nothing about it. He was asleep. Yes, he slept through a revolution. And one of the great liabilities of life is that all too many people find themselves living amid a great period of social change, and yet they fail to develop the new attitudes, the new mental responses, that the new situation demands. They end up sleeping through a revolution."

Dr. King would be 90 years old today; and his words still hit home. He understood the cyclical nature of history—the patterns that repeat, over and over, until we learn the lessons they hold. My hypothesis is that all existence is cyclical. War and peace are part of a greater cycle of human understanding and misunderstanding. I like to say, "master patterns, master life." We are living through a repeating 50-year cycle of racial and cultural tension, and it will keep returning until we reconcile it.

Today feels very much like the 1960s, when a new consciousness, voiced by Dr. King, disrupted the old order. The result? Bloodshed, violence, resistance. We're seeing the same resistance today because we still haven't learned to stop "othering" one another. Until we do, this cycle will continue, repeating itself over and over like some form of social Groundhog Day.

This cycle also signals the start of major social, political, and technological changes. History will look back on our time and call it a cultural revolution. Thomas Kuhn described these moments as paradigm shifts—when old systems fall and new ones emerge. So, if you are working for social justice, if you are fighting for systemic change, you are part of *Team Paradigm Change*. You're helping to usher out the dying old order and bring in something new. We've been here before—think about what followed the chaos of the 1960s: black mayors were elected, civil rights expanded, and society began to change.

But just as progress was made, the forces of resistance responded. What would Dr. King say to us today, those of us who are still working for progress, diversity, and inclusion? He might remind us that the cycle isn't over. Progress doesn't follow a straight line. It moves forward, and then it faces resistance. That's the nature of the struggle for equality–three steps forward one or two steps back. But onward we go.

We can't say we were asleep after 2008. We had a moment of jubilation—when it felt like progress was inevitable. The election of the first Black president seemed like a huge step forward. But what followed was a backlash (black-lash), the pendulum swung in the opposite direction. The 2016 election brought a man to power who was the complete opposite of Barack Obama in character, leadership, and spirit. That cycle of action and reaction is familiar, isn't it? It's a pattern that repeats on our journey toward freedom. It happened in the

1960s, and it's happening again today.

We can't afford to fall asleep again. This time, we are wide awake, determined to keep Dr. King's dream alive. But how do we do better? How do we help? How can we make a real impact?

The first step is to recognize the patterns. See the pieces of the puzzle in life and how they affect you—your community, your country, your world. It's time for reflection, not finger-pointing. Now is the time to ask hard questions and take responsibility for the world we've helped create. We are part of the global 1%, and we have a hand in shaping the systems of injustice we're fighting against. As Gandhi said, "Change yourself and you change the world."

How do we create real change? We prioritize. Political campaigns spend over $8 billion to elect people who promise us better wages, lower inflation, more jobs, and relief for the middle class. But can't they see that the money used for elections could achieve those very things? Imagine what we could accomplish if we redirected those billions toward the actual problems we face—poverty, healthcare, education, and community investment. The solution is right in front of us, but we're too caught up in the same cycles to see it. The kingdom stands at the door and knocks, but no one answers.

This is our moment to reconcile our thoughts, words, and deeds. We have to stop doing the same things over and over, expecting a different result. Yes, a rock will ripple as far as it can go, but we hold the power to change the course of that ripple. With love, with intention, we can transform the very direction of our world.

History shows us that every 50 years, we're pulled back into a cycle of racial and political tension. Look at 2019: racial strife, hate crimes, mass shootings, the rise of social media fueling division—doesn't it feel like we've been here before? Go back to 1969: civil rights movements, assassinations of leaders like King and Kennedy, Vietnam, widespread protests. Or take 1919: just after World War I, the Tulsa Race Massacre, and violent backlash against Black progress. And 1869? The Civil War had just ended, Reconstruction was beginning, and the KKK was rising.

This cycle stretches back even further—to 1619, when the first enslaved Africans arrived on these shores. For over 400 years, we've been trapped in this repeating loop of progress met by resistance, of hope followed by hatred. It's a pattern so ingrained in our history that it feels inevitable. But it doesn't have to be. This time, we can break the cycle. We can see the pattern for what it is—a call to change the course, to stop repeating the mistakes of the past, and to build something new–a cyclical that is more compassionate and less violent.

We are not powerless to these repeating patterns. The ripples of our thoughts, intentions, and actions create our reality. We can choose to break the patterns of the past.

Emotional literacy is essential—we must learn to truly see ourselves, flaws and all, and recognize how our emotions, judgments, and resentments shape the world around us. Emotional literacy means being able to name what we feel and understanding how those feelings influence our behavior —especially when it comes to issues like race, privilege, and justice. It's the ability to step back, take stock of our own biases, and notice when fear or anger is driving us to shut down, lash out, or stay silent.

Without emotional literacy, we can easily become defensive when confronted with uncomfortable truths about ourselves or our role in maintaining systems of oppression. We might think we're neutral, but by failing to question our assumptions, by avoiding difficult conversations, we become complicit in injustice. This kind of literacy forces us to ask: *How are my thoughts, my words, and my actions contributing to the very systems I say I want to change?* It also allows us to move beyond guilt and shame, which often paralyze people, into a space of accountability and growth. Emotional literacy empowers us to confront our own discomfort, to admit when we're wrong, and to do the inner work necessary to create outward change. When we build this capacity, we can better listen, empathize, and respond—creating the ripples of change that start within and spread outward into our communities. It's through this emotional honesty that we begin to dismantle the subtle ways we participate in and perpetuate oppression, even when we don't realize it.

So, don't panic. We've been here before. People of color have been living with fear for centuries, and now others are feeling that same fear. But change comes when enough people are impacted. This is our time to be part of the change.

Dr. King once dreamed of a beloved community. We still dream of that world, where all people are valued and affirmed. But dreaming isn't enough. We must live that dream daily—first in our minds, then in our actions. War and peace may be the story of human history, but we don't have to be slaves to that cycle. We can remain awake during this great revolution, knowing that we are not powerless but empowered to be the change we wish to see. Amen.

References:

1. Dr. Martin Luther King Jr.'s sermon *"Remaining Awake Through a Great Revolution"*, delivered at the Washington National Cathedral on March 31, 1968. This sermon is where King addresses the dangers of being complacent during times of great social change and highlights the interconnectedness of humanity.
2. Thomas Kuhn's concept of paradigm shifts, from his influential book **The Structure of Scientific Revolutions**, where he explains how major changes in thought, science, and society occur when old paradigms are replaced by new

ways of understanding the world.

3. Mahatma Gandhi's quote, "Change yourself and you change the world," is a well-known expression of his belief in personal responsibility and the power of individual transformation to effect broader social change.

4. The Tulsa Race Massacre of 1921, one of the worst incidents of racial violence in American history, where a prosperous Black community in Tulsa, Oklahoma, was destroyed by white mobs, provides historical context for the cycles of racial violence in the United States.

5. The establishment of the Ku Klux Klan in 1866 and its rise during the Reconstruction era, following the Civil War, as a reactionary force against Black freedom and progress.

6. The arrival of the first enslaved Africans in America in 1619, marking the beginning of the transatlantic slave trade and the systemic racial oppression that has continued for centuries.

7. Resmaa Menakem's **My Grandmother's Hands: Racialized Trauma and the Pathway to Mending Our Hearts and Bodies**, which explores how the trauma of racism impacts both Black and white bodies, and offers tools for healing from that trauma.

8. Robin DiAngelo's **White Fragility: Why It's So Hard for White People to Talk About Racism**, which discusses how emotional defenses, such as guilt and defensiveness, prevent many white people from engaging in conversations about race and systemic oppression.

9. Isabel Wilkerson's **Caste: The Origins of Our Discontents**, which examines America's racial hierarchy through the lens of caste systems, showing how deeply ingrained social structures perpetuate inequality.

34. THE POOR PEOPLE'S CAMPAIGN REVISITED

I want to take us back to a moment in history that still calls out to us today. The year was 1968. Dr. Martin Luther King Jr. was leading a movement that spoke not only to the injustices of racism but to the crushing weight of poverty. He called it the Poor People's Campaign—a vision for economic justice, for a world where the poor and the marginalized would be seen, heard, and uplifted. He called us to understand that poverty was not just an economic issue—it was a moral one.

We're here today, more than fifty years later, and the need for this vision has only deepened. Yes, we've made progress. But look around, and you'll see the undeniable truth: the poverty that Dr. King fought against is still with us. It's evolved, entrenched itself deeper into our institutions, our policies, and even into the minds of those who don't realize their own participation in maintaining this system. The Poor People's Campaign was about more than just feeding the hungry and clothing the naked. It was about demanding systemic change. It was about justice.

And so we revisit that campaign today. We revisit it not as a historical event, but as an ongoing movement—a call for moral revival, for systemic change, and for justice that extends to every single one of God's children.

Now, we have to ask ourselves the difficult questions: *Have we done enough?* Is poverty still racialized? Does it still disproportionately impact Black and Brown communities, women, Indigenous people, and immigrants? The answer is yes, it does. It's right in front of us, in our communities, in our streets, in the lives of the people we serve.

But there is hope. Hope in the form of a new generation of leaders who are once again carrying the torch of this campaign. Rev. William Barber and Rev. Liz Theoharis are leading the resurgence of this movement, calling us to a "moral fusion," uniting people of all races, religions, and backgrounds to fight against the evils of poverty, racism, and environmental degradation. Their message is the same as Dr. King's: poverty is not an accident. It is the result of choices—policy choices. But those policies can be undone. Those systems can be dismantled.

This is where we come in. As people of faith, we are called to be the ones who challenge these systems. Our faith teaches us that we are all interconnected. Our seventh principle affirms respect for the interdependent web of all existence. Poverty is a tear in that web. When our brothers and sisters are excluded from economic participation, when they are denied healthcare, housing, education—when they are denied dignity —our web is weakened. We all suffer.

Dr. King knew that. He understood that poverty isn't just about a lack of money—it's about a lack of opportunity, a lack of justice. Poverty, he said, is violence. It's a violence against the soul, a violence against the spirit, a violence against our shared humanity. And it's a violence that is perpetuated every day by systems that prioritize profit over people.

So what are we going to do about it? I believe we are called to rise to this challenge, to confront these systems with the same courage and boldness that Dr. King did. This means advocating for living wages, for healthcare as a human right, for affordable housing, and for quality education for all. It means recognizing that charity is not enough. Charity addresses the symptom, but justice addresses the root. And we, as a people of faith, are called to be agents of justice.

Let me be clear: justice is hard work. It's messy. It's uncomfortable. It requires sacrifice. But it is necessary. Justice is not something we ask for; it is something we demand. Justice is love in action. It is faith in action. The Poor People's Campaign, both then and now, calls us to embody that love, that faith, in the way we fight for a more just world.

Now, let's not get it twisted. This is not just about the poor. This is about all of us. Poverty dehumanizes us all. It cheapens the soul of a society. And if we allow it to persist, we are complicit in the injustice. We must be willing to do more than just give out of our abundance. We must be willing to change the very systems that create poverty in the first place.

This is why Dr. King called for a revolution of values—a shift in the way we think about poverty, wealth, and the worth of every individual. He challenged us to look beyond material wealth and to see the inherent worth and dignity in every human being. He reminded us that the measure of a society is not how it treats its wealthy, but how it treats its poor.

I challenge each of us to reflect on our role in this fight. Are we advocates for justice? Are we willing to be uncomfortable, to challenge the status quo, to speak truth to power? Are we willing to love the poor, not just with our charity, but with our demand for justice?

This is the call. This is the work. And this is the time. The

Poor People's Campaign is not just a relic of the past—it is a living movement, and we are its hands and feet. Together, we can make Dr. King's vision a reality. Together, we can build a society where poverty is no more, where every person is treated with dignity, and where "justice rolls down like water and righteousness like a mighty stream."

May it be so.

Amen.

References:

1. **Bolden, Tonya.** *M.L.K.: Journey of a King.* New York: Abrams Books, 2007.
   This biography covers Martin Luther King Jr.'s life and work, including the Poor People's Campaign, providing a detailed look into his vision for economic justice and equality.
2. **King, Martin Luther Jr.** *Where Do We Go from Here: Chaos or Community?* Boston: Beacon Press, 1967.
   Dr. King's seminal book, written during the last years of his life, outlines his thoughts on poverty, racial inequality, and the need for a "revolution of values" in America. It directly informs the principles behind the Poor People's Campaign.
3. **Barber, William J., and Liz Theoharis.** *The Revived Poor People's Campaign: An Intergenerational Movement to End Poverty.* Poor People's Campaign, 2018.
   This source is key for understanding the contemporary resurgence of the Poor People's Campaign, led by Rev. William Barber and Rev. Liz Theoharis. It discusses modern efforts to continue King's legacy through advocacy for economic justice, racial equality, and systemic change.
4. **Harrington, Michael.** *The Other America: Poverty in the United States.* New York: Simon & Schuster, 1962.
   This classic text on poverty was instrumental in shaping the discourse around economic inequality in America and had a direct influence on the formation of the Poor People's Campaign in the 1960s.
5. **Theoharis, Liz.** *Always with Us? What Jesus Really Said about the Poor.* Grand Rapids, MI: Wm. B. Eerdmans Publishing, 2017. Theoharis, a co-leader of the current Poor People's

Campaign, explores the biblical and theological roots of the movement, drawing connections between faith, poverty, and justice.

6. **King, Martin Luther Jr.** *Testimony before the Senate on the Poor People's Campaign.* Senate Committee on Government Operations, Washington D.C., 1968. Dr. King's testimony before the U.S. Senate sheds light on his vision for the Poor People's Campaign and the moral imperatives behind it.

7. **Poverty USA.** *Poverty in America: Understanding the Problem.* United States Conference of Catholic Bishops, 2020.
A useful resource for current data on poverty in the United States, discussing the intersection of race, gender, and class in modern poverty.

8. **West, Cornel.** *Race Matters.* Boston: Beacon Press, 1993.
This book addresses race and poverty in America, with insight into how systemic racism perpetuates economic injustice. It is highly relevant to understanding the modern context of the Poor People's Campaign.

9. **Dorrien, Gary.** *Breaking White Supremacy: Martin Luther King Jr. and the Black Social Gospel.* New Haven, CT: Yale University Press, 2018.
Dorrien's work explores the theological and social justice roots of Dr. King's activism, particularly his late-career focus on economic justice and the Poor People's Campaign.

10. **Smith, Preston H.** *Racial Democracy and the Black Metropolis: Housing Policy in Postwar Chicago.* Minneapolis: University of Minnesota Press, 2012.
This book analyzes how housing policy contributed to poverty in postwar Black urban communities, connecting to King's broader concerns about economic inequality.

35. POWER OVER OR POWER WITH: SHAPING A JUST HUMANITY

Norman Cousins once said, "I am interlocked with other human beings in the consequences of our actions, thoughts, and feelings." Those words resonate deeply with me, as they speak to our undeniable interconnectedness. Frances Ellen Watkins Harper, the bold African American abolitionist, suffragist, poet, and Unitarian, expressed a similar truth when she declared, "We are all bound together in a great bundle of humanity." Harper's words remind us that our shared human experience is not just a social condition but a profound, cosmic struggle for moral order. It is a battle over narratives—who is good, who is evil, and whose way is right. Since long before the time of Jesus, humans have been locked in this fight for power: the power to control the story, to decide who eats first, and to determine who is worthy of love and justice. I want to talk about power.

As an Affiliate Faculty member at Meadville Lombard Theological School, I am privileged to work with remarkable thinkers like Dr. Mike Hogue and Dr. Sharon Welch. Recently, Dr. Hogue delivered a transformative lecture on the nature of power—how it is perceived, wielded, and distributed. He challenged us to rethink power's role in shaping history, emphasizing that if we want to move toward greater justice, equity, and compassion, we must confront not only the ruling powers but the deep-seated ideologies that sustain them. He highlighted two Latin concepts of power: *potestas*—the power to dominate and control—and *potentia*—the power to connect, transform, and uplift.

Power as *potestas* is the power we know all too well—it dominates, controls, and imposes. It's a hierarchical power rooted in scarcity, fear, and the relentless belief that power must be wielded over others to maintain order and security. This power structure is embedded in the fabric of our history; our founding fathers, for instance, openly spoke of laws to secure control, often favoring the interests of the "Masters of men" over the common good. It is a power based on exclusion, conquest, and the illusion of superiority, manifesting in systems that prioritize the few over the many. This kind of power has shaped the world for centuries, driving empires, colonization, systemic racism, and social hierarchies. Its legacy is evident in the corruption, inequality, and injustice that pervade our institutions and societies today. *Potestas* thrives on the idea that resources, rights, and privileges are limited and must be guarded fiercely, often at the expense of others.

Power as *potentia*, on the other hand, represents a fundamentally different approach. It is a relational power that emphasizes connection, collaboration, and shared potential. Rather than exerting control over others, *potentia* invites us into a collective dynamic where power is not a zero-sum game but a shared force that grows through mutual engagement. This power is transformative because it encourages us to act together, leveraging our diverse strengths to create new possibilities. It is the power of empathy, dialogue, and cooperation that seeks to uplift rather than suppress.

Potentia is not about who has the upper hand but about how we can use our combined energies to change the narrative of domination. It calls us to move beyond competition and fear, inviting us to imagine and work toward a world where power is distributed, where every voice matters, and where true justice can flourish. While *potestas* clings to the past and seeks to maintain control through division and fear, *potentia* is the power of the future—an evolving force that has the capacity to heal relationships, build communities, and reshape societies. It is the power of "we" rather than "me," the power that recognizes our interconnectedness and strives to create a world where we all rise together.

Our struggle lies between two opposing forces: the entrenched power of domination and the emerging power of collective action. To engage with these dynamics, we must be vigilant and intentional, recognizing that every effort toward transformation will inevitably encounter resistance. As history shows us, the dialectic of progress—a concept explored by the philosopher Hegel—suggests that each significant shift in power triggers a counter-response. Dr. Sharon Welch reminds us that "resistance is never a straight path; it's a winding road marked by setbacks and surges forward." When monumental changes occur, such as the election of an African American president, an antithesis often emerges, pushing back against progress. However, through this ongoing tension, a new synthesis is born, gradually shaping a more just and equitable society.

Dr. Hogue speaks of *Countervailing Resonances*—a term that captures the idea of offsetting power by creating something equally impactful, something that vibrates through humanity, raising our consciousness. This resonance is formed through grassroots movements grounded in compassion, empathy, and love. We see these resonances emerging today as new movements challenge the prevailing power structures. Even amidst the pain and struggle, these moments mark a time ripe for systemic change.

Consider the old Christmas story: a time when power-with emerged, threatening the prevailing powers so much that King Herod sought to destroy it. Yeshua—Jesus—embodied a force opposite to the status quo, offering teachings that challenged the powerful few. His words in the Beatitudes were revolutionary, emphasizing humility, compassion, and love. His life and ministry were a profound example of countervailing power that still inspires us today.

Throughout history, from the American Revolution to the Civil Rights Movement, and now with movements like Black Lives Matter, we see the ongoing struggle between power-over and power-with. These patterns—of oppression and resistance, progress and pushback—teach us that while the road is long and fraught with setbacks, the moral arc does indeed bend toward justice.

Today, we stand at a pivotal moment, not merely as observers of history but as active participants in its unfolding. As people of faith, we are called to engage, to resist, and to be the countervailing resonances that disrupt the narrative of domination and control. Our task is to embody a new way of being—one rooted in relational power, mutual respect, and our shared humanity. Dr. Sharon Welch challenges us with these words: "Our courage lies in the small, persistent acts of solidarity and defiance that weave together the fabric of a new world." Let us be bold and unwavering in our commitment to this vision. By embracing our interconnectedness and acting with purpose, we can help shape a future where justice, equity, and compassion are not just ideals but lived realities. Together, let us be the resonant voices that bend the arc of history toward love.

May it be so.

Amen.

References

1. **Cousins, Norman.** *Human Options: An Autobiographical Notebook.* New York: W.W. Norton, 1981. This book provides insights into Cousins' reflections on humanity and interconnectedness.
2. **Harper, Frances Ellen Watkins.** *Complete Poems of Frances E.W. Harper.* New York: Oxford University Press, 1988. A collection of Harper's work, emphasizing the interconnectedness of humanity.
3. **Hogue, Mike.** *American Immanence: Democracy for an Uncertain World.* New York: Columbia University Press, 2018. Hogue's exploration of democracy, power, and ethical responses to societal challenges.
4. **Hogue, Mike.** *The Promise of Religious Naturalism.* Lanham, MD: Rowman & Littlefield, 2010. This book delves into religious naturalism and how it can inform contemporary ethical and ecological challenges.
5. **Welch, Sharon.** *Communities of Resistance and Solidarity: A Feminist Theology of Liberation.* Maryknoll, NY: Orbis Books, 1985. Welch explores the dynamics of power, liberation, and ethical responsibility.
6. **Welch, Sharon.** *A Feminist Ethic of Risk.* Minneapolis, MN: Fortress Press, 1990. This work challenges readers to consider ethical action amid uncertainty and power struggles.
7. **Hegel, Georg Wilhelm Friedrich.** *The Phenomenology of Spirit.* Oxford: Oxford University Press, 1977. Hegel's exploration of dialectics and the moral progression of history.
8. **Martin Luther King Jr.** *Strength to Love.* New York: Harper & Row, 1963. King's reflections on power, justice, and the ongoing struggle for civil rights.
9. **Hanh, Thich Nhat.** *Peace Is Every Step: The Path of Mindfulness in Everyday Life.* New York: Bantam Books, 1991. A spiritual and ethical guide that underscores

interconnectedness and the power of collective mindfulness.

10. **Parker, Palmer.** *Healing the Heart of Democracy: The Courage to Create a Politics Worthy of the Human Spirit.* San Francisco: Jossey-Bass, 2011. Palmer emphasizes the importance of relational power and the role of individuals in transforming society.

36. JUSTICE IS LOVE IN ACTION

Preached at the Sunday Morning Worship Service at the Unitarian Universalist Association General Assembly, 2012

We are here on a very special Sunday, this is General Assembly Sunday where we come to worship and give thanks. But we are also here because we are very concerned about the State of Arizona, and how it treats some of its people. Amen? We expressed our concerns privately and publicly this week. We've been loud in our opposition. We are certainly letting Governor Brewer and her sheriff know that these beautiful brown people down here are here to stay. [APPLAUSE]

Perhaps they haven't gotten the memo. They too are God's people. And as they say in my neighborhood, "God don't make no junk". We are here to let them know not to play politics with people's lives. We are here to tell them to embrace instead of erase. Learn how to love instead of hate. Learn how to, as

Dr. King said so well, live together as sisters and brothers, or perish as fools.

We made some progress this week. They know we're here. In fact, the sheriff, I think, shut down the jails for visitors because we're here. And we've made progress, but 'the road is rough, the going gets tough, and the hills are hard to climb." We've still got a long way to go and I just want to encourage everyone here to go home and start a little trouble.

[APPLAUSE]

In the name of justice–start some good trouble. For indeed, the justice we seek–beloved community becomes manifest from our persistent marching, our letter writing, our continuous public witnessing, our one-on-one conversations proclaiming that we stand on the side of love and on the side of justice. You know something, we do whatever we choose to do in life. And I want to be honest with you this morning, we have the world we have because enough of the right people have not stepped up to renounce human tragedies.

[APPLAUSE]

We can collectively speed up the day to beloved community, but first we have to dedicate and rededicate ourselves to this work. And we have to look in the mirror and be honest with ourselves and say "self, you know what, I have not done enough for the underprivileged, marginalized, and oppressed." I do understand that learning how to take a stand is a process, it is a growth process.

To take a stand on anything important we have to be convicted. Our conscience must be pricked in some small or great way. There has to be a moral imperative that holds us captive and moves us from hibernation to participation. It takes courage and faith to stand in the face of ignorance which oftentimes can cost you your time, your peace, and your sleep. I'm being real with you. There is a price to pay if we want justice to roll down and history is wrought with examples.

One example for me, many of you may or may not know, but in an early sermon, long before his Ware Lecture here at GA in 1966, Dr. King shared the moment when he chose to stand on the side of love, accepting his call to lead in spite of the difficulties. It was sometime in 1955 during the Montgomery bus boycott. Listen to these lengthy words of the then 26-year-old Martin Luther King:

> "I came home and my wife was in the bed and I immediately crawled into bed to get some rest so I could get up early the next morning. And then immediately the telephone started ringing and I picked up the phone. On the other end was an ugly voice. And that voice said to me in substance, 'nigger, we're tired of you and your mess now. And if you aren't out of this town in three days, we're going to blow your brains out and blow up your house.' I had heard these things before, but for some reason that night it got to me. I was frustrated, bewildered.

> Then I got up and went back to the kitchen and started warming some coffee, hoping the coffee would give me a little relief. Then I started thinking about many things. I pulled back on the theology and philosophy that I had just studied in the universities trying to give philosophical and theological reasons for the existence and the reality of sin and evil, but the answer didn't quite come there. I sat there and thought about a beautiful little daughter who had just been born about a month earlier. She was the darling of my life. And I'd come in night after night and see that little gentle smile,

and I sat at that table thinking about that little girl and thinking about the fact that she could be taken from me at any minute.

And I started thinking about a dedicated, devoted, and loyal wife who was over there asleep. And she could be taken from me, or I could be taken from her. And I got to the point that I couldn't take it any longer. I was weak. And something said to me, you can't call on daddy now, he's up in Atlanta 175 miles away. You can't even call on momma now. You've got to call on that power that can make a way out of no way. And I discovered then that religion had to become real to me. And I bowed down over that cup of coffee—I'll never forget it—and oh yes I prayed a prayer, and I prayed out loud that night.

I said, Lord, I'm down here trying to do what's right. I think the cause that we represent is right, but Lord I must confess that I am weak. I'm faltering. I'm losing my courage. And I can't let the people see me like this because if they see me weak and losing my courage they will begin to get weak. And it seemed, at that moment, that I could hear an inner voice saying to me, Martin Luther, stand up for righteousness. Stand up for justice. Stand up for truth and lo I will be with you even until the end of the earth."

[APPLAUSE]

Powerful words that we now know now as Dr. King's "Kitchen Call." It was a major impetus in moving him forward socially, and I'm sure he had that conversation with his God many times in his ministry when the road got rough. And his call, we know, was extraordinary. Most of us won't have that kind of call, but even still the world is calling, do you hear what I hear? The world is calling, do you hear what I hear?

AUDIENCE: Yeah!

Good. The spirit is calling you. It is calling us to wake up and understand the game that is being played. It is asking us to learn the game of life and get into it ready to play. Now currently in this game, we're witnessing a paradigm shift in many societies and many are uncomfortable and afraid. This game is called modern tribalism.

Let me break this down to you, just focusing here on America. We are all living in a constructed or created reality, the American dream. This is what I'm talking about. We've collectively created it and we can collectively change it. It's not that simple, though, because it works quite well for a few gamers who get lots of incentives to keep the game a certain way.

Now, in this game there is no alien at work, only the tragic human condition with all of its prejudices and biases, virtues and vices, various stories, mores, folklores, et cetera. We create meaning. We've created things we love. And we've created things we hate.

Now we're all in this game for better or for worse. And we all sort of create meaning out of all of this chaos and ambiguity. Now, within the game those with massive incentives have created, what I'm calling, the societal quintessential of privilege.

Now, here's what that looks like. If you're looking at a dartboard, in the center, the bullseye, in the center, that represents ultimate privilege. Now what does this center of that bullseye look like in its purest form? It's a white man. He's tall. He's fit. He's blonde, blue eyed. He's a CEO. He's Protestant.

226

He's straight. He's a man of the house. He's married and he's the best dad in the world. He has 2.5 kids, a dog, and a cat. He's wise and patient, so loving. He lives in a lovely home in the suburbs. He has great genes. His spouse, his wife, is also tall. She's fit. She's blonde and blue eyed, a supportive homemaker. She makes the best apple pie too. She's Protestant, straight, mild tempered, innocent, a little bit naive. By golly, it's June Cleaver!

[LAUGHTER]

And let me not forget she walks around in high heels and pearls. She's always so nice. Her home is in the suburbs. It's always tidy and clean. She's perfect. She has superb genes.

Now this game of privilege empowers and provides incentives to those who get closest to the center of that dartboard of which I've just described. If you have all of the things mentioned, step to the center. If you don't, take a step back for everything that you don't have. But let me say, the makers of this game doomed it from the start. It wasn't honest about what this country and world is. This is the dream of some, a few, but it is not my America. This is not the game that I would like to play.

Perhaps to some it is the America that you want and that's fine, but this has never been my America. And, sadly, it is the facade many strive toward but few ever get close to. I'm being real with you this morning. We are a diverse world. We have many kinds of families. We're not only white but we are black. We are Latino. We are Latina. We're gay. We're straight. We're bisexual, lesbian, transgender. We're Asian Pacific Islander. We are so many things and so much more. And that is my point.

[APPLAUSE]

The problem with immigration is the same problem that some people have with an African American United States President, which is the same problem they have with same sex marriage, and woman's reproductive rights, and overall empowerment, which is the same problem that I have with the mass incarceration system that locks up too many blacks and Latinos. It is all one big problem. Maybe two, actually.

[APPLAUSE]

One, America is getting too brown, too fast. And those who control the dartboard don't like it. They fear they are losing power. Two, the traditional family myth is being challenged and changed before their eyes. O- M- G.

[APPLAUSE]

What is happening to my America? Where's the baseball and apple pie? The sky is falling! The world is coming to an end! My stocks! My country! My Social Security! What am I to do? Thank God the story is changing!

[APPLAUSE]

There's nothing wrong with the Leave it to Beaver story, that was one of my favorite shows growing up, I have to tell you. But the reality is that this current homogeneous paradigm has marginalized and oppressed far too many non-white people for centuries. And it is only presented to us one reality which is good and that's just not true.

That my friends is the issue of what's going on right now. That is the lie that is being sold to us in movies, in politics, on television, it's everywhere and we have sort of bought into it somehow as if it is some beautiful and perfect mono-cultural masterpiece.

We've never been a homogeneous nation. We've always been a heterogeneous nation made up of many kinds of people. The Census figures tell us that 36% of Americans are minorities. In a few decades the minorities of America will probably equal or surpass the European-American majority. Some are shuttering at this reality and working like hell to redistrict and suppress votes, and for the sake of what? The betterment of humanity? I say embrace the change. Embrace the change!

[APPLAUSE]

We are religious liberals, that's what we do. We evolve and resolve. We embrace not erase. And I say that you should tell some of your friends or family members in a very loving way to—how do I say this—grow up.

[APPLAUSE]

I'm a first and seventh principle preacher, which means that my faith calls me to fight to participate in the game. This struggle is too important and too many lives are at stake. When I think about the worth and dignity of all in the interdependent web of existence of which we are all a part, I cannot see another's woe and not be in sorrow too. I cannot see another's grief and not seek for kind relief. I cannot see a falling tear and not feel my sorrow's share. I cannot see my faith as just for the privileged either.

I don't want to see my faith or my church as some mono-cultural experience. I cannot see my immigrant brothers and sisters dying in the desert and not get very upset.

[APPLAUSE]

I can't and I won't. I cannot look at our principles or our historic legacy as Unitarian Universalists, how we've been with the downtrodden and oppressed, and then do nothing. To me, that is a counterfeit faith, a kind of paltry piety. Justice is love in action. Justice is not just in what we say, it is in what you're willing to do.

[APPLAUSE]

However, a lot of us don't like choosing a side. You know, when we choose a side, it's like when we were growing up. I was always short and my sister, she's tall, she would always get chosen on the basketball team ahead of me. They would choose her before me. And it always made me feel bad. Some of us don't like choosing sides because it makes us feel bad. We feel like we're the loser. They're the winner, we're the loser. So we don't really like choosing a side. I understand that. I do. And we've seen the world, how bruised and beat up it is from people choosing sides, creating all kinds of dichotomies and false dichotomies, one tyranny leading to another tyranny. I hear you. I get it.

But I have a litmus test that helps me decide whether to stand. Maybe it will help you. Does my stance lift up the worth and dignity of all? Does my choice eventually join one to another, or continue tearing us further apart? Does my choice move us toward our beloved community, to a world with mutuality and reciprocity? Does it recognize the namaste, the holy, in others? Does it create the us against them mentality, or the we are together reality? I ask myself these questions before I decide to take a stance. Perhaps you, too, could ask yourself some of these questions.

Standing up is also about changing bad legislation. Amen?

AUDIENCE: Amen!

Dr. King mentioned how important moral legislation is in bending that moral arc toward justice. I think he was on to something. As King said, "you may not like me, but the law can keep you from lynching me." We need solid, moral laws. They protect us from ourselves. But when I think about the laws, past and present, in America it has quite often occurred to me that just because some things are legal, does not make them moral or ethical.

[APPLAUSE]

Sometimes we have to work real hard to get rid of very bad laws that keep the world separate and unequal. Slavery was legal at one point. Hello? And to stand against it meant you were breaking the law. That seems crazy for most of us today but it was legal for a very long time. And so my belief is that sometimes we have to go against the norm so that the circle of privilege can be widened and shared by more people. We have to be collectively maladjusted to speed up the freedom of all the earth's people.

Reverend Bill Sinkford would always say we have to afflict the comfortable and comfort the afflicted. And when we fail to act there are repercussions that occur, historical happenings that have been the result of our acquiescence. And I'll offer as an example for you, early America, in Virginia specifically, when immigrants from England and Africa came over to the New World. You may not know this, but at first, all who came over were indentured servants, white and black, Native American, alike. This was before the transatlantic slave trade. As long as a person professed to be a Christian upon their arrival to Jamestown, they were promised land and a few other things if they worked as indentured servants for around seven years.

This was, of course, in the 1600s but as time passed and the labor force changed, the law changed to reconcile what had become a lack of workers in early America. Now you've got to pick up a history book to get all the details. But at first, as long as you were Christian you were okay. But in 1705, about 100 years later, the law was amended in the Virginia General Assembly to state this—now watch the power of the law here my friends—"all servants imported and brought into the country who were not Christians in their native country shall be accounted and shall be slaves. All Negro, mulatto, and Indian slaves within this dominion shall be held to be real estate. If any slave resists his master correcting such slave and shall happen to be killed in such correction, the master shall be free of all punishment as if such accident never happened." The Virginia General Assembly declaration, 1705.

And now many states followed suit with Virginia leading

the way. America was now going to be a country defined by slavery, defined by black and white, defined by red and blue states. This unethical, immoral law in 1705 still lives with us today. The vestiges of it. We live with its ramifications. It was there in the Dred Scott case. It lived and created the Civil War, lived during Jim Crow, lived in Brown v. Board of Education, lived during the Voting Rights Act, and the Civil Rights Movement. This bad legal decision has shaped American history as we know it. It has shaped our relationships with each other.

[APPLAUSE]

But thank God for conscientious people who stood up and said, you know what, this is not right. Legal does that mean ethical or moral.

[APPLAUSE]

History is replete with examples of how when we don't respond so many innocents suffer, but I'm telling you this morning the world is calling us. Calling the gentle, angry people. Calling the justice-seeking people. That is why we have to continue to stand up in opposition to any legislation that treats our brown immigrants and other sisters and brothers as if they're not fully human and fully divine.

[APPLAUSE]

I'm so clear this morning. I can see clearly. I can see clearly now the rain is gone. It's so clear to me when looking at history and the legal system why we must stand up for the human rights of immigrants in America. It's clear to me that advocating for those who are of the same sex and desire marriage, that's a no-brainer. It's clear to me why the mass incarceration system is jacked up and needs an overhaul. It's clear to me why conservation and ecological responsibility are required for humanity's sustenance. It's clear to me that the medical system is corrupt.

[LAUGHTER]

It's clear to me that the few still dictate how the many eat. Is clear to me that we have a lot of work to do. Get in the game! Come on! Get in the game!

[APPLAUSE]

There are too many Josselines out there. We need to let them know that we're not giving up on them. That we, Unitarian Universalists, are not giving up on you. We refuse to give in to this exclusive dream. No, we will not give in to this myth. We can change the myth. It's a mental choice we must make.

I'm not going to live with a mind of fear and scarcity. That's a mental choice that I'm making. I'm going to choose to see God in others. That's a mental choice that I'm making. I'm going to keep marching and keep praying and keep meditating and writing letters and working with the UU advocacy organizations because I believe that we have the power to change human history to something that is truly welcoming and affirming.

[APPLAUSE]

Amen! Do you believe it? I believe. You believe. We can speed up today to justice. You see, when the spirit is working inside of you, you want to share and care and give and nurture. When the great spirit moves and challenges you, you can't look at others without seeing yourself. When you are truly living a meaningful life you just want to give your life away. When spirit lives inside of your heart, you want relationships based on trust. That's the world that I dream of. That's the world that I dream of.

I don't know about you this morning but I'm still a yes we can kind of guy. I'm going to keep believing in the dream and in my faith that it can manifest its greatness in this life. Because you see, I, like Langston Hughes, *"Dream a world where [all] will know sweet freedom's way. Where greed no longer saps the soul nor avarice blights our day. A world I dream where black or white, whatever race you be, will share the bounties of the earth, and every [soul] is free. Where wretchedness will hang its head and joy, like a pearl, attends the needs of all [humankind] of such, I dream! My world!"*

Amen!

[Standing ovation]

References

1. **Martin Luther King, Jr.: A Life** by Marshall Frady – Covers King's personal moments of struggle, including the "Kitchen Table Prayer," which reflects his commitment to justice during the Montgomery Bus Boycott.
2. **A Call to Conscience: The Landmark Speeches of Dr. Martin Luther King, Jr.** edited by Clayborne Carson and Kris Shepard – This book includes King's pivotal moments and speeches, highlighting his calls for justice and personal conviction.
3. **Strength to Love** by Martin Luther King Jr. – King's philosophy of justice as an active form of love, emphasizing moral courage and social responsibility.
4. **Where Do We Go from Here: Chaos or Community?** by Martin Luther King Jr. – Explores King's vision of a just society, emphasizing the importance of love in action.
5. **The Radical King** edited by Cornel West – Includes King's famous quote, "The arc of the moral universe is long, but it bends toward justice," and emphasizes the moral imperative of action.
6. **Stamped from the Beginning: The Definitive History of Racist Ideas in America** by Ibram X. Kendi – Provides a historical look at how racist ideas have been perpetuated in America, linking to the societal structures you critique.
7. **The New Jim Crow: Mass Incarceration in the Age of Colorblindness** by Michelle Alexander – Alexander's work provides insight into systemic racism, mass incarceration, and the continued impact of discriminatory laws.
8. **The Warmth of Other Suns: The Epic Story of America's Great Migration** by Isabel Wilkerson –

Chronicles the migration of Black Americans, revealing the systemic injustices they faced, aligning with themes of marginalization and justice.

9. **Why We Can't Wait** by Martin Luther King Jr. – King's powerful arguments for immediate action against injustice, capturing the urgency of the civil rights movement.

10. **The Fire Next Time** by James Baldwin – Baldwin's work delves into racial struggles and the need for systemic change, echoing the moral imperative you describe.

11. **God of the Oppressed** by James H. Cone – A foundational text in Black Liberation Theology, exploring the intersection of faith and justice for marginalized communities.

12. **Jesus and the Disinherited** by Howard Thurman – Thurman explores the social and spiritual dimensions of justice, emphasizing the need to stand with the oppressed.

13. **The Souls of Black Folk** by W.E.B. Du Bois – A classic examination of racial inequality and the quest for justice, deeply resonant with your themes.

14. **America's Original Sin: Racism, White Privilege, and the Bridge to a New America** by Jim Wallis – Discusses the historical roots of racism and the moral call to action, connecting with your points about societal change.

15. **Pedagogy of the Oppressed** by Paulo Freire – Freire's examination of education as a tool for social justice aligns with the need to stand against oppressive systems.

SECTION 6: NATURE, SCIENCE, AND PHILOSOPHY

37. YOU ARE THE EARTH: TRANSFORMING OUR THINKING ABOUT NATURE

Our planet is in crisis, but we have the power to heal it. The key lies in transforming how we think about our relationship with nature—from something we conquer and subdue to something sacred that we must protect, like parents caring for their children. It is about moving from domination to collaboration, recognizing that we are not above nature but part of it.

Our disconnection from nature began when we moved away from our hunter-gatherer selves. In those early days, we were more collectivist, more connected to the earth and to one another. But as we evolved, we organized ourselves into cities, became agrarian, and developed more complex social structures. With civilization came class hierarchies and patriarchy. We became cultured, sophisticated, and distanced from the natural world. In the process, we lost something profound.

The privileged among us created myths to justify our place in this new world. We told stories—big, colossal epics—about how we got to where we are. These stories, passed down through generations, explain why things are the way they are, often providing a moral rationale for the dominance of one group over another. The stories tell us who is in control and who is not. One of the most significant stories, especially in the Western world, comes from the Bible: the creation story of Adam and Eve.

In the book of Genesis, we find the narrative of how everything came to be. Adam, meaning "humanity," and Eve, meaning "life-giver," are created in a perfect garden, living in harmony with nature. But that harmony does not last. Just two chapters into the Bible, they are cast out of paradise for breaking a rule—eating fruit from the tree of knowledge. As a result, they are condemned to a life of labor. Adam must "till the soil" to eat, and Eve will experience pain in childbirth. This is a powerful metaphor for how humanity has experienced separation from nature and each other.

One part of this story is particularly telling. In Genesis 2:19-20, we read:

> *"Now the Lord God had formed out of the ground all the wild animals and all the birds in the sky. He brought them to the man to see what he would name them; and whatever the man called each living creature, that was its name. So the man gave names to all the livestock, the birds in the sky, and all the wild animals."*

This passage signifies that men were given authority to name the animals—as if they were ours to control. This notion of dominance over the natural world is deeply problematic.

Then, in Genesis 1, we find a different creation account. Here, the language is even more explicit: "Let us make MAN in our image." Women are excluded. "Let *him* have dominion over" nature. Men—not women—are told to "subdue" the earth. This is the patriarchy at work. In essence, the earth is ours (meaning men's) to do with as we please. This idea of dominion has shaped our entire worldview. It has justified the exploitation of natural resources, the destruction of ecosystems, and the mistreatment of animals. It has also justified the subjugation of certain groups of people.

This is not just an environmental issue, but a gender issue as well. The very idea that men were given dominion over the earth ties back to the historical oppression of women. Patriarchy and environmental degradation are intertwined in these stories. And as long as we cling to these outdated narratives, both the earth and women will continue to suffer.

But we need to stop telling this story—or, at the very least, reframe it. The old narrative of domination is no longer serving us. In fact, it is killing our planet. It may have been necessary in an earlier time, but now it is outdated. We need a new story, one that reflects our interconnectedness with nature, our responsibility to protect it, and our shared destiny with all living beings.

My stepson, Parker, a few years ago, saved up some money, bought a van, and traveled across the country with his dog. One of his stops was the Redwood Forest in Northern California, home to some of the largest trees on earth. These sequoias, some up to 30 feet wide and 300 feet tall, are ancient —some are over 3,000 years old. Parker described standing among these giants, feeling like an ant. He was surrounded by trees that had witnessed countless generations come and go. "They were here long before me, and they'll be here long after I'm gone," he said. He was mesmerized by the beauty, the stillness, and the sense of being part of something much greater than himself.

I asked him, "Didn't you wish you had someone there to validate what you were experiencing other than your dog?" He responded, "No way. I didn't feel alone at all. I felt safe, complete, whole—a small part of something much bigger than me."

Parker had what I would call a divine experience. It was a moment of unity consciousness, of recognizing that he was not separate from nature but a part of it. This is the kind of transformation we all need. We must have our own divine experiences with nature to truly understand that we are not above it. WE ARE NATURE. We are it and it is us.

You can't teach this feeling. You have to experience it. When you do, you realize that every living thing—plants, animals, trees, even the earth itself—is sacred. You realize that you cannot destroy what is sacred. You cannot exploit it, oppress it, or harm it. When you understand that we are all part of the same web of existence, it changes you. You become more compassionate, more forgiving, more connected.

And this is what the world needs today. We need a collective awakening, a moment of unity consciousness, to heal our planet. We must recognize that the destruction of our environment is tied to the destruction of our own humanity. The more disconnected we become from nature, the more disconnected we become from ourselves and each other.

Our Native American kin understood this. They revered nature as part of themselves. They lived in harmony with the land for thousands of years, and while their societies were not perfect, they respected the earth in ways that we have forgotten. When European settlers arrived, they brought with them a different story—one of domination and exploitation. Christopher Columbus himself wrote in his journals that the Native people he encountered were peaceful and had no weapons. He saw them as easy to conquer, and this mindset led to their decimation.

This story of conquest has continued for centuries, and it has brought us to where we are today. We have advanced technologically, but we have failed to advance morally. We have learned how to control nature in some ways, but we have forgotten how to live in harmony with it.

To heal the planet, we need to transform our thinking. We must move away from the old narratives of domination and exploitation. We must tell new stories—stories that honor the sacredness of all life, that recognize our interconnectedness, and that inspire us to protect the earth as we would protect ourselves.

On this Earth Day Sunday, I leave you with a prayer. It is a Native American prayer that speaks to the deep wisdom of living in harmony with nature:

> "Earth teach me stillness as the grasses are stilled with light. Earth teach me suffering as old stones suffer with memory. Earth teach me humility as blossoms are humble with beginning. Earth teach me caring as the mother who secures her young. Earth teach me courage as the tree which stands all alone. Earth teach me limitation as the ant which crawls on the ground. Earth teach me freedom as the eagle which soars in the sky. Earth teach me resignation as the leaves which die in the fall. Earth teach me regeneration as the seed which rises in the spring. Earth teach me to forget myself as melted snow forgets its life. Earth teach me to remember kindness as dry fields weep with rain."

May it be so.

References

1. **Genesis 1-3.** *The Holy Bible, New International Version.*
These chapters from the Bible contain the creation stories of Adam and Eve, the dominion mandate, and humanity's separation from nature. The language of dominion and the exclusion of women is central to the sermon's discussion of patriarchy and environmental degradation.

2. **Ruether, Rosemary Radford.** *Gaia and God: An Ecofeminist Theology of Earth Healing.* San Francisco: HarperSanFrancisco, 1992.
Ruether explores the intersection of ecological destruction and patriarchy, arguing for an ecofeminist theology that sees nature and women as sacred, rather than objects of control.

3. **Merchant, Carolyn.** *The Death of Nature: Women, Ecology, and the Scientific Revolution.* San Francisco: Harper & Row, 1980. Merchant's classic work discusses how the Scientific Revolution redefined nature and women as passive, subordinate entities, laying the groundwork for environmental and social exploitation.

4. **Armstrong, Karen.** *A Short History of Myth.* New York: Canongate, 2005.
Armstrong examines how myth has shaped human consciousness, especially myths of creation and domination.

5. **Shiva, Vandana.** *Staying Alive: Women, Ecology, and Development.* London: Zed Books, 1989.
Shiva critiques the impact of Western patriarchal and capitalist systems on both women and the environment, offering a perspective that aligns with the sermons critique of patriarchy and environmental destruction.

6. **Tucker, Mary Evelyn, and John A. Grim.** *Ecology and Religion.* Washington, D.C.: Island Press, 2014.
This book provides an overview of how different religious traditions address ecological issues and calls for a new, interreligious narrative that treats the earth as sacred and interconnected.

7. **Ruether, Rosemary Radford.** *Integrating Ecofeminism, Globalization, and World Religions.* Lanham, MD: Rowman & Littlefield Publishers, 2005. In this book,

Ruether explores the relationship between patriarchy, environmental exploitation, and global economic systems, providing a theological and feminist critique.

8. **Columbus, Christopher.** *The Diario of Christopher Columbus's First Voyage to America, 1492-1493.*
Columbus's journals, where he describes the Native Americans he encountered as peaceful and easy to conquer, provide historical context for the colonization narrative and its implications for both Indigenous peoples and the environment.

9. **Berry, Thomas.** *The Dream of the Earth.* San Francisco: Sierra Club Books, 1988.
Berry's work calls for a new ecological spirituality, one that recognizes humanity's place within the larger web of life.

10. **Chief Seattle.** "Speech to Governor Isaac Stevens, 1854."
Chief Seattle's famous speech emphasizes the sacredness of nature and the interconnectedness of all living things, reinforcing the Native American wisdom you referenced.

11. **Keller, Catherine.** *Face of the Deep: A Theology of Becoming.* London: Routledge, 2003.
Keller offers a feminist reading of creation, challenging traditional interpretations of Genesis and advocating for a more inclusive and ecological vision of the divine.

38. THE AMERICAN BUFFALO: A LESSON IN HUBRIS

Today, my sermon is a lamentation. To lament is to express deep grief and sadness, and that is where we are in our world. I am reminded of the Book of Jeremiah in the Hebrew scriptures: "A voice is heard in Ramah, lamentation and bitter weeping. Rachel is weeping for her children; she refuses to be comforted for her children, because they are no more." Too often, this is the cry of people mourning loved ones lost to war and violence. But it is not only humans who deserve our lament. Today, I want to talk about the American Buffalo, whose suffering mirrors our own. They, too, deserve a voice. For centuries, they have lamented, and their story provides a powerful lesson about what happens when we fail to live with compassion and empathy.

In mourning the buffalo, I cannot help but also mourn for the Native American tribes who revered them. As the buffalo suffered, so did the indigenous people who depended on them for survival.

Ken Burns has a new documentary about the buffalo. It's two parts and nearly four hours long, but worth watching. The lesson I hope to share is that human hubris—our exaggerated pride and unbalanced ego—can lead to great destruction if not guided by a theology of interdependence, reverence, and compassion for all living beings. This mindset is sorely needed today, given the many tragedies we see in the news.

Before 1800, there were 60 million buffalo roaming North America, from Canada to Alaska and as far south as Mexico. One Lakota elder said the buffalo were as plentiful as fish in the sea. It's hard to imagine. But for the buffalo, this was their Garden of Eden. They thrived for hundreds of years, long before Americans encountered them. But when frontiersmen arrived, their heaven turned into hell. In just 100 years, the buffalo were almost exterminated—by 1900, only 300 remained.

Think about that: 60 million to 300 in a century. What kind of narrative plays out to make that level of destruction possible? Humans have the power to wreak such havoc for the sake of space, money, power, and sport. And think of the impact on the psyche of the animals and the souls of the indigenous people who revered them. For various Native American tribes, the buffalo were sacred. They provided food, clothing, warmth, and a sense of purpose. The indigenous only killed what they needed to survive, ensuring the buffalo's population remained stable.

When the buffalo were nearly wiped out, it marked the end of the indigenous people's Garden of Eden and the beginning of decades of trauma, abuse, and inhumanity that continue today. My lament is for them as well.

This is a story not just about animals but about humans, too. It's the story of what happened to many beings—human and non-human—under the banner of "manifest destiny," the belief that America was given to Europeans by God to do as they pleased. And they did just that. In their quest to conquer nature, they also conquered the people who revered the buffalo. That is the sad reality of our human condition today.

But something happened with the buffalo. Some people decided to care. A restoration took place. President Theodore Roosevelt, who had once contributed to the problem, eventually took action to protect the buffalo from extinction. He created national parks and enacted laws, and other nonprofits joined in. Slowly, the buffalo's numbers grew. By 2016, there were an estimated 400,000 buffalo—far from the original 60 million, but a sign of hope nonetheless.

What we pay attention to can grow and thrive. When we meet the world with compassion and empathy, we can create beauty and preservation. But when we dehumanize others or see animals as mere objects, we are capable of great harm.

The buffalo is the mascot of many colleges and universities, but Howard University stands out to me. Howard, a predominantly Black institution, chose the buffalo or bison as its symbol. This is significant: the marginalized and oppressed, like the buffalo, are at risk of becoming extinct unless human will and compassion ensure their survival. The buffalo represents resilience, strength, and power—along with suffering and brutality.

So many cultures can relate to the buffalo. Look at the Jewish people in Europe or Israel. Their history, like the buffalo's, is one of resilience mixed with domination and brutality. And we cry out, "These people deserve to be free!" I lament with my Jewish kin today.

Look at the Bedouins, Palestinians, and Muslims—people whose lands have been shrunk, their populations confined. Again, we cry, "This is wrong! These people deserve freedom!" I lament for my Muslim and Palestinian kin.

This story of domination is global, and it's tragic. Rodney King once asked, "Why can't we all just get along?" It was a profound question. And the answer is this: we don't have a theology of reverence and interdependence.

Interdependence means trust and support between and among all living beings, not just humans. It is a sacred, holy trust that includes animals and the earth itself. A theology of reverence means holding life sacred, understanding that we are all connected in a giant web of consciousness. As Chief Seattle said, "The earth does not belong to us. We belong to the earth."

Therefore, we cannot bomb into dust what we are truly connected to. We cannot starve what we love. We cannot destroy what we hold sacred. The problem is that not enough of us live by this theology. Instead, our god is the ego, which creates an illusion of separation. This illusion is at the heart of our violence and destruction.

Martin Luther King said something profound about hubris in his sermon, "Why Jesus Called a Man a Fool." He spoke of a man who believed he was self-sufficient, superior to others, and in control of his own destiny, not realizing how deeply he depended on the labor and lives of others. King said:

> *"Something should remind us before we can finish eating breakfast in the morning that we are dependent on more than half of the world. We get up in the morning and go to the bathroom and reach over for a sponge, and that's handed to us by a Pacific Islander. Then we reach over for a bar of soap, and that's given to us at the hands of a Frenchman. And then we reach up for our towel, and that's given to us by a Turk. And then we go to the kitchen for breakfast, getting ready to go to work. Maybe this morning we want to follow the good old American tradition, and we drink coffee. That's poured in our cups by a South American. Or maybe we are desirous of having tea. Then we discover that it's poured in our cup by a Chinese. Or maybe we want*

cocoa this morning, and then we discover that that's poured in our cup by a West African. Then we reach over for a piece of toast, only to discover that that's given to us at the hands of an English-speaking farmer, not to mention the baker. And so before we finish eating breakfast in the morning, we are dependent on more than half of the world."

King concluded: "And any man who fails to see the interdependent structure of reality is really a fool."

By King's account, we are living in foolish times. We are continuing the cycle of violence, oppression, and war, ignoring the truth of our deep interdependence. And now, people are taking sides. But choosing sides based on power or domination is not the answer. The only side I will take is the side of love.

I am reminded of the Apostle Paul's words in 1 Corinthians 13, which remains one of the most profound reflections on love ever written. Paul lived in violent times, too, but his vision was rooted in hope and compassion. As I close, I share these powerful words from Paul:

"If I speak in the tongues of [humans] or of angels, but do not have love, I am only a resounding gong or a clanging cymbal. If I have the gift of prophecy and can fathom all mysteries and all knowledge, and if I have faith that can move mountains, but do not have love, I am nothing. If I give all I possess to the poor and give over my body to hardship that I may boast, but do not have love, I gain nothing.

Love is patient, love is kind. It does not envy, it does not boast, it is not proud. It does not dishonor others,

*it is not self-seeking, it is not easily angered, it keeps
no record of wrongs. Love does not delight in evil but
rejoices with the truth. It always protects, always trusts,
always hopes, always perseveres. Love never fails."*

May we all side with love, now and forever.

Amen.

References

1. **King, Martin Luther Jr.** *A Knock at Midnight: Inspiration from the Great Sermons of Reverend Martin Luther King, Jr.* New York: Warner Books, 1998.
   This book includes the sermon "Why Jesus Called a Man a Fool," where Dr. King discusses the themes of hubris, interdependence, and the illusion of self-sufficiency. The extended quote in your sermon is sourced from this collection.

2. **Genesis 1-3.** *The Holy Bible, New International Version.*
   The biblical creation stories from Genesis are central to understanding themes of dominion, human relationships with animals, and the loss of Eden.

3. **Burns, Ken (Director).** *The American Buffalo: A Story of Survival.* PBS, 2023.
   This documentary by Ken Burns provides a comprehensive look at the history of the American Buffalo, their near extinction, and their revival. It offers context for understanding the buffalo's significance to indigenous people and the impact of human greed and exploitation.

4. **Flores, Dan.** *American Serengeti: The Last Big Animals of the Great Plains.* Lawrence, KS: University Press of Kansas, 2016. Flores examines the historical significance of the buffalo and other animals in North America, discussing their extinction and the impact of colonialism.

5. **Isenberg, Andrew C.** *The Destruction of the Bison: An Environmental History, 1750–1920.* Cambridge: Cambridge University Press, 2000. Isenberg's work explores the environmental and economic factors that led to the near

extinction of the buffalo, emphasizing the relationship between humans, land, and wildlife. It provides a critical lens for understanding how the buffalo's decline mirrored the suffering of indigenous peoples.

6. **Chief Seattle.** "Speech to Governor Isaac Stevens, 1854."
Chief Seattle's famous speech speaks to the deep connection between Native American peoples and the land. His words, "The earth does not belong to us. We belong to the earth," echo the themes of reverence and interdependence in the sermon.

7. **Paul, The Apostle.** *The First Epistle to the Corinthians, Chapter 13. The Holy Bible, New International Version.*
This passage is where the famous "Love is patient, love is kind..." quote is found, used in your sermon to emphasize the power of love and compassion in healing relationships and addressing conflict.

8. **Deloria, Vine Jr.** *God Is Red: A Native View of Religion.* Golden, CO: Fulcrum Publishing, 2003.
Deloria's work explores the differences between Western and indigenous spiritualities, particularly the reverence for nature and interdependence with the land that is central to Native American traditions.

9. **West, Cornel.** *The Radical King.* Boston: Beacon Press, 2015.
West compiles some of Dr. King's most radical sermons and speeches, offering context for understanding King's broader critiques of American society, hubris, and the interconnectedness of all life.

39. EVOLUTION: ARE WE DEVOLVING?

This morning's reading took us into a serene moment in the life of a young boy, enraptured by the stillness of nature. The imagery paints a powerful picture of connection: the dark green water, the stillness of the lake, the fish floating between the grasses. Have you ever had such an experience? Sitting by a lake, walking through the woods, gazing up at the stars, and suddenly realizing you are part of something vast, something awe-inspiring, beyond your control or understanding?

These moments of awe bring us into a space of deep reverence for life. Whether it's the birth of a child, the slow drifting of clouds, or the mesmerizing sound of waves lapping the shore —these experiences remind us that life is more than the rush of our daily routines. It's moments like these when we feel a deep connection to something beyond ourselves, something mysterious, something transcendent.

Have you ever witnessed the awe-inspiring in your life— something that seemed to stop time? Perhaps it was the synchronicity of an unexpected coincidence that changed your perspective. Maybe it was the simple act of watching a baby sleep, say their first words, or take their first steps. These moments remind us of life's deep mysteries. For me, it's the beauty of music, the resonance of a song by Joshua Long, *We Are Earth,* that can bring me to tears, as I'm sure many of you have experienced. These moments speak to something beyond words. They bring us in touch with the presence of the divine. For those who are humanists or follow another path, this might be described as the sublime, the unnameable essence of life.

This is what the Tao Te Ching teaches in its opening verse: *"The Tao that can be told is not the eternal Tao. The name that can be named is not the eternal Name. The unnamable is the eternally real."* In a world filled with chaos and violence, these experiences can seem fleeting, even unreal. But the Tao reminds us that these are the moments when we are closest to reality. These moments of awe, wonder, and transcendence are real and available to us all if we take the time to notice them. They surround us in the natural world, in the stars, in the rhythm of life.

I am reminded of the story of a man who was struggling with the state of the world. He couldn't understand why there was so much violence, pain, and suffering. Then one night, he had a dream. In this dream, an angel took him into space and asked, "What do you see?" The man looked out and saw endless darkness, sprinkled with countless stars all perfectly placed. He marveled at the beauty and order of it all. The angel then took him above the earth and asked him the same question again: "What do you see?" The man saw a beautiful white, blue, green, and brown sphere rotating effortlessly, everything in perfect harmony. The angel said to him, "Thou art that. Everything is exactly as it should be. The earth, the stars, the planets—everything operates in harmony. Its design is perfect, its math pristine, its geometry sacredly designed."

The angel continued, "Listen as the earth sings a harmonious tune to its sun, and the solar system joins in the universal orchestra. The earth and the stars are doing what they are supposed to do. All is well. Do not get caught up in the illusion. This is reality. And you are part of that reality."

The man woke up, and the dream stayed with him for the rest of his life. When things got hard, he would return to the lesson of the dream: that there is order and beauty beyond the chaos we often see.

This story is deeply Taoist in its worldview. It reminds us to see life as yin and yang, not as two opposing forces at war with each other, but as complementary forces in balance. In Taoism, cause and effect are part of the same whole; they work together. Dualism, however, is a Western concept, influenced by the religion of Zoroastrianism and the philosophy of Plato, that has deeply impacted the three major religions—Judaism, Christianity, and Islam. In dualism, the world is viewed as a battleground between good and evil, light and darkness.

This dualistic mindset still dominates much of our worldview today, especially in Western cultures. We see it in our politics, in our media, in our relationships. The world seems divided into camps of good and bad, right and wrong, with very little room for nuance or complexity. And when we look at the state of the world, it can feel as though evil is winning. The earth seems to be on fire—literally, with wildfires spreading uncontrollably, and metaphorically, with the fiery rhetoric of world leaders and the violence we witness in conflicts around the globe.

It feels like we live in a time where, as the philosopher Nietzsche put it, "We have the highest values devalue themselves." Hypocrisy runs rampant. People in power speak of justice, peace, and unity, but their actions often betray those very ideals. We seem unable to work together to solve the pressing issues that could lead to our extinction: climate change, nuclear threats, systemic injustice. It is all so depressing.

But perhaps we are a both/and species. Perhaps *we operate under both dualism and Taoism simultaneously,* navigating between the two as we make sense of the world. The Taoist view invites us to see the world's natural balance and trust in the order of things. The dualist view compels us to fight for justice, to stand up for what is right. These two perspectives exist in tension with each other, and finding balance is not easy.

This tension is particularly challenging when we see children starving in Ethiopia or Somalia, or people running from bombs in Gaza. I am not homeless, unemployed, or incarcerated, so I must always measure my philosophical perspective with the reality of the suffering I see in the world.

John Wesley, the founder of Methodism, offers a powerful reminder: *"Do all the good you can, by all the means you can, in all the ways you can, in all the places you can, at all the times you can, to all the people you can, as long as ever you can."* We are each called to make a difference, to do good in the world. But there is a risk. If our passions, our sense of justice, or our empathy are triggered too often, we can become burned out, overwhelmed, and lose our sense of balance. This is why the wisdom of the East reminds us to look up at the stars and out into nature. Nature offers us balance. It reminds us that we are part of a larger whole, that life is not all chaos and suffering, but also beauty and harmony.

We are part of this world, and it is part of us. We must not lose ourselves in the social, political, or religious struggles of our time to the point that we forget the awe-inspiring beauty that surrounds us. Yes, we must deal with the awful, but we must also celebrate the awesome.

This brings us to the dualistic framework that dominates much of our world today. This "us versus them" mentality has created deep divisions in our society. We categorize people, places, and things into rigid boxes: good or evil, right or wrong, saved or damned. And once we've placed someone in the "bad" category, it becomes easy to dehumanize them, to see them as the enemy.

But life is not so simple. Dr. Martin Luther King Jr. reminds us, *"In the worst of us, there is some good, and in the best of us, there is some evil."* Perspective is everything. We cannot reduce people to these binary categories. Life is complex, and so are people.

This is why I have such great respect for Charles Darwin. Darwin's work on evolution changed the way we understand life on this planet. His theory of natural selection was revolutionary, and it came into direct conflict with the religious teachings of his time. Darwin's view was that all living organisms, including humans, evolved over time, adapting to their environments to survive. This idea challenged the belief that humans were created by God in a fixed, perfect form, separate from the rest of the natural world.

Darwin's work was groundbreaking because it showed that life is not static. It is constantly evolving, changing, and adapting. But his work was also deeply misunderstood by some. Over time, powerful individuals distorted Darwin's ideas into the concept of "survival of the fittest," using it to justify social hierarchies, racism, and white supremacy. This misinterpretation of Darwin's work fueled the eugenics movement and the belief in the superiority of certain races. Even today, these corrupted ideas persist in white nationalist movements.

But Darwin never intended for his work to be used in this way. As Rev. Fred Muir has often reminded me, Darwin's work teaches us that the species that are most adaptable to change, not the most powerful, are the ones that survive and thrive. His theory of evolution was about adaptability, not domination.

The paragraph conveys your ideas clearly, but it could be expanded to provide more depth and emphasize the complexity of human progress. Here's an expanded version:

The question then arises: Are we, as humans, devolving? Are we slipping backward, becoming less compassionate, less connected, and less evolved? I don't believe that's the case. Instead, certain aspects of our society—such as white supremacy, patriarchy, and the winner-take-all mentality—are what's devolving. These harmful systems are relics of the past, no longer sustainable in a world moving toward inclusivity, justice, and equality. As humanity evolves, these outdated structures are being weeded out because they cannot adapt to the future we are collectively building.

That said, progress is not a linear journey. It's a winding path, often with obstacles, setbacks, and detours. While it may seem at times like we are regressing, the overall trajectory is forward. We may take three steps forward and one or two steps back, but each setback serves as a reminder that change requires persistence. Despite the challenges, we press on toward the goal of individual and collective freedom, knowing that with every effort, we get closer to a more compassionate and just world.

White supremacy, for example, is in its death throes. It is devolving because it cannot survive in a world that is moving toward greater equality, inclusion, and diversity. This is why the world feels so chaotic right now. We are witnessing the death of old systems and ways of thinking that are no longer viable. The social order is adjusting to a new way of being, one that is more inclusive, more adaptable, and more aligned with the values of compassion and justice.

The conqueror mindset that has dominated human history is a holdover from our primitive brain, the amygdala, which is responsible for our fight-or-flight response. But as we evolve, the more rational, compassionate parts of our brain are developing. We are learning that cooperation, not domination, is the key to survival.

We are animals, but with higher consciousness, bringing with that higher responsibility. Yes, animals kill for survival, but as humans, we are capable of reason, empathy, and compassion. Murder and violence are not inherent to our nature; they are remnants of an old way of being that no longer serves us. Our higher consciousness allows us to transcend those instincts and move toward a more compassionate and peaceful existence.

In World War I, it was reported that many soldiers never fired their weapons. Even in the heat of battle, they could not bring themselves to kill another human being. It was unnatural to them. Today, modern warfare is fought from a distance, with drones and bombs, making it easier to kill without feeling the weight of it. But the fact remains: killing another human being goes against our nature.

Our work, then, is to weed out these old, destructive behaviors and cultivate the qualities that will allow our species to thrive: empathy, compassion, cooperation, adaptability.

As Unitarian Universalists, we are part of a living tradition, one that is constantly evolving. We are not bound by dogma or the past. We are free to adapt, to change, to grow. This is what it means to be part of a living faith. And it is also what it means to be human.

We are evolving. We are moving from competition to collaboration, from either/or to both/and. We are transcending the rigid binaries of race, gender, and power. We are evolving toward a world where collaboration, interdependence, and compassion are the guiding principles.

And as we evolve, we will look back on this time and wonder: How did we ever live like that? How did we ever believe that one race was superior to another? How did we ever justify the destruction of the planet for the sake of profit? Our descendants will look back and be amazed at how far we've come.

That day is coming. We are on the cusp of a new age, an age of evolution, compassion, and unity. Our work is to help bring that day closer, to be the catalysts for this new era of humanity.

As we move forward, may we align ourselves with the power of evolution, with the awe-inspiring force of life itself. May we do all we can to weed out outdated ideas, beliefs, and practices that no longer serve us. And may we work together to create a world that is more just, more compassionate, and more evolved.

May it be so.

Amen.

References

1. **Muir, Fredric.** *The Whole World Kin: Darwin and the Spirit of Liberal Religion.* Boston: Skinner House Books, 2010. This book explores the connection between Darwin's theory of evolution and liberal religion, emphasizing interdependence, adaptation, and the evolving nature of human consciousness.
2. **Darwin, Charles.** *On the Origin of Species.* London: John Murray, 1859.
   Darwin's seminal work on evolution, natural selection, and adaptation is central to the themes of human progress, adaptation, and the evolution of society.
3. **Marx Hubbard, Barbara.** *Conscious Evolution: Awakening Our Social Potential.* Novato, CA: New World Library, 1998. Barbara Marx Hubbard's work on conscious evolution offers a vision of humanity evolving toward greater compassion, interconnectedness, and higher consciousness.
4. **Tao Te Ching.** Translated by Stephen Mitchell. New York: Harper & Row, 1988.

The Tao Te Ching provides a philosophical framework for understanding balance, yin and yang, and the interconnectedness of all things. Its teachings on the Tao, and seeing beyond dualism, are referenced.

5. **King, Martin Luther Jr.** *Strength to Love.* Minneapolis: Fortress Press, 1963.
   This collection of King's sermons explores the balance between good and evil, as well as the importance of compassion and love in overcoming violence and injustice. King's idea that "in the worst of us, there is some good" is central to the message on perspective and human nature.

6. **Wesley, John.** *The Works of John Wesley, Volume 14: Do All the Good You Can.* Nashville: Abingdon Press, 1984.
   Wesley's famous call to action, "Do all the good you can," speaks to the moral responsibility highlighted— the need for continuous effort toward social justice and compassion.

7. **Zoroastrianism.** *The Zend-Avesta.* Translated by James Darmesteter. Oxford: Clarendon Press, 1880.
   The teachings of Zoroastrianism, particularly its influence on dualism, provide historical context for the dualistic thinking that has shaped Western religion and philosophy.

8. **Hawking, Stephen.** *The Grand Design.* New York: Bantam Books, 2010.
   This book discusses the laws of the universe, order, and balance, much like the angelic vision in the sermon. Hawking's exploration of the interconnectedness of the cosmos parallels the sermon's themes of universal harmony.

9. **Nietzsche, Friedrich.** *Thus Spoke Zarathustra.* Translated by Walter Kaufmann. New York: Penguin, 1966.
   Nietzsche's philosophy, particularly his ideas about the "devaluation of the highest values," reflects the moral and ethical challenges addressed in the sermon.

10. **Hubbard, Ruth.** *The Politics of Women's Biology.* New Brunswick, NJ: Rutgers University Press, 1990.
    This work explores the misuse of evolutionary theory, particularly in terms of gender and social hierarchies, which ties into the discussion of how Darwin's theories were distorted to justify oppression.

40. CIVILIZATIONS: COLLABORATION, COOPERATION, CONQUEST

We live in the Age of Narcissism—a time when the focus on our individual self-image, or what I like to call "somebody-ness," is front and center. It's no longer enough to simply be—now we feel this pressure to project our curated selves to the world, to declare our importance and uniqueness. Social media, our modern culture, it all amplifies this need to be seen, to be liked, to be validated. We've become experts at self-promotion, often without stopping to think about the impact this has on those around us. What's sold to us as self-empowerment is, in many ways, a distraction from something deeper—our communal responsibilities, our shared well-being.

This isn't new. Human civilization has *always* been preoccupied with seeking comfort—whether it's social, emotional, or physical comfort—and we've often sought it at the expense of others. Throughout history, whether it was through class structures, colonialism, or economic systems that favor the few over the many–the "tyranny of the minority"--comfort has been bought by marginalizing others.

We build walls—literal and figurative—to keep our discomfort at bay. This, my friends, is spiritually immature behavior. It's underdeveloped. And it's a mindset that has driven both cooperation and collaboration *and* conquest.

For centuries, civilizations have advanced by taking—taking land, taking resources, taking autonomy from others. Whether it was the expansion of empires or the rise of corporate monopolies, the pursuit of comfort for one group has often required the subjugation of another. Conquest is always about taking—taking power, taking wealth, taking even identity. It's about imposing one group's will over another, usually through violence or coercion.

However, cooperation and collaboration don't *have* to come through conquest. The problem isn't the desire to collaborate; it's the way collaboration has historically played out. Too often, "collaborating" has really meant *dominating*. If one group works with another, it's usually to assimilate or overpower, not to uplift or share.

And this is where we've got to grow up. As a species, we are still caught in the adolescence of our development. We act like we believe that in order to succeed, we've got to compete, dominate, or subdue. We see ourselves as separate from each other, each striving for individual gain instead of collective progress. This is the mindset that has driven wars, exploitation, environmental degradation—you name it.

But what if we could evolve? What if we could move past the conquest mindset? What if, instead of seeking comfort by dominating others, we found comfort in coexisting peacefully, in working toward shared goals where there doesn't have to be a winner and a loser?

To mature beyond conquest, we've got to face the root of violence—both physical and psychological violence. Violence, at its core, is a failure of connection. When we can no longer see the humanity in another person, when we forget that their struggles are tied to our own, that's when violence becomes possible. This applies not only to the violence of warfare but also to the subtler violence of exclusion and marginalization. When we can't imagine ourselves in someone else's shoes—when we fail to see their pain, their needs—that's when violence becomes justifiable. That's when it becomes normalized.

This has been the mindset for much of our history, but it doesn't have to define our future. Moving beyond violence means developing a capacity for empathy—real empathy. It means seeing the world through another's eyes and recognizing that their well-being is directly connected to ours. We have to redefine what success means. It can't just be about conquering or accumulating more; it must be about creating environments where *all* can thrive. That's the key to a successful future.

If we can embrace this new paradigm, we'll start to see cooperation not as a way to advance at someone else's expense, but as a way to enrich *everyone's* experience. True collaboration happens when we build something that benefits all parties without needing to sacrifice or marginalize anyone in the process. This is what it means to mature. This is the adult way of being, recognizing that we are all interconnected and interdependent.

In this new world we're striving for, success won't be measured by how much wealth or power we accumulate but by how much peace, justice, and understanding we can foster. In short, we've got to move from a mindset of conquest to a mindset of connection—from this paradigm of "somebody-ness" to one of shared humanity. That's how we grow up as a species.

Civility, kindness, sharing—these beautiful, powerful words are often driven by our need for comfort. Even love, for many of us, is conditional, based on whether we feel comfortable or uncomfortable with a person, a place, or a thing. For these values to really flourish, there has to be unity. There's a word in science for this—*entrainment*. It's the alignment of an organism's rhythm with its environment. That's why we, as Unitarian Universalists, are covenantal. We know that covenanting through our principles, agreeing on how we're going to *be* together, is what holds us together in community.

But today, we lack that rhythm. There's disharmony—at home, at work, among friends. Why? Because we're stuck in old, undeveloped ways of being. We haven't grown into adults, as a species. We are still adolescents.

Think about adolescence. In its early stages, there's a clumsiness as bodies grow, a preoccupation with certain parts of ourselves. As we grow older, the voice changes, identity starts to form, and there's emotional instability. This is how I see our current civilization—confused, unsure of our identity, irritable, inconsistent, but full of promise. We're still finding our collective voice.

Way back, 12,000 years ago, during the Agrarian Age, we shifted as a species. Before that, for 99% of our time on this planet, we lived as hunter-gatherers, in small, cooperative groups. These societies were less violent because there was space, and we didn't have to fight for resources. But when agriculture began, we started to protect land. Villages became towns. Towns became cities. And the cycle of conquest began.

From 5000 BCE to 1000 BCE, it was the most violent time in human history, even though today's world feels chaotic. Steven Pinker, in *The Better Angels of Our Nature*, says we live in the least violent time. It doesn't feel that way, but the data says it's true. Back then, many of the skeletons archaeologists dug up have skull fractures—evidence of normalized violence.

This is what the PBS documentary *Civilizations* calls "destructive creation." From Mesopotamia to Egypt, from

Rome to Mesoamerica, the pattern repeats: conquest, domination, and then collapse. Today, when people get desperate, they revert to that base survival mode. But this mindset of hubris, of cultural superiority, is unsustainable. As history shows us, all great empires fall.

But we don't have to keep repeating this cycle. We can grow beyond it. We can shift from destructive creation to constructive creation.

The key is to rewrite the story—our human story. A story that embraces all of us, not just some of us. The mature among us are already rewriting this narrative. Look at what Lin-Manuel Miranda did with *Hamilton*—rebranding the American Revolution. We need to do this kind of reimagining across every sector of society. We must move beyond the conqueror's narrative if we're going to survive.

The new story is about safe connections, egalitarian cooperation, compassionate engagement, and bold collaborations.

When we connect with each other's humanity, when we recognize that my needs are your needs, we create safe connections. When we work as a unit with a common purpose, we accomplish more together than we ever could apart. It's like in soccer—the team that passes the ball more wins. That's egalitarian cooperation.

Compassionate engagement is about empathy—about understanding that every person you meet is struggling in some way, just by being alive on this planet. Compassionate engagement reminds us that we're all in this together—8-billion strong.

Finally, bold collaborations are about justice-making, about working with people who are willing to retell the story of humanity in a way that's sustainable, healthy, and balanced. It's about creating a new narrative where power-*with* replaces power-*over*.

We can do this, friends, one day at a time. We can move from destructive creation to constructive creation. We can be a place of safe connections, egalitarian cooperation, compassionate engagement, and bold collaborations.

I'll leave you with these words from Daniel Coyle in *Culture Code*:

"Culture is a set of living relationships working toward a shared goal. It's not something you are. It's something you do. High-purpose environments don't descend on groups from on high; they are dug out of the ground, over and over, as a group navigates its problems together and evolves to meet the challenges of a fast-changing world."

Amen.

References

1. *The Better Angels of Our Nature: Why Violence Has Declined* by Steven Pinker (2011) – This book explores the history of violence and argues that humanity is currently living in its least violent era, despite perceptions to the contrary.
2. *Civilizations* by David Olusoga (PBS Documentary, 2018) – This documentary series traces the history of art and culture across human civilizations, emphasizing the interplay of creation and destruction.
3. *Guns, Germs, and Steel: The Fates of Human Societies* by Jared Diamond (1997) – A deep exploration of how geography, agriculture, and technology have shaped the fate of civilizations, often through conquest and domination.
4. *The Rise and Fall of Ancient Egypt* by Toby Wilkinson (2010) – This book examines the cycles of creation and destruction in one of the world's greatest early civilizations and how power dynamics led to the fall of empires.
5. *Sapiens: A Brief History of Humankind* by Yuval Noah Harari (2011) – Harari explores the cognitive revolution

and the rise of agricultural society, which fundamentally changed human civilization from cooperative bands of hunter-gatherers to conquest-driven societies.

6. ***Culture Code: The Secrets of Highly Successful Groups*** by Daniel Coyle (2018) – A study of how groups create successful cultures through shared goals and the ongoing process of relationship-building, applicable to modern organizations and ancient civilizations alike.

7. ***The Dawn of Everything: A New History of Humanity*** by David Graeber and David Wengrow (2021) – This book challenges conventional ideas of early human history, arguing that many societies were more egalitarian and less violent than previously believed, offering an alternative to the narrative of conquest.

41. 2: THE POWER OF YIN/YANG (LEFT/RIGHT BRAIN BALANCE)

On December 10, 1996, Jill Bolte had a stroke—a major stroke. She had a tumor on the left side of her brain, the size of a golf ball, pressing on the language center of her brain. She recounts this day, which profoundly changed her life, in both her book and her TED Talk, both titled My Stroke of Insight—a title I love because it perfectly describes the incident and its impact on her life.

Jill's left brain began short-circuiting that day—the side that is logical, rational, the "Dr. Spock" side. As it began hemorrhaging, Jill remembers feeling strange—her reality started to shift. As her left brain went offline, she became increasingly aware of her body, and everything seemed to slow down. She entered an altered state of consciousness where she could observe herself from outside, like an actor in a play. She could no longer tell where she began and where she ended. Her left brain eventually went completely offline, and her mind became silent.

In that silence, Jill felt something extraordinary: expansiveness. She described feeling enormous—as if she was a part of something larger, blending into the walls of her home, with no boundaries between herself and the world. There was no stress, no past or future—only the present moment. It was still, quiet, peaceful. In that moment, she didn't feel the "I" anymore—she only felt the "we."

As her left brain began to come back online, she struggled to process the experience, but it changed her life forever. She says she metaphorically died that day and was reborn with a new mission: to advocate for brain health and to discuss the importance of stimulating and using the right brain. Her TED Talk has been watched by millions of people!

One of those who has followed Jill's work is member Dr. Scott Eden, who is currently doing research on this topic. I want to thank him for sharing some of his research with me and introducing me to information that aligns so closely with my worldview and theology. I want to share with you what I've learned, as I agree with both Scott and Jill that these insights can profoundly change human society—if we embrace them.

What makes Jill's story particularly cool is that she's a neuroanatomist—a brain doctor who studied at Harvard University, or as I like to call it, "Dr. Spock University." (I'm just kidding—I'm not picking on Harvard. Most educational institutions are logic-based.) But today, I want to talk about how that logic-based, left-brain rationality is, in some ways, harming our capacity for equity and equality.

The left brain is all about the "I," and this is good. The "I" says, "I AM." "I am somebody." "I exist. I have agency." That's beautiful! It is the home of the ego, and it's what makes humans unique. It gives us intelligence, creativity, and the ability to design mechanisms for survival. We would not be where we are today without our left brain. It's how we've learned to understand the universe—through math, numbers, and equations. It allows us to look at the past and plan for the future. It helps us protect ourselves from danger. It gives us language, the beautiful words and diverse languages we speak around the world.

But here's the thing: in our current world system, which is left-brain dominant, all these virtues can become vices if they're not balanced by the creativity and expansiveness of the right brain.

In a book Scott recommended to me—*The Master and His Emissary: The Divided Brain and the Making of the Western World*—the author talks about how research shows that the left brain is slightly larger than the right. They believe this is due to overuse but can't fully confirm it. What this means is that we tend to use the reasoning side of the brain more than the creative side, and if that's true, then what are we missing out on? Jill Bolte tells us about another reality—one very different from the one we live in. A reality of unity, tranquility, and love.

The right brain is where the "I" disappears, and the "we" emerges. It's the side where oneness is the norm. It's the side where we find rhythm in music—not just counting the beats (which the left brain does), but *feeling* the music. The right brain is about living in the present moment, being here *now*. It's the side that sees in pictures rather than words. That's why when we witness something awe-inspiring—like a grand lake or a towering mountain—we often find ourselves speechless. That's a right-brain experience. It's an experience of perfection, Nirvana, heaven on earth, bliss.

Where the left side of the brain is linear—thinking in straight lines—the right side is non-linear, multidirectional. The left brain is dual; the right brain is non-dual. The left is *either/or*, while the right is *both/and*. The left is about details, and the right brain is about vision.

269

The point is, both hemispheres are needed for us to function successfully. But as humans, we tend to over-function with our left brain. We get caught up in deadlines and to-do lists, and we get "crispy"—burned out—trying to meet arbitrary goals. That's why balance between both sides is so crucial. This quest for balance, I believe, is the purpose of our species—both individually and collectively. When we become more balanced within, the changes we yearn for on the outside will start to manifest.

And that brings me to my sermon title: "2."

The number 2 shows us something fundamental about balance. The number 1 symbolizes unity, oneness. It stands alone, needing nothing. It can symbolize God. It can mean singularity. And yet, 1 yearns for a companion—2. 2 brings challenges. 2 brings duality, contrast, conversation, and expression. That's the beauty of 2: it gives us the ability to experience life fully, through interaction and relationship.

If you look at your body, you are split right down the middle—from head to toe. You were once 1 embryo that became a zygote (2). One became two, on its way to becoming fully human. You are a "two," born to experience and learn. You have two brain hemispheres, two ears, two arms, two shoulders, two hands, two legs, and two feet. If you look closely at yourself, it's as if something stitched the two sides of you into one.

I saw this up close with my wife's surgery. When I looked at the stitches they put in, the doctors aligned the staples almost exactly down the middle of her body. There's a natural line there.

So one becomes two, and two must become one. That's the journey. We are born into duality—into tension, drama, and angst. But the grand spiritual game is to take the two and make them one again. This is the secret that both nature and spirituality have been teaching us all along: balance.

Plato wrestled with this understanding. He said, "A soul is like a pair of winged horses and a charioteer joined in natural union." Plato was talking about his own struggles with his left and right brain—his internal struggle to live virtuously. He was also describing the corpus callosum, the part of the brain that connects the two hemispheres and allows them to communicate.

In the Gnostic Gospel of Thomas, written in the 90s CE (common era) there's a saying attributed to Jesus that also speaks to this idea of union between the left and right brain. It says:

> *"Jesus said to them, 'When you make the two one, and when you make the inside like the outside and the outside like the inside, and the above like the below, and when you make the male and the female one and the same, so that the male not be male nor the female not be female; then you will enter the kingdom.'"*

This passage supports the idea that two must become one. This is our goal as human beings—to reconcile the dichotomies in our mind that arise from being dual, seemingly conflicted beings. This is a lifelong struggle, but it's at the heart of all dis-ease we experience. "Listen if you have ears."

Church is a place where the right brain is given more prominence. It's where we work on expanding our capacity for compassion and equity. What churchgoers do on Sundays is mostly a right-brain experience. Our time of sharing, our monthly themes, our prayer/meditation; the music we listen to during worship—these are right-brain activities. Worship revives us. Preaching (I sure hope) inspires us. Small group ministries invigorate us. Being in a community of people who share our values affirms us. All right brain stuff.

271

We live in a world dominated by the left brain—a world where people don't pause to reflect on their behavior or relationships. As a result, we become a society that over-judges, over-moralizes, and declares others "not good enough." We live in a society where fear—a left-brain behavior—reigns, and where gratitude and generosity—right-brain qualities—are seen as weaknesses. The left brain is overworked and exhausted.

So what does balance look like for me, Rev. John? Good question.

There is nothing wrong with reason and science—these are left-brain activities. In fact, these, as mentioned, are part of what makes humans special. However, for every left-brain activity we engage in, we need to balance it with a right-brain one. If you've spent an hour categorizing and organizing, spend some time being creative. If you've spent an hour watching the news, spend another hour watching nature. If you've spent three hours talking about financial matters, spend three or more hours talking about or engaging in activities that help you appreciate your community.

Take walks, go for hikes, take naps, listen to music—these activities help you get out of your head and into your heart. They lift the fog when life gets cloudy. Indeed, it was the right-brain music of the spirituals that carried my ancestors to the promised land of freedom. Music moves us so deeply—it is connected to our interdependence–the right brain.

I want to touch on equity now as it relates to this message. Equity is about fairness, about doing what's just and right. I believe the world will become fairer when people learn to expand the limitless capacities of the right brain. I think that in our desperate need to survive over thousands of years, we've overdeveloped our left brain, which has become the master controller for most of us. Our ability to give more power to the right brain will determine whether we reach our highest potential as human beings. Ceding more power to the right brain will determine whether we can create the beloved community on this planet.

All the "-isms" and inequities we see today—racism, sexism, patriarchy, and environmental degradation—are a result of imbalanced left-brain processing. The left brain functions from a place of fear, survival, and scarcity. It operates with an "I-IT" mentality—us versus them. The right brain, on the other hand, embraces an "I/THOU" mentality—one of unity consciousness, expansiveness, and collaboration. It recognizes that there is enough for everyone if we share.

Jill Bolte was reborn in 1996 when a tiny blood vessel exploded in her head which woke her up to the reality that she was more than she ever imagined. You are more than you imagine. You are the Big Bang. You come from that one force. I dare say, you *are* that one force. The "I" and the "we" are one. And you, like the billions of people who've come before you and the billions alive today, decided to awaken on this planet to learn, grow, and evolve. The one became two.

You are a special creation of the cosmos. You are the cosmos contemplating itself. You are the one that became two. And the two must become one.

Amen.

References

1. *My Stroke of Insight: A Brain Scientist's Personal Journey* by Jill Bolte Taylor (2008) – Jill Bolte Taylor recounts her personal experience of having a stroke, which led to her insights about the right and left hemispheres of the brain and the importance of balance between them.
2. *The Master and His Emissary: The Divided Brain and the Making of the Western World* by Iain McGilchrist (2009) – This book delves into the history and function of the left and right brain hemispheres and how the imbalance between them has shaped Western civilization.

3. *The Gospel of Thomas* (c. 90 CE) – This ancient text contains sayings attributed to Jesus, including teachings on the importance of unity and balance, such as the idea of "making the two one."

4. *The Tao Te Ching* by Lao Tzu (c. 4th century BCE) – A foundational text of Taoism, this work discusses the balance of opposites, such as yin and yang, which ties into the themes of unity and duality present in your sermon.

5. *Plato's Phaedrus* by Plato (370 BCE) – In this dialogue, Plato uses the metaphor of the charioteer and winged horses to describe the tension between different aspects of the soul, which can be understood as an analogy for the left and right brain hemispheres.

6. *The Divided Self: An Existential Study in Sanity and Madness* by R.D. Laing (1960) – This psychological study explores the division within the self, particularly how modern society fosters imbalance in the human psyche, relevant to the left-right brain.

42. FIBONACCI, AHIMSA, THE BUDDHA, AND YOU

You are born into an environment of kill or be killed. Earth is a place of violence. Millions of species are eating each other alive. You feel something is wrong. The flame of expectancy ignites. The monumental struggle to overcome the limits of the mammalian condition begins. You invent tools, language, religion, art, agriculture, science, industry, and technology, striving for something more, something new. Great beings appear, telling you to expect a new condition, a new state of being in which we feel ourselves connected to all life, admonishing us to love one another as ourselves. But most of us do not listen. It is not yet time.

We humans become highly successful. Like the single-celled beings, we consume the nutrients of our Mother Earth. We use her resources, destroy her species. We migrate, we populate, we pollute. Our societies become over-complex, overextended, unmanageable. We sense the finiteness of our planet and the impending limit to growth. The situation has become critical once again.

Something new is about to happen.

1945 marks the next turn on the spiral. Our minds have penetrated the heart of matter and discovered how to use the power of the atom. We rapidly gain even greater capacities to transform or destroy our world. Through genetics, cybernetics, and astronautics, we gain the power to build new life forms and little new worlds in space. We move outward into the universe of our origins, seeking to find new resources, new knowledge, and new life, just as our predecessors once colonized the barren earth.

Oxygen requires the single cells to cooperate. Now, nuclear power forces warring peoples to seek peaceful means of conflict resolution. You now know that we must cooperate or die. Your planet is being integrated into one whole living system. The same force that drew atom to atom and cell to cell is now drawing you to other humans in a new pattern. Your environments, your communication systems, and your ecology are all destined to integrate into a whole body. **-Barbara Marx Hubbard**

5 00 years before Jesus, there was another person of color in India who went on a spiritual quest to find answers to questions about life. Notice, I said "another person of color." It's a fact that all the major world religions were started by people of color–non-European peoples. When some realize Jesus was a brown Jew and Buddha was a brown Indian, it gives

them pause, especially considering the false constructs we live within today. Interestingly, we're discussing "centering people of color" in our congregations, and this aligns with the history of major religions. Christianity, Judaism, Hinduism, Islam, Taoism—all these great religions had founders who were not from Europe.

But I digress... that's not what this message is about—but context is important.

Let's talk about Siddhartha Gautama, who became the Buddha. His story, while filled with myth and legend, is also archetypal —a story of human evolution and one man's journey toward awakening. It's the classic coming-of-age narrative—a hero's journey, as Joseph Campbell would say—and when you read it, you find yourself in the story. We've all had some of these experiences.

Siddhartha was 29 when he left his life of luxury and wandered in the wilderness, living off the land. Like the stories of Moses and Jesus, Buddha also had a wandering experience with temptations. His is a universal story about finding yourself—about searching in all kinds of people, places, and things, only to realize that the answer lies within.

If you don't know much about Buddhism or the story of Lord Buddha, I highly recommend watching a documentary on Prime Video titled *Buddha*. It's outstanding. This one man's discovery changed the world, and today there are over 500 million Buddhists globally.

Siddhartha's story is about all of us and our search for inner peace, how we wrestle with making sense of the destruction and inhumanity we see in the world. His journey—from being a prince indulging in luxury, to becoming a monk and experiencing deep despair and deprivation—mirrors our own struggles to find satisfaction in life. He lived at life's extremes on his way to becoming a Buddha—an awakened one, "one who woke up." He believed the world was filled with sorrow and despair, but by going deep within and facing his shadows, dragons, and fears, he found serenity.

He described this as "suffering," but we can understand it today as angst, dissatisfaction, uneasiness, anxiety. It's that feeling when you can't calm down, when you can't get that inner voice to shut up, when you can't stop worrying.

What I love about his story is that Siddhartha found his answers through *experience*, not through conversion by someone else. He was an existentialist, finding his purpose through his own journey, and his teachings remain therapeutic for us even today.

This brother came from royalty but chose poverty. He nearly died, taking himself to the bitter edge of life. He learned from the ascetic Vedic priests' techniques of deprivation and long hours of meditation. They believed higher consciousness could be achieved by denying the body food and water. And what we now know is: *this is true*. We also know that we can achieve altered states of consciousness through practices like psilocybin. Johns Hopkins has conducted studies using mushrooms to help patients overcome addiction, trauma, and severe anxiety. This approach will likely become part of modern medicine.

The magic happens when we allow the mind to let go. We can access higher forms of connection or consciousness, enabling us to relax, be present, and find happiness. We also know that altered states of awareness can be reached through hedonism. When groups become tribal in war, sports, or politics, or even through sex, we raise awareness toward something bigger, but often in a narcissistic, exclusive way.

Buddha, however, didn't find his answer to suffering through pleasure or deprivation. *Extremes lead to extremes.* Extremes destroy life. But, ironically, his close brush with death did open his mind—like a near-death experience. Buddha realized that extremes weren't the answer; he wanted to live.

Buddha's breakthrough came while sitting in nature under a tree. (Remember that—it was *in nature* where he had his epiphany.) As he sat in silence, memories flooded back. He remembered a spring festival with his father, and the joy of watching people dance and celebrate. He remembered the small insects he'd watched that day, marveling at their unity and purpose. Even when those insects were trampled by a passerby, they re-organized and continued their work. Nature was resilient, and he saw the awful and the awesome as one continuous dance. There, under the bodhi tree, he realized his connection to everything. He understood the underlying workings of nature, including human nature—the permanence and impermanence of life.

"There is joy in the brokenness," he thought. He chose life that day, under the bodhi tree. Soon after, a young woman mysteriously appeared and nourished him back to health with a meal that reminded him of his childhood. This was another affirmation that he'd found his answer. Life speaks to us when we decide to say "yes" to life.

Buddha realized the middle way was the best path—the path of balance. He had been wound too tightly, and the extremes could not be sustained. His message became the first humanist and moderate one the world had ever heard.

When he opened his Sangha, he allowed women to join and live as equals. There was no caste in his school. Buddha believed that everyone was destined to awaken, to make peace with fear, anxiety, aging, illness, and death—the things that cause suffering. When we transcend suffering, Buddha taught, we experience Nirvana—heaven within and without. The kingdom within.

Buddha broke with the traditions of his time. He was a universalist before UU existed. The Vedic tradition was male-centric, ritualistic, and cast in a rigid system (pun intended). Buddha found it ineffective, so he changed it. His simplicity, originality, and inclusiveness attracted many followers, even the men who had initially taught him.

Back then, the world wasn't so different from today. People were losing interest in traditional religious practices, poverty and social injustice were rampant, and the caste system was enforced with violence. And yet, Buddha emerged with his middle way—his answer to suffering. "Living means suffering. To end suffering, end desire."

I translate that as: if you want to relieve your anxiety, stop being a control freak. Let go. See the bigger picture and release the need to control everything. Let it go, and engage again when you're able to see clearly. Step back. Look from a distance, and you'll see the holiness and unity in it all.

Do this with compassion—AHIMSA. Be nonviolent. Walk mindfully, knowing that all living things have worth. They are you, and you are them. When we do harm to others, we do harm to ourselves. This, Buddha taught, is the way to transcend the illusion of separateness that causes suffering. His message is as relevant today as it was 2,500 years ago.

This teaching of Ahimsa—nonviolence—is central. When we move with compassion, when we see the divine spark in all beings, we begin to understand that every person we meet is on the same journey. They will eventually awaken, just like us. The suffering we feel is because we cling to the illusion of separateness. We try to power through things that are beyond our control, and we suffer as a result. But Buddha's message is simple: let go.

It's a high-level teaching. It's advanced spirituality. So simple and yet it eludes so many. When you experience the highs and lows of life and don't become vengeful or spiteful, when you move toward acceptance and look at things honestly and objectively, you begin to see that much of life is gray—not black and white. Much of what we experience as conflict is fear and misunderstood perception. You transcend the dichotomy, learning to manage ambiguity.

Look at the yin and yang symbol in Taoism—black and white, opposites, yet containing a bit of each other. Now spin it fast, and it becomes gray. That's the reality of life. We are both— black and white, yin and yang, good and bad, joy and suffering. When we understand this, we stop clinging to rigid views and embrace the complexity of life.

Buddha knew this. He understood that all of life is a continuous, interconnected cycle. When you rise above the "us versus them," mentally you find the "we are together" reality. You begin to see the underlying patterns in nature, the rhythms and structures that guide the universe. You see life as a Fibonacci sequence—a sacred geometry, an ancient mathematical pattern that reveals itself in everything from the smallest seed to the largest galaxy. Life *is* math. It is a set of patterns and cycles that continually unfold, guiding everything toward balance and growth.

Think about it: the same sequence exists everywhere in nature, in the spirals of galaxies, the arrangement of petals in a flower, even the structure of our DNA. The Fibonacci sequence isn't just a human discovery; it's nature's blueprint. Every number in the sequence builds upon the previous ones, expanding outward, spiraling upward—never static, always evolving. From the micro to the macro, this pattern is woven into the very fabric of existence.

The Fibonacci sequence isn't just a mathematical curiosity; it's a visual representation of the universe's continuous push toward expansion and evolution. Life, in all its forms, is designed to expand outward—growing from the simplest to the most complex, from the unconscious to the deeply aware. This mathematical precision mirrors our own spiritual journeys. Just as the Fibonacci spiral begins at a single point and gradually grows into a larger and more complex form, so too does human consciousness evolve. We are not meant to stay small; we are meant to grow, to spiral outward, to transcend our limitations and expand into something greater. This math is more than just numbers—it's the pulse of the universe.

In that growth, we humans are destined to awaken, just like Buddha. We are on a journey to live with greater awareness, sensitivity, compassion, and love. We're destined to evolve beyond our primitive, survival instincts into something more. Maybe this is what the gods and goddesses of ancient myths represent—our future selves, a more advanced version of humanity.

And this brings me to the great Barbara Marx Hubbard. She believed humanity is evolving into something greater —something that will eventually transcend our current limitations. In her book, *Suprasexual rEvolution*, she describes the human journey as one of continuous growth, like the Fibonacci sequence. We are expanding outward, moving toward something bigger, something more enlightened.

It might seem naive to believe this, especially in light of the suffering and injustice we see in the world today, but Barbara Marx Hubbard was optimistic. She believed that at the edge of disaster is where humans take their greatest steps forward. And she was right—history shows that we've survived and thrived in the face of hardship. We've gotten creative, we've adapted, and we've progressed.

She believed that we're heading toward a time of great awakening, where humanity will become kinder, gentler, and more evolved. We are moving toward being a global, borderless, and even galactic humanity. Technology is advancing at a rapid pace, and gene editing is one of those breakthroughs that may even allow us to rid the world of diseases like cancer and sickle cell in our lifetime.

Of course, with these advancements come ethical questions—who gets access to these technologies? Who controls them? But the point remains: we are becoming god-like in our capacities. We are evolving.

Barbara Marx Hubbard believed in the power of this evolution and saw it as a natural unfolding. She saw the gray—the balance of opposites—and believed that, through this balance, humanity would find its way forward.

Life is gray. It's black, it's white. It's all of these things. Accept the ambiguity as part of the spiritual journey. Embrace different perspectives and recognize that growth requires us to see beyond our own limitations.

When we move beyond duality, when we step into the gray, we enter divine spaces of compassion, nonviolence, and unconditional love. We come into acceptance—acceptance of life's highs and lows, of its beauty and brokenness. We begin to live with balance, managing our extremes and finding the middle way. We become co-creators of a more just, compassionate world, one in which we no longer suffer from the illusion of separateness.

Buddha said, "When I awaken, all awaken." He knew that his insight would become humanity's insight because we are all connected. We are all becoming Buddha.

Dear friends, as you continue on your own journey toward awakening, remember to do as little harm as you can. Be mindful of your intent and impact. Encourage others to do the same. And remember the lesson of the Buddha: all things in moderation. Avoid the extremes. Find your way back to unconditional love when you've strayed. Acceptance is liberation, and liberation is Nirvana.

Namaste, and Amen.

References

1. ***Buddha (PBS Documentary)*** directed by David Grubin (2010) – A powerful visual exploration of Siddhartha Gautama's life, spiritual quest, and the foundational teachings of Buddhism, including Ahimsa and the middle path.

2. ***The Dhammapada*** (c. 3rd century BCE) – A collection of sayings attributed to the Buddha, emphasizing his teachings on suffering, nonviolence (Ahimsa), and the middle way as key principles for spiritual and social balance.

3. ***My Stroke of Insight: A Brain Scientist's Personal Journey*** by Jill Bolte Taylor (2008) – This book recounts Jill Bolte Taylor's experience with a stroke, highlighting the themes of consciousness and the integration of the brain's hemispheres, which align with your sermon's discussion of balance between rationality and spirituality.

4. ***The Middle Length Discourses of the Buddha*** translated by Bhikkhu Ñāṇamoli and Bhikkhu Bodhi (1995) – A key text from early Buddhism, offering discourses on the Buddha's teachings about the middle way and the practice of Ahimsa.

5. ***The Heart of the Buddha's Teaching: Transforming Suffering into Peace, Joy, and Liberation*** by Thich Nhat Hanh (1998) – This modern work explains the Buddha's teachings on suffering and mindfulness, as well as the importance of nonviolence (Ahimsa) as part of personal and collective healing.

6. ***The Master and His Emissary: The Divided Brain and the Making of the Western World*** by Iain McGilchrist (2009) – This book examines the left-right brain divide and its impact on Western thought, connecting to your sermon's theme of finding balance between the logical and spiritual aspects of consciousness.

SECTION 7: SOCIETY, CONFLICT, AND HUMAN BEHAVIOR

43. BELOVED COMMUNITY EXPLAINED

Beloved community isn't just an idea we aspire to—it's a reality we live into, moment by moment. It's the ground we stand on when we commit to love, justice, and equity. It's the foundation we build together through relationships that matter—relationships rooted in care, compassion, and mutual respect. When we talk about beloved community, we're talking about a place where everyone is truly valued. It's a place where love is at the center, guiding everything we do. It's about creating a community that reflects our highest selves and calls us to be better each day.

Now, let's talk about what it means to *be* in a beloved community. How do we live it out? What values does it hold dear? And, most importantly, how do we know we're experiencing it when we see it?

Love at the Center

First and foremost, love is at the heart of beloved community. I'm not talking about that warm and fuzzy feeling we sometimes associate with love—I mean the kind of love that *moves* you to act. The love that pushes you to care for others, to listen deeply, and to show up even when it's uncomfortable.

This love is active; it's intentional. It calls us to examine ourselves and ask: "Are my words and actions aligned with love? Am I making space for others to thrive?"

When love is truly at the center of beloved community, everything changes. We start asking different questions. We don't just focus on what's fair for us—we look at what's just for everyone. We shift our thinking from "me" to "we." This is where justice, equity, and interdependence come in.

Justice, Equity, and Interdependence

Justice in beloved community means we don't just settle for surface-level fairness. It means we roll up our sleeves and get to work dismantling the systems that keep people from thriving—whether that's racism, sexism, homophobia, or any other form of oppression. It's about creating a space where *everyone* can flourish, not just a few. Equity goes hand-in-hand with that, because we know that fairness isn't about giving everyone the same thing—it's about meeting people where they are and making sure they have what they need to thrive.

Interdependence is what ties it all together. In beloved community, we recognize that we're all connected. What happens to one of us affects all of us. We understand that our well-being is wrapped up in the well-being of others, and we commit to taking care of each other because we know we can't go it alone.

What Beloved Community Looks Like

How do we know beloved community when we experience it? What does it actually *look* like?

It feels like being welcomed just as you are—without needing to hide, without needing to perform. You show up, and people see *you*, for real. It's a space where you don't have to downplay any part of your identity, and where diversity is embraced, not just tolerated. It's a community where people actively work to make sure everyone has a seat at the table.

It's also a place where there's a shared sense of purpose. You know you're not just here for yourself, but for the good of the whole. You're not competing with others— you're collaborating. That's what beloved community feels like: working together, side by side, because we're all in this together.

And trust me, *beloved community isn't conflict-free*. That's not the goal. The goal is to handle conflict in ways that deepen relationships rather than break them apart. It's a place where we can disagree and still stay connected because we're committed to something greater than ourselves. We handle conflict with grace, seeking reconciliation and repair.

Practicing Beloved Community

Let's dig into the practices that sustain beloved community. These aren't abstract ideas—they are the tools we use to build the world we want to live in.

1. **Be a Community of Communities**
   This is a concept by my dear friend, Paula Cole Jones. We are a collection of smaller communities that come together to form the whole. Each of us has our own purpose and identity, but we prioritize the well-being of the entire community. This is how we build resilience—by leaning on each other and understanding that our connections make us stronger.
2. **Embrace a Multicultural Paradigm**
   Beloved community celebrates *differences*. We reject dominant cultural norms that tell us there's only one right way to be. Instead, we actively create liberatory spaces where all people can bring their full selves, knowing that our diversity is our strength.

3. **Create Covenantal Relationships**

   This community isn't about transactions—it's about relationships. We are in covenant with one another, which means we're committed to care, accountability, and repair. When harm happens— and it will—we don't run. We stay, we talk, and we heal.

4. **Move at the Speed of Trust**

   This has recently been made popular by adrienne maree brown. Trust is the foundation of any beloved community. Without it, we can't grow. We build trust by being vulnerable, by showing up honestly, and by being consistent in our actions. Trust doesn't happen overnight, but once it's there, it transforms everything.

5. **Build Resiliency and Self-Care into Our Systems**

   Here again, brown says that life has its ups and downs, and so do relationships. Beloved community acknowledges this and builds in time for rest and reflection. We take care of ourselves and each other so we don't burn out. Self-care isn't an afterthought —it's central to sustaining our work.

6. **Decentralized Leadership**

   This is brown again. She says, and I agree, that leadership in beloved community is shared. Every person is invited and encouraged to lead in their own way. This keeps the community dynamic and prevents burnout. We recognize that leadership isn't about one person—it's about the collective.

7. **Focus on What We Want to Grow**

   This is an old business adage and it is apropos. In beloved community, we put our energy into what we want to see flourish. We focus on justice, love, and equity, knowing that what we feed will grow. We don't waste time on division or negativity—we build up the values that unite us.

8. **Collaborate Instead of Compete**
   Collaboration is key. When we work together, we create something far greater than what we could accomplish alone. In beloved community, we don't compete—we lift each other up. Collaboration is how we show love in action.

9. **Commit to Emotional and Spiritual Literacy**
   Finally, we commit to understanding ourselves and others better. We practice emotional and spiritual literacy by learning to express our feelings and needs with care. We know conflict is part of life, but we work through it with kindness and grace, because at the end of the day, love is what holds us together.

Beloved Community is Possible

Beloved community is not some distant dream—it's something we can live into *right now*. It takes practice. It takes commitment. But it's possible. When we live out these values—when we center love, practice justice, and honor our interdependence—we experience beloved community. We see it. We feel it. And we help it grow.

May we continue to build beloved community, together, with love at the center of all we do. Amen.

References:

1. **Paula Cole Jones** is the creator of the 8th Principle, which calls on Unitarian Universalists to commit to dismantling racism and other oppressions in ourselves and our institutions. The 8th Principle aligns with the values of equity, justice, and liberation that are essential to building beloved community. For more on the 8th Principle, visit: https://www.8thprincipleuu.org/

2. **adrienne maree brown**, in her book *Emergent Strategy: Shaping Change, Changing Worlds* (2017), emphasizes the importance of moving at the "speed of trust," embracing collaboration, and decentralizing leadership, all of which are foundational to beloved community. Her focus on

fractals, where small actions reflect and create larger systems of change, directly connects to the practice of building beloved community. See: brown, adrienne maree. *Emergent Strategy: Shaping Change, Changing Worlds.* AK Press, 2017.

3. **Rev. Dr. Martin Luther King Jr.** popularized the concept of beloved community, which is deeply rooted in nonviolence and justice. His vision calls for a world where poverty, hunger, and homelessness are not tolerated because the human spirit is recognized and honored in every person. His framework provides historical grounding for modern-day beloved community work. See: King, Martin Luther Jr. *Where Do We Go from Here: Chaos or Community?* Beacon Press, 1967.

4. The **Unitarian Universalist Association (UUA)** has adopted core values such as interdependence, pluralism, and equity that provide guidance for living out the principles of beloved community. These values are integral to building communities that are just, inclusive, and transformative. For more information: "Values and Covenant," Unitarian Universalist Association, https://www.uua.org/.

44. SEX & WAR

Let's talk about the basics. The primal forces that drive humanity, the things we don't always like to admit control us, yet they run underneath our everyday lives. Two forces—sex and war—have shaped our societies, our structures, and our stories since the beginning of time. In this sermon, I want to explore what's behind these forces, particularly male domination, and how, despite our evolutionary past, we must rise above these instincts to create a more just and peaceful world.

Jane Goodall, a British primatologist who spent 45 years studying chimpanzees in Tanzania, once believed that chimps were peaceful, cooperative creatures. Over time, though, she witnessed a different side of them. The males, especially, exhibited extreme violence. She saw how male chimps teamed up to destroy weaker groups, sometimes without any clear reason other than perceiving the others as a threat. These stronger chimps would kill the males of the other group and take their females. Why? It was instinctual. It was a way to expand territory, claim resources, and preserve their tribe's survival. The alpha male, of course, mated with whomever he chose, ensuring his genes continued through the strongest possible offspring.

Why does this matter for us? Because, according to authors Malcolm Potts and Thomas Hayden in their book *Sex and War*, this behavior points to the root of our own human aggression. They call it a "Stone Age mentality," an inherited predisposition toward violence, particularly in men. Our distant cousins, the chimpanzees, are 98% genetically similar to us. And while we've built civilizations, governments, and laws, we are still carrying these ancient behaviors within us. Men, in particular, have inherited what Potts and Hayden call "war genes"—a behavioral predisposition toward violence.

Now, I know this sounds bleak. I know it may feel like a heavy burden to carry, especially for men. But acknowledging this doesn't mean we're stuck in it forever. It means we need to understand it so we can transcend it.

Let me be real with you: I know this aggression personally. I've felt that testosterone-driven need to prove myself, especially when I was younger. Testosterone is a powerful hormone, and it plays a big role in this story. Young men, in particular, are swimming in it. It's part of the reason why they pay higher car insurance, why they're more likely to die from violent crime, and why they're often the ones sent to war. Testosterone pushes young men to prove themselves, to fight, to dominate. They're like those young chimps, eager to climb the ranks and claim the top spot.

But here's the thing—we are more than our hormones. We can't just let testosterone run the show. This aggression, this drive for dominance, it doesn't serve us in the world we're trying to build. It may have had its place in the Stone Age, but today, it causes more harm than good. It fuels wars, drives inequality, and perpetuates violence, especially against women.

We see this aggression play out in so many ways—sometimes in subtle ways, like when men feel the need to dominate a conversation or take up more space than necessary. Sometimes it's more overt, like when boys and men engage in violent behavior. And yes, women can be complicit in this worldview, but when we look at the world—politically, economically, sexually—it's clear that we live in a male-dominated paradigm.

We need to be honest with ourselves about the rewards society gives men for this aggression. From a young age, boys are taught that aggression will get them what they want—whether that's status, power, or money. But at what cost? We need to redefine what we reward in men. Instead of celebrating domination and violence, we should be lifting up qualities like compassion, collaboration, and emotional intelligence.

This is where we need to change. We need a shift in leadership, in power structures, and in how we value certain behaviors over others. I believe that a more balanced society—one that includes more female leadership—can help us address these global issues of war, aggression, and resource scarcity. Men and women are both capable of leading, but history shows us that male-dominated leadership often results in war and conflict. It's time for a more balanced approach.

Women, when they step into leadership, bring something different to the table. And it's not that women are inherently better or more peaceful, but they tend to lead with more empathy, compassion, and a focus on collaboration. This is the kind of leadership we need to solve the problems we're facing today—whether it's climate change, poverty, or global conflicts over resources. It's time to move toward a balanced power structure that values feminine qualities like nurturing and collaboration alongside the masculine qualities of strength and protection.

Now, I'm not saying that we need to suppress all aggression or deny that testosterone exists. There's a place for masculine energy, for strength, and for protection. But we need to evolve beyond the Stone Age mentality that tells us the only way to survive is through domination and violence. We are not chimpanzees, bound by instinct alone. We have the ability to reflect, to choose, and to change.

Rising above this inherited aggression means harnessing it for good. It means recognizing when we're falling into those old patterns of domination and choosing a different path. It means teaching young boys that strength isn't about hurting others or proving superiority—it's about standing up for what's right, protecting the vulnerable, and using their power to build, not destroy.

I want to leave you with this: we have the capacity to change. As human beings, we are not locked into one way of being. We can evolve. We can rise above the violence and aggression that's been passed down to us. But it will take work. It will take conscious effort, and it will require us to let go of outdated ideas about what it means to be a man or a leader.

I believe the future of leadership is one where men and women work together—where both masculine and feminine energies are valued and celebrated. We need the strength and courage of men, yes, but we also need the compassion, creativity, and collaboration that women often bring. Together, we can create a world where war is no longer the first option, where domination is replaced with cooperation, and where all people can thrive.

So let us rise above our less-evolved nature. Let us embrace the fullness of our humanity, both its strength and its tenderness. And let us work together to build a world that reflects the best of who we are, not the worst of what we've inherited.

Amen.

References

1. Jane Goodall, *In the Shadow of Man* (1971) – Goodall's groundbreaking work on chimpanzee behavior, including male aggression and territorial dominance.
2. Malcolm Potts and Thomas Hayden, *Sex and War* (2008) – A study on the biological roots of human warfare, linking male aggression to evolutionary traits.

3. Sharon Welch, *A Feminist Ethic of Risk* (1990) – Explores how compassion, justice, and risk-taking can help overcome systemic violence and domination.
4. Riane Eisler, *The Chalice and the Blade* (1987) – Examines the shift from partnership to domination models in human societies, focusing on gender dynamics and power.
5. Carol Gilligan, *In a Different Voice* (1982) – Discusses how traditional psychological theories have often overlooked the moral and ethical perspectives of women, emphasizing relational approaches to ethics.
6. Rev. Dr. Martin Luther King Jr., *Where Do We Go from Here: Chaos or Community?* (1967) – King's reflections on violence, justice, and the potential for nonviolent social change.

45. FANATICS (EXTREMISM)

We all worship something, don't we? It doesn't matter what you believe about God or religion. At the core of human nature, we are drawn to something bigger than ourselves. We look for meaning, something to give us purpose. But here's the kicker: not everything we worship is good for us. As David Foster Wallace pointed out in his famous 2005 commencement address at Kenyon College, everyone worships something. The only real question is, what are we worshiping?

David Foster Wallace, a brilliant mind and celebrated writer, spoke to something deep within us—this idea that what we focus on, what we give our energy to, will ultimately shape us. And tragically, Wallace, like so many who've come before him, wrestled with these big questions in ways that led him to despair. He took his own life in 2008, after a long battle with depression. But before he left this world, he left us with a gift—wisdom about what we worship, and how it can either give us life or eat us alive.

Wallace said, "There is actually no such thing as atheism. Everybody worships. The only choice we get is what to worship. And the compelling reason for maybe choosing some sort of god or spiritual-type thing to worship [...] is that pretty much anything else you worship will eat you alive."

Think about that for a moment. Whatever we give our attention to, whatever we obsess over, has the power to control us. And the truth is, most of us have no idea we're doing it. We live in a world full of distractions, filled with messages about money, power, beauty, and success. And if we're not careful, we fall into default settings. We become fanatics without even knowing it.

What is a fanatic? Simply put, it's someone who is consumed by excessive zeal or passion for something. Fanaticism comes from having an obsessive interest or enthusiasm for an idea, a belief, a cause, or even a lifestyle. Now, zeal isn't necessarily a bad thing. Passion, enthusiasm, and devotion can drive us toward meaningful lives. But when we cross the line into fanaticism, it can begin to harm us—and others.

In today's world, fanaticism is everywhere. You see it in politics, religion, and even in personal lifestyles. But here's the question I want you to wrestle with: What are *you* fanatic about? What are you worshiping in your life, and how is it shaping you? In many ways, Wallace's words echo the existential thoughts of great philosophers like Friedrich Nietzsche, who observed the rise of nihilism—the belief that life is meaningless. Without something meaningful to devote ourselves to, it's easy to slip into a place where nothing matters. And this sense of meaninglessness is creeping into our Western culture, leading more people to feel lost, disconnected, and empty.

But here's the good news: We have a choice. We don't have to fall into that pit of nothingness. We can choose to devote our lives to something that lifts us up and gives us purpose.

Wallace warned us about what happens when we worship the wrong things. If you worship money and material things, you'll never have enough. If you worship beauty and physical appearance, you'll always feel inadequate. If you worship power, you'll end up feeling weak and afraid. And if you worship your intellect, you'll feel like a fraud, always on the verge of being found out. The problem isn't that these things are inherently bad—it's that they have the power to consume us without us even realizing it.

The world we live in today won't discourage us from chasing these false idols. In fact, our culture thrives on it. We live in a world where the worship of self, of personal freedom, of power and achievement, runs rampant. We are told that the key to happiness is getting more, achieving more, and being more. But this is a trap.

Here's the real truth: The most important kind of freedom isn't the freedom to do whatever you want. It's the freedom that comes from attention, awareness, and discipline. The kind of freedom that Wallace spoke of is the freedom to *care* about other people and to *sacrifice* for them. It's the freedom to get outside of yourself and to live for something greater than your own ego.

Look around, and you'll see fanaticism taking hold in all areas of life. From political zealots who believe their way is the only way, to religious extremists who are convinced their version of truth is the only truth, to social media influencers whose obsession with self-promotion distorts reality. This kind of fanaticism isn't just dangerous—it's exhausting.

When we become fanatics, we lose our ability to see the bigger picture. We become trapped in a cycle of needing more—more power, more recognition, more validation. And in the process, we forget what really matters. We forget that real meaning in life comes from connection, compassion, and humility.

So, what's the alternative? How do we live a life of passion and zeal without falling into the trap of fanaticism?

The answer lies in balance. It lies in mindfulness, in choosing what we focus on and being aware of what we give our energy to. We need to ask ourselves: Are we worshiping something that brings us life, or are we worshiping something that's slowly eating us alive?

I'm not here to tell you what to worship—that's a decision each of us has to make. But I will tell you this: Whatever you choose, make sure it gives you the freedom to love, the freedom to grow, and the freedom to serve others. Because real freedom comes from living a life that's not just about you. It's about being part of something bigger, something more meaningful.

Wallace said, "The really important kind of freedom involves attention and awareness and discipline, and being able truly to care about other people and to sacrifice for them over and over in myriad petty, unsexy ways every day." That's where real meaning is found. Not in the grand gestures, but in the small, everyday acts of kindness and service.

So, as we move into this three-part series on fanaticism, I want you to think deeply about what you are fanatical about. What are you worshiping in your life? Is it something that brings you life, or is it something that's slowly consuming you?

We all worship something. The only choice we get is what to worship. Choose wisely, my friends. Choose something that lifts you up and connects you to others. Choose something that gives you the freedom to love, to serve, and to live with purpose. Because in the end, that's the only kind of worship that will truly set you free.

Amen.

References

1. David Foster Wallace, *This Is Water: Some Thoughts, Delivered on a Significant Occasion, about Living a Compassionate Life* (2009) – The text of his 2005 Kenyon College commencement speech, which emphasizes the importance of choosing what to worship in everyday life.
2. Friedrich Nietzsche, *The Will to Power* (1888) – Explores the concept of nihilism and the human search for meaning, relevant to the discussion of fanaticism and worship.
3. Sharon Welch, *A Feminist Ethic of Risk* (1990) – Provides insights into the ethics of responsibility and the dangers of excessive zeal, emphasizing the importance of mindfulness and care.
4. Søren Kierkegaard, *Fear and Trembling* (1843) – Offers a philosophical exploration of faith, zeal, and the human condition, which can inform the understanding of fanaticism in a spiritual context.
5. Thomas Merton, *New Seeds of Contemplation* (1961) – Merton's reflections on the role of awareness and mindfulness, which are essential in combating the unconscious worship of harmful things.
6. Viktor Frankl, *Man's Search for Meaning* (1946) – A foundational text in existential thought, highlighting the importance of finding meaning in life and avoiding the pitfalls of nihilism and fanaticism.
7. Erich Fromm, *Escape from Freedom* (1941) – Examines how individuals can unconsciously submit to authoritarianism and fanaticism as a way to escape the anxiety of true freedom and responsibility.

46. OUR CIVIL WAR–
A WAR FOR CIVILITY

T his government shutdown is affecting our household. My wife, a federal worker, is feeling the effects firsthand. This is the longest shutdown in history—absurd, really, because it's supposedly over a wall. Yet, it's not just about a wall. It's about division, a deepening of the polarization that's tearing our nation apart. And as I prayed for this country, I realized none of this is new. Polarization, people choosing sides, even against their best interest, has been happening for centuries. It's not new to religion or politics. It's not new to America. It's not new to human history.

We are still engaged in a Civil War in this country—a war that didn't end in 1865. The Civil War might have physically concluded then, but spiritually and mentally, it continues. More than 600,000 people died in that conflict, and yet here we are, still fighting a war for the soul of this nation.

I believe this war has always been mental and spiritual—about what kind of country we want to be. But this struggle didn't begin with the Civil War; it began in 1776 when our founding fathers boldly declared their independence from England. They claimed that all men are created equal, but we've been struggling ever since to define who "all" includes. From the beginning, freedom, access, and opportunity were battlegrounds, and those same issues fuel division today. If you do the math, it's been 264 years—an infant nation still grappling with its identity.

While America gained its independence, it also inherited England's sins—chiefly, the practice of buying and selling human beings. America grew wealthy through this immoral practice, as did England and Europe. But they all failed miserably in one key area: you cannot proclaim freedom while simultaneously denying it to others. Freedom for some is not true freedom.

This great sin of "othering" is part of our national DNA. We marginalize those who are different, and that inherited sin runs through every problem we face today.

If you've seen the musical *Hamilton*, you know it uses the genre rap to tell the story of America's early struggles for freedom. It's the music of revolution, the cry of people wanting to be free. That's what early America was—a nation rapping against oppression. But as Lin-Manuel Miranda beautifully illustrates, not everyone was in the room when the founding fathers made their decisions. They didn't consider women, people of color, or the poor. Our founders were flawed, just like us—products of their time and place.

In 1833, England abolished slavery, which placed immense pressure on young America, claiming freedom while holding millions in bondage. This hypocrisy led to the Civil War, a conflict ostensibly over states' rights but truly over the moral issue of slavery. We fought, killed each other, and "othered" each other—those in chains, those in power, and those who simply feared change.

The Civil War officially began in 1861, but the tension had been building for decades. America struggled with the addition of new states, balancing free states and slave states. This fragile harmony was maintained out of fear. Fear, as it always does, leads to division, to othering. When Abraham

Lincoln ran for president, he did so on a platform against the expansion of slavery. He won the election with just 40% of the vote and no support from the southern states. Sound familiar?

But Lincoln wasn't a saint, nor was he a pure abolitionist at heart. He was a brave man in a polarizing time, but his priority was preserving the Union, not ending slavery. He even considered sending freed Black people back to Africa—a plan to rid the country of its "Negro Problem." Othering still haunts us today, as we see in the treatment of immigrants at the border, racial tension, and economic inequality.

Emancipation came in 1865, but true freedom did not. While slavery ended legally, its remnants lived on through sharecropping, low wages, segregation, and systemic oppression. Some might say the vestiges of slavery still persist today. Southern landowners, after the war, feared losing their wealth and power. They spread fear, telling their communities that Black people would take their jobs and leave them destitute. Sound familiar? Much has changed, but much remains the same.

We've seen this pattern of othering throughout history. It was there when the KKK emerged in the 1860s. It was present during the Tulsa riots of 1921, when jealousy of Black prosperity led to violence. And it was there in the 1950s when Rev. Martin Luther King Jr. rose to lead the civil rights movement. The seeds of othering are deeply embedded in the American story.

King, a young pastor at Dexter Avenue Baptist Church in Montgomery, Alabama, stood on the same steps where the Confederacy was born and declared, "How long? Not long." In the very place where white supremacy had been formalized, King led the fight for equality. It's as if some divine power was showing us again: you're all on the same team. We are all made in the image of God, and "we must learn to live together as brothers and sisters—or perish as fools." as King would say.

But we don't learn from history. We're stubborn. We don't analyze it enough. We don't see the larger pattern at play. From the Revolutionary War to the Civil War to the civil rights movement, we've been engaged in the same game. The British and other European powers created loyal subjects by subjugating people, teaching them the toxic pattern of "othering." When America broke from the monarchy, it could have broken from slavery too, but it didn't. That failure continues to haunt us today.

We're all products of our culture, of the virtues and vices passed down to us. We say we want diversity and inclusion, but we must confront the fears that hold us back—the fears that make us other those who are different from us.

This ongoing Civil War is not fought with guns, but with a lack of civility. This new, yet old war is now *a war on civility.* Can we put aside our tribalism for the higher cause of community, peace, and justice? This war for civility is about healing the damage that's been done, repairing relationships, and moving beyond us versus them.

We face a huge spiritual abyss in this nation—a deficit caused by our inability to see the divine in each other. We've won some battles, but the war for true freedom and equality is ongoing. Freedom isn't just about ending chains; it's about being bold enough to hope, to believe in a better future, and to act with courage.

Despite the evidence, I still have hope. I see progress in the regress, and I know that forces, seen and unseen, are guiding us toward justice. We must continue to wake up, challenge our assumptions, and reject the divisions that separate us.

I want to leave you with three things. First, be more civil in our public and private discourse. Be kinder and, as Maya Angelou says, "listen more, read more and think more." Second, we cannot lose hope. Like the spiritual "Motherless Child," which often ends on a minor note, we must choose to end on a major note of hope, even when it feels out of place. Hope is not a naive wish, but a bold act of defiance in the face of despair.

Thirdly and lastly, I want to share the words of Rev. Fred Kaan, who understood what it meant to hold onto hope in the darkest of times. As a man who lived through the Nazi occupation and saw his family suffer unimaginable hardship, he dedicated his life to peace and reconciliation. He penned Hymn 137, *We Utter Our Cry*, which I believe is the perfect prayer for our time. I close with his words:

> *We utter our cry: that peace may prevail,*
> *that Earth will survive, and faith must not fail.*
> *We pray with our life for the world in our care,*
> *for people diminished by doubt and despair.*

> *We cry from the fright of our daily scene*
> *for strength to say "No" to all that is mean:*
> *designs bearing chaos, extinction of life,*
> *all energy wasted on weapons of death.*

> *We lift up our hearts for children unborn;*
> *give wisdom, O God, that we may hand on,*
> *replenished and tended this good planet Earth,*
> *preserving the future and wonder of birth.*

> *O Creator of Life, come, share out, we pray,*
> *Your Spirit on Earth, revealing the Way*
> *to leaders conferring 'round tables for peace*
> *that they may from bias and guile be released.*

Let this hymn be our guide and our prayer as we continue to fight for that love supreme that connects us to a future where the walls between us come down, and we live in a true beloved community. May be so. Amen.

References

1. **The Souls of Black Folk** by W.E.B. Du Bois (1903)
   This foundational text offers a profound exploration of race and identity in America. Du Bois's concept of "double consciousness" reflects the internal struggle of being both Black and American, providing historical and emotional context to the legacy of the Civil War and ongoing racial tensions.

2. **A People's History of the United States** by Howard Zinn (1980)
   Zinn's book tells the story of American history from the perspective of marginalized groups, including African Americans, Indigenous peoples, and laborers. His perspective underscores the long-standing issues of "othering" and systemic oppression in the U.S.

3. **Team of Rivals: The Political Genius of Abraham Lincoln** by Doris Kearns Goodwin (2005)
   This biography delves into Lincoln's leadership during the Civil War, highlighting his political acumen and moral complexity. It provides context for your discussion of Lincoln's priorities and how they shaped the war and post-war era.

4. **The Civil War: A Narrative** by Shelby Foote (1958-1974)
   Foote's three-volume work covers the Civil War in detail, illustrating both the battlefield and the social dynamics that continued long after the war. This reference is key for understanding the Civil War as an ongoing mental and spiritual struggle in America.

5. **The Radical King** by Martin Luther King Jr., edited by Cornel West (2015)
   This collection of King's most radical speeches and writings demonstrates his lifelong fight against systemic injustice. King's vision of a "beloved community" and his

challenge to othering deeply resonate with your sermon's themes.

6. **Hamilton: The Revolution** by Lin-Manuel Miranda and Jeremy McCarter (2016)
   This book details the making of the *Hamilton* musical and how its narrative connects the American Revolution to modern struggles for freedom. It helps frame your reference to *Hamilton* as "the music of revolution" that parallels today's cries for justice and inclusion.

7. **Jesus and the Disinherited** by Howard Thurman (1949)
   Thurman's spiritual classic challenges readers to consider how the teachings of Jesus offer a blueprint for the oppressed. His focus on love, nonviolence, and human dignity directly supports your message of embracing the "other" and rejecting hatred.

8. **The New Jim Crow: Mass Incarceration in the Age of Colorblindness** by Michelle Alexander (2010)
   Alexander's book highlights how racial inequality, particularly through mass incarceration, is a continuation of America's long history of racial oppression. It underscores the enduring legacy of slavery and systemic racism, which you discuss in your sermon.

9. **Caste: The Origins of Our Discontents** by Isabel Wilkerson (2020)
   Wilkerson's examination of caste systems, including America's racial hierarchy, provides a powerful framework for understanding how the Civil War's aftermath created entrenched social divisions that persist today.

SECTION 8:
SPIRITUALITY
IN PRACTICE

47. TATTOOS FROM THE HEART

I want to talk about putting faith into practice. There is an amazing social entrepreneur here in Annapolis you may have met—Elizabeth Kinney. She has done so much to transform lives by using her privilege as a vehicle for social change. Elizabeth is the founder of the Annapolis LightHouse Homeless Prevention Center, the LightHouse Bistro, and the new Rise and Shine Bakery. She started these social enterprises to assist the unemployed, underemployed, and marginalized in finding a career path. She helps get them off the street, trains them, and then hires them. Countless lives have been transformed by her work.

During our last conversation, Elizabeth gave me a book that transformed her thinking: *Tattoos on the Heart* by Gregory Boyle. I see her ministry and Father Boyle's work as examples of how we can put progressive values into practice to transform society.

Father Gregory Boyle is a man with a huge heart, able to see beyond prejudice and stereotypes. Known simply as "G," Boyle is a Jesuit priest who built his ministry, serendipitously, in Boyle Heights, California—a neighborhood often referred to as the "gang capital of the world." This area, populated primarily by Mexicans and Native Americans, has about 22 gangs within a community of 100,000 residents.

What makes Father Boyle special is his ability to see abundance instead of scarcity, to have faith instead of fear. Called to Delores Mission Church in 1988, Boyle realized his limitations and the needs of the community. He ventured into social entrepreneurship, creating jobs, dignity, and opportunities for gang members, providing them a way out of the dead-end lifestyle. His vision began with the simple act of offering jobs and removing unwanted tattoos. Over the last 30 years, his organization, *Homeboy Industries*, has grown, helping hundreds leave gang life and find new paths.

Father Boyle's leadership has brought rival gang members together as friends, helped families heal, and inspired privileged communities to see the worth and dignity in the working poor. He reminds us that one person can make a difference.

At *Homeboy Industries*, they started with a bakery and now offer employment services, tattoo removal, case management, legal and educational services, mental health support, and training in areas like solar panel installation. Their *Homegirl Cafe*, catering service, and food truck bring gourmet food to the community while providing jobs and hope.

For me, this is social justice at its best—programs that provide housing, jobs, and "soft skills." There's a scripture that says, "Let them know us by our works." Not by our words or education, but by our actions—our generosity and our willingness to see ourselves in others. When we spend time with people who are different from us, we start to truly see them. Once we see them, our fear disappears, and we can engage in real relationships.

Father Boyle's success comes from his ability to SEE people. He knows their names, drives them around, counsels them, and loves them. He says, "I know you." In the Hebrew scriptures, to "know" someone is a deep expression of intimacy. Namaste: "I see God in you. Can you see God in me?"

This is a story about compassion. It hasn't been easy—Boyle has seen too many die from gang violence, too many babies born into a world of limited opportunities. But he persists.

And that's what we're called to do: persist in the face of despair. Our vision at UUCA is large—to create an emotionally literate, multicultural congregation that lives its principles both inside and outside these walls. It's a big vision, and the road is rough, but we must persist. There is so much to gain, so many lives to touch, and so much hope to bring.

If we could be more like Father Boyle, perhaps we could dream bigger, with generous hearts. We can partner with those working to bring communities together—like the LightHouse, which has evolved into a social enterprise helping people find jobs through culinary training. They're working with me to establish a program to teach "soft skills"—emotional literacy, professionalism, and a positive attitude.

I challenge us to think BIG—not just about our budget, but about our ministry. We are not a for-profit company or a federal agency. We are a church, a congregation, a sacred space where people of faith gather.

"Faith is belief that is not based on proof," and "confidence or trust in a person, thing, or deity." Our faith—our dogma— is our first principle: the inherent worth and dignity of every person. It is a belief that implicitly calls us to action. At UUCA, our vision says we "exist to create the Beloved Community by inspiring and empowering all to live bold and compassionate lives." This is both a faith and an action statement.

The world has many dark places, but together, we can turn the world around. We build a new way by imagining a planet where people, regardless of culture, gender, race, or sexual orientation, can pursue happiness in a fair and equitable way. It is our ongoing work from generation to generation.

And that's why we're here. That's why we bring our children here and why we give financially—to support a vision that sees the world transformed. We are doing planet-saving work. Some of us still fuss over music selections or a $100 line item in the budget—give me a break! Is that why we are here? We are here to be a lighthouse, a beacon of hope.

So, I ask: What do you want to do? Let's do it.

Amen.

References

1. *Tattoos on the Heart: The Power of Boundless Compassion* – Gregory Boyle
   A key inspiration for the sermon, this book by Father Gregory Boyle shares stories from his work with gang members in Los Angeles, offering lessons in compassion and redemption.
2. **The Bible, James 2:18 (NIV)** – "But someone will say, 'You have faith; I have deeds.' Show me your faith without deeds, and I will show you my faith by my deeds."
3. **The Hebrew Scriptures** – References to the concept of "knowing" someone deeply, as discussed in the context of intimacy and relationship-building.
4. **Homeboy Industries** – www.homeboyindustries.org
   The organization was founded by Father Gregory Boyle that provides employment and social services to former gang members, emphasizing social justice and transformation.
5. **Unitarian Universalist Principles** – The First Principle: "The inherent worth and dignity of every person."

48. INVITATION AS SPIRITUAL PRACTICE

What do I mean when I say "Invitation as a Spiritual Practice?" First, we need to ask: what is a spiritual practice? A spiritual practice is anything I do with my mind or body that aligns or realigns me with my highest calling to do good in the world. It's that daily or weekly action, that sacred pause, that ritual that brings me back to my core values, to what I love, and to what gives my life deep meaning and purpose. It's what moves me from despair to hope, from feeling stuck to feeling seen, affirmed, and okay with life—just as it is.

A spiritual practice is a bridge from the noise and busyness of life to a place of calm—a place where we're not just surviving but thriving. It's what grounds us to the Ground of Being, anchoring us to that BIG S SELF—the truest part of us that isn't driven by ego, status, or ambition, but by a deep, centered knowing. That place where wisdom and peace live. Some examples? Meditation, prayer, yoga, journaling, mindfulness, volunteering, nature walks, running, exercise, reading sacred texts, chanting, or (my favorite—singing). And coming to church on Sunday is a spiritual practice that realigns our souls.

So, now that I've defined spiritual practice, let's talk about what I mean by invitation as a spiritual practice. To be more inviting means opening the spaces in your heart and the physical spaces you occupy. It means creating a vibe where others feel comfortable, valued, and included. It's extending yourself in a way that says to others, "I see you. I hear you. You are welcome here." It's an act of love that shows up through our words, our actions, and just being present.

Being inviting is not just about being polite or friendly. It's deeper than that. It's about embodying a generous spirit that sees the Namaste—the divine—in the other person. It's about empathy; it's about being willing to share your time, your attention, your resources. It's not just sitting back, waiting for folks to come to you, but stepping out, reaching out, including, and engaging. It's about being available and present, creating not just space, but a true sense of belonging.

Spiritually, being inviting means recognizing the inherent worth and dignity of every person. It's understanding that we're all connected. It's about lowering our walls and widening our circles because when we all feel included, we all thrive.

I've got two quick stories about invitation that I want to share—moments that weren't exactly warm and fuzzy. In one, someone invited me into their space; in the other, I had to let the spirit of invitation guide me forward. And in both moments, the simple act of inviting turned into a blessing— not just for me, but for the other person too.

Before I was called to this congregation, I was a member and later the minister of another Unitarian Universalist Church. I went from being a member to a board member, to a candidate for ministry, to the Director of Outreach, and then to the co-minister and eventually the solo minister over eight years. As my position and power changed, so did the temperature in the room. Comments emerged that were racial and mean. After I became co-minister, one member told me her husband was leaving the church because, "I don't like what he's doing. He's trying to turn this into a Black church." That got to me. We sang some gospel and R&B now and then, but that was too much for him. So, he left... for two years.

But his wife kept coming to church, loving the music, the community, and the energy we were building. She'd go home and tell him about everything he was missing and challenge him on his racism and biases. Slowly but surely, he started coming back. Then one day, he invited me to hit some golf balls at a driving range. We went, and I was terrible, but we laughed, had lunch, and bonded. By the end of the day, he shook my hand, apologized, and said, "I was wrong about you." He came back to church and fell back in love with his community. That invitation? It was healing for both of us.

And then there was George. Good old George. George was one of the biggest givers in the church, but he did not like me. He did not want me to be a minister at HIS church. He criticized everything I did—my clothes, my diction, my sermons, my singing. One day, when he was dying, I didn't want to visit him. But something inside said, "Go. You want to be a minister? Love the unlovable." I showed up nervous but brought a gift basket as a peace offering. He complained a lot, but after I prayed with him, he thanked me. Before I walked out the door to his room, George called my name, "John." "Yes George" I said. "You're alright with me. Thank you for coming." His wife later told me that my visit meant a lot to him.

That time of invitation changed us both. He saw me, and I saw him.

When you live a life of invitation, you recognize that no one is a stranger; we are all journeying together through the peaks and valleys of life. Invitation is a radical spiritual practice because it calls us to be courageous, vulnerable, and authentically ourselves. It challenges us to say "yes" to life, to step into the unknown, and to connect deeply with one another.

So let us be bold in our invitation. Let us open our hearts wider than ever before, reaching out to those we know and those we have yet to meet. Let us break down the walls that divide us and create a community where all are seen, valued, and loved. Because when we do, we are not just building a welcoming community; we are transforming the world.

May this sacred practice of invitation ignite a fire within us, leading us to deeper connections, greater courage, and a love so profound that it reshapes our lives and the lives of all we touch. This is our calling. This is our work. And together, we can change everything.

Amen.

References

1. **The Art of Spiritual Practice: A Guide to a Fulfilled Life** by David A. Cooper - This book explores the various forms of spiritual practice and how they align individuals with their highest aspirations.
2. **The Book of Joy: Lasting Happiness in a Changing World** by Dalai Lama, Desmond Tutu, and Douglas Carlton Abrams - This book discusses practices like meditation, gratitude, and forgiveness, which can be seen as ways to realign with joy and purpose.
3. **The Power of Now: A Guide to Spiritual Enlightenment** by Eckhart Tolle - Tolle discusses the importance of grounding ourselves in the present moment, which is central to many spiritual practices like mindfulness and meditation.
4. **The Gifts of Imperfection: Let Go of Who You Think You're Supposed to Be and Embrace Who You Are** by Brené Brown - This book emphasizes authenticity and vulnerability, traits that are essential to practicing invitation as a spiritual act.
5. **The Hidden Life of Trees: What They Feel, How They Communicate** by Peter Wohlleben - This book underscores the interconnectedness of all life, paralleling how being inviting is about recognizing the inherent worth of others.
6. **Sacred Texts: The Bible, The Bhagavad Gita, The Tao Te Ching** - These texts provide wisdom on how spiritual

practices help individuals align with a higher sense of purpose and being.

7. **Namaste: The Spirit of Hospitality in India** by Phyllis S. Morgan - This book explores the concept of "Namaste" and how it embodies an inviting spirit, seeing the divine in others.

8. **No Man is an Island** by Thomas Merton - Merton discusses the interconnectedness of humanity and the spiritual call to embrace others with an open and inviting heart.

49. FINAL WORDS AND CONTACT INFORMATION

We have come to the end of our journey together. Through these pages, we have delved into the complexities of the human spirit—the triumphs, the challenges, the deep questions, and the moments of grace that define our existence. This book has been a testament to the power of faith, the resilience of hope, and the transformative force of love. We have journeyed together through stories of personal growth, spiritual awakening, and the pursuit of justice, and we have celebrated the beauty of our shared humanity.

Each sermon is more than just words on a page; they are invitations to engage, to reflect, to feel, and to live more fully. They are calls to action, to kindness, to courage, and to the unyielding pursuit of truth, justice, and compassion in our lives and communities.

We began with reflections on personal growth and self-awareness, exploring the courage to live authentically, face our fears, and embrace resilience. We delved into concepts of self-identity, mindfulness, and the power of our words, recognizing the profound impact they have on shaping our lives and the world around us.

From there, we ventured into spirituality and inner wisdom, drawing from a rich tapestry of beliefs and traditions. We explored Buddhist teachings on mindfulness and right speech, the wisdom of ancient philosophies like Taoism and the spiritual insights of Hinduism and its emphasis on interconnectedness and surrender. We examined the transformative power of mysticism, the Kabbalistic insights from Jewish thought, and the reflections of Islamic spirituality on divine will and the human heart. We also connected with indigenous spiritual practices that honor the earth, water, and nature's rhythms, reminding us of our deep connection to the world around us.

Our journey continued with reflections on Christianity and its teachings on love, forgiveness, and redemption, as well as the symbolism found in the stories of Jesus, including the parable of the Prodigal Son. We explored my chosen faith, Unitarian Universalism and its roots in Christian theology while celebrating its evolution into a faith that embraces wisdom from all sources.

We explored the philosophies of American Transcendentalism, delving into the thoughts of Emerson and Thoreau, and we connected with the ancient wisdom of Greek Stoicism, which calls us to embrace resilience, virtue, and self-discipline. We engaged with the ethical principles of Eastern philosophy, the moral challenges presented by existentialism, and the quest for enlightenment found in Zen Buddhism. We examined the mystical elements of Hermeticism and alchemy, celebrating the journey of turning the lead of life's struggles into the gold of spiritual transformation.

We also confronted the urgent call of social justice, drawing on the prophetic voices of figures like Dr. Martin Luther King Jr., whose theology of love and justice continues to challenge and inspire. We examined the revolutionary power of liberation theology, the ethical demands of humanism, and the courage required to dismantle systems of oppression and build a beloved community where all are free.

Through it all, we returned again and again to the themes of interconnectedness, compassion, and the necessity of mindful engagement with the world. We were reminded that our words and actions matter—that we have the power to shape our reality and the responsibility to use that power wisely. We were called to be careful with our words, intentional in our choices, and courageous in our convictions.

As we close this book, I hope you leave these pages feeling seen, challenged, and inspired. I hope that something here has sparked a new idea, offered comfort in times of uncertainty, or reminded you of the sacredness of your own journey. My deepest wish is that these reflections have served as a companion on your path—lifting you up, offering wisdom, and calling you to live more fully in alignment with your values.

We are all pilgrims, traveling onward and upward, each carrying our own burdens and blessings. We are the alchemists of our lives, turning our experiences into wisdom and love. The journey doesn't end here; it continues in every conversation, every act of kindness, and every moment of reflection and connection.

Thank you for walking this path with me. May we continue to grow, to question, to seek, and to love with all our hearts. May we be bold in our actions, gentle in our judgments, and steadfast in our commitment to creating a world where justice, equity, and compassion guide the way. Onward we go.

Amen.

Reverend John Thomas Crestwell, Jr.
jcrestwell@uuannapolis.org

50. BENEDICTION:

As you leave these pages, may you carry within you the love that binds us all—the love that knows no bounds, no limits. May hope be your companion on this journey of life, guiding you through the unknown, lighting your path when the way seems unclear.

Go forth, then, not as you were, but transformed by what you've encountered here—wiser, more courageous, more free. Live these words, let them take root in your heart, and may your life be a testament to the power of truth, justice, and compassion.

You are not alone on this journey. We are all interconnected, bound by a common destiny, striving toward a beloved community.

With love, with hope, and with the knowledge that you are capable of greatness—go, live fully, and let your light shine. Amen.

SECTION 9: QUOTES
FROM BOOK

Chapter 1: Authenticity— Freedom—Pain–Pleasure

Section: Personal Growth and Self-Awareness

1. "There is no authenticity, no freedom, no joy without enduring some pain. To live authentically is to face the crucifixion before the resurrection."
2. "Authenticity isn't about self-promotion; it's about quiet strength rooted in humility, where your presence testifies to the truth within you."
3. "Our nation's journey mirrors our personal quests for authenticity. We will never be an authentic people until we confront the contradictions in our story."
4. "Authenticity, freedom, pain, and pleasure are the threads of our human experience, teaching us that redemptive pain pushes us to grow, evolve, and become our truest selves."

Chapter 2:
Conquering Fear

Section: Personal Growth and Self-Awareness

1. "Fear paralyzes, but courage is the force that moves us forward. We may not conquer all fear, but we can rise above it with faith, hope, and love."
2. "We fear not because the danger is real, but because we doubt our ability to survive it. The true battle is with our own mindset."
3. "Every time you confront your fears and move beyond them, you help heal the world. Faith calls us to be brave truth-tellers."
4. "Spiritual people do not let fear guide them but faith, hope, and love. Holy boldness keeps us focused on unity and truth."

Chapter 3: Happiness: A Journey

Section: Personal Growth and Self-Awareness

1. "Happiness isn't something you chase; it's something you cultivate in the everyday moments, finding joy in the journey, not just the destination."
2. "Happiness is always there, standing at the door, knocking. You decide when to let it in."
3. "Even in the darkest of times, happiness is a choice we make—like Nelson Mandela, who found joy even behind bars by embracing hope and forgiveness."
4. "Joy is in the mess, in the rain, and in the sunlight that comes after the storm. It's always waiting for us, if we choose to open the door."

Chapter 4: Becoming Nobody

Section: Personal Growth and Self-Awareness

1. "I had to unbecome before I could truly become. The journey to becoming my best self meant embracing my humanity, flaws, and mortality."
2. "I am nobody because I am everybody. I am special, but not that special. I choose to be love in all its expressions."
3. "True awakening isn't about rejecting dogma or becoming more progressive—it's about surrendering the ego and embracing our interconnectedness."
4. "We live in an age of narcissism, but the real challenge is to overcome the fixation on self and rediscover our common humanity."

Chapter 5: Blink: Improving How We Judge Others

Section: Personal Growth and Self-Awareness

1. "Our rapid judgments can be insightful or flawed. To judge wisely, we must approach each moment with the curiosity of a child and the wisdom of an elder."
2. "The less we know about someone's story, the more likely we are to misjudge them. Real understanding requires us to become perpetual students of life."
3. "Improving our judgments requires humility—the courage to admit what we don't know and to challenge our biases head-on."
4. "Does this idea or action call me to courage and growth, or does it push me toward fear and division? This question guides our journey toward justice and connection."

Chapter 6: Lemons to Lemonade

Section: Personal Growth and Self-Awareness

1. "Life will keep handing us lemons, but how we handle them is our choice. When bitterness creeps in, we can reach for sweetness, calm, and connection."
2. "We are the alchemists of our lives, transforming the sour moments into something sweet and nourishing with love, kindness, and compassion."
3. "Making lemonade out of lemons isn't about avoiding the sour moments—it's about discovering the sweetness within them."
4. "What kind of lemonade are you making today? Are you letting the sourness take over, or are you finding ways to sweeten your mix?"

Chapter 7: Forgive 70x7

Section: Personal Growth and Self-Awareness

1. "Forgiveness isn't about excusing the wrong—it's about releasing the power it has over us, so we can step out of the shadow of the past and into the light of healing."
2. "Jesus' call to forgive 70 x 7 isn't about counting offenses—it's a reminder that forgiveness is a boundless resource, meant to liberate us, not the offender."
3. "Forgiveness transforms how we hold memories. The hurt may remain, but its control over our emotions and actions fades away, freeing our spirit."
4. "Forgiveness feels like liberation. It's a release, a lightness—a step into a new reality where grace, mercy, and humility guide us."

Chapter 8: Care-Full
and Care-Less

Section: Personal Growth
and Self-Awareness

1. "Fear's power lies in its ability to make us look back too long. We must learn when to care-fully and when to care-less to protect our peace and well-being."
2. "Not everything that scares us deserves our energy. Sometimes, we need to say, 'Cancel, cancel, cancel. I'm not taking that in.'"
3. "We cannot build a beloved community without compassion. Caring fully means knowing when to hold on and when to let go."
4. "Compassion isn't passive; it's the vehicle for connection that moves us beyond fear, bringing us closer to the world we're meant to create."

Chapter 9: Wordsmithing - The Power of Words

Section: Personal Growth and Self-Awareness

1. "Words have power; they 'spell' things into existence. They can inspire, heal, or harm—so be careful of the words you say, for you never know which ones you'll have to eat."
2. "The magic of words lies in their ability to shift perspective, change hearts, and inspire action. They create energy in motion—emotion—that moves us."
3. "We must become effective wordsmiths, choosing language that builds up rather than tears down, words that lift us up and draw us closer to our best selves."
4. "Words that embody humanity's sacred values—love, vulnerability, non-violence—are the incantations that cast a spell of love upon our world."

Chapter 10: The Alchemist

Section: Spirituality and Inner Wisdom

1. "Life, like alchemy, is about transformation—turning the lead of our everyday experiences into the gold of wisdom, compassion, and understanding."
2. "The journey itself is the real treasure. It's not about the destination, but about the courage to follow our hearts and the resilience to keep going."
3. "Sometimes, being lost is the only way to truly be found. Our missteps and struggles are essential steps toward growth and self-discovery."
4. "You are the Alchemist of your own life. The treasure you seek is not outside of you—it's something you will uncover within."

Chapter 11: Choiceless Awareness

Section: Spirituality and Inner Wisdom

1. "When we practice pure awareness, we are no one. We are unity, the zero point where healing occurs and we connect with the all-encompassing force of existence."

2. "True freedom is found within, away from judgment and expectation. It's an inner knowing that we are connected to all things, seen and unseen."

3. "Imagine the universe is participating with you. When you suspend judgment and simply become aware, you are in communion with the divine."

4. "Choiceless awareness reminds us that we are more than our titles, our accomplishments, or our failures —we are pure potentiality, capable of our own healing, transformation, and freedom."

Chapter 12: The Hindu Trinity: The Number 3

Section: Spirituality and Inner Wisdom

1. "Life moves in three dimensions: creation, preservation, and dissolution. To find peace, we must learn to dance with these cycles, embracing their highs and lows."
2. "The number 3 is a symbol of completion, perfection, and enlightenment, reminding us that every ending makes way for a new beginning."
3. "Creation, love, and loss are always in motion. When we learn to flow with these rhythms, we discover the wisdom of life's cosmic dance."
4. "The dance of Shiva calls us to radical acceptance of life's cycles—inviting us to create, love, and let go, knowing that even in loss, there is renewal."

Chapter 13: Water Metaphors

Section: Spirituality and Inner Wisdom

1. "Water sustains, nourishes, and connects us. Sixty percent of what makes us human is water, and without it, we would not be here. We are water."
2. "In Hollywood, any time you see a character stepping into the rain or wading in water, they are about to be reborn into a new character with a new outlook. Like them, we are having a death and resurrection experience."
3. "Water, whether in the form of rain, flood, or tears, is a harbinger of change. It's not here to drown us but to lead us toward liberation."
4. "Wade in the water, children, God's gonna trouble the water. It's a reminder that when life's waters become turbulent, they lead us to transformation and freedom."

Chapter 14: The Seven Spiritual Laws

Section: Spirituality and Inner Wisdom

1. "Mentalism reminds us that everything begins with thought. When you realize your thoughts shape your experiences, you become empowered to create the life you want."
2. "The Law of Correspondence teaches us that everything is interconnected. Just as the cycles of nature reflect the cosmos, our inner and outer worlds are in constant dialogue."
3. "The Law of Vibration tells us that everything is in motion, even if we can't see it. Raise your vibration by cultivating love, joy, gratitude, and peace."
4. "The Law of Polarity shows us that everything has its opposite, yet these opposites are just different degrees of the same experience."
5. "The Law of Rhythm reminds us that everything flows, rises, and falls. Appreciate the rhythm of life —knowing that tough times won't last forever, and neither will the good."
6. "The Law of Cause and Effect reminds us that we are active participants in the unfolding of our lives. If you want change, become the cause of that change."
7. "The Law of Gender teaches us balance—the masculine and feminine energies exist in everything. True harmony comes when we bring these energies into alignment."

Chapter 15: The Law of Surrender

Section: Spirituality and Inner Wisdom

1. "Be like water, rolling with life's punches, adjusting and readjusting without exhausting yourself."
2. "Real surrender is about letting go of control and trusting the flow—moving with life rather than forcing it."
3. "Taoism teaches that when you're rigid, you're working against the natural flow of the universe. Peace comes when we embrace the dance of life."
4. "Focus on how you live the process, not on controlling the results. Life gives and takes, but the journey is what matters."

Chapter 16: Be Invictus

Section: Spirituality and Inner Wisdom

1. "Life will bring its dark moments, its shadow teachers, but I give thanks when they arrive. I am Invictus—unconquerable. I will not give up on myself, even when I feel lost."
2. "The shadow, far from being evil, is a necessary part of our growth. It's the teacher that presents challenges, reminding us that life's players—our relationships, experiences—are all part of our journey toward awakening."
3. "In times of darkness, we are given the chance to see reality without the distortions of blame or projection. We recognize that all humans, at some point, feel vulnerable, weak, and in need of healing."
4. "I am responsible for my life. I will not let the judgments of others, or my own projections, dictate my reality. I am the master of my fate. I am the captain of my soul."

Chapter 17: Heaven & The Afterlife

Section: Spirituality and Inner Wisdom

1. "I believe our fear of death and our need to survive are among the most powerful driving forces in the world."
2. "Energy doesn't die; it just changes form. And we, my friends, are energy."
3. "Heaven is not just a place; it is a promise—an unfolding journey where our spirits continue to evolve, endlessly and beautifully."
4. "Maybe we get what we desire most after we die. I think that our souls know what we most deeply desire, and that's what we go toward when we die."

Chapter 18: Does God Exist?

Section: Spirituality and Inner Wisdom

1. "GOD is not confined to a church, mosque, or temple. GOD isn't even confined to a name. GOD is beyond our words, beyond our limited human understanding."

2. "When I say GOD is energy, I mean that GOD is the life force that flows through all creation. It's the pulse that beats in your heart, the gravity that holds the planets in orbit, and the inspiration that sparks your creativity."

3. "GOD is not about fear or punishment. It's not about rules and restrictions designed to keep you in line. GOD is about love, connection, and living your highest good."

4. "It's easy to get caught up in the noise of life, to be overwhelmed by the demands and distractions that pull us away from our center. But GOD or LOVE is always calling us back, inviting us to return to that place of stillness, that place of truth."

Chapter 19: The Aquarian Gospel, Eschatology, and the New Age

Section: Spirituality and Inner Wisdom

1. "The world waits for sages and saviors, but we forget to see ourselves as the harbingers of hope and peace. We look outside of ourselves when we think about peace, assuming it's something someone else will deliver."

2. "What if there's no grand beginning or end? What if that day is today? What if heaven is not a distant place but a present possibility, created within us?"

3. "We are the creators of our own heavens and hells, shaping our reality with every thought, every choice, every breath."

4. "Stop searching outside yourself. Open the windows of your heart and let that light pour in. Be the light that turns toil into joy, the light that makes the ordinary sacred."

Chapter 20: Samhain and the Origins of Religion: Wicca, Paganism, Magic, Spells, and Harry Potter

Section: Spirituality and Inner Wisdom

1. "At its core, magic is about intention—using thoughts, words, and phrases to manifest desires. While there can be a darker side, most magic aims to do good, to heal, and to make the world better."
2. "Early humans created rituals around the four elements—earth, air, fire, and water—which they saw as magical forces of life. The dirt where things grow, the invisible air we breathe, the warming and transformative power of fire, and the life-sustaining gift of water—all were sacred."
3. "All religion is fundamentally astro-theological—of the stars and the earth. When we approach sacred texts with this perspective, it becomes clear how much we share across our diverse faith traditions."
4. "We are all moving toward Spirit, God, the Cosmos, or whatever we call the divine, from different paths, but with one shared longing—for home, for understanding, for community."

Chapter 21: Easter: The True Meaning of Resurrection

Section: Faith, Religion, and Spiritual Reflections

1. "The resurrection is a powerful metaphor for transformation—a call to die to the old self so the new self can be born."
2. "The story of Jesus' resurrection teaches us about hope in tomorrow and belief in our ability to be the best version of ourselves."
3. "To embrace resurrection is to believe that no matter how many times we stumble, we can get back up, renewed and ready to start again."
4. "Resurrection is not just Jesus' story—it's our story. It's the story of believing in tomorrow, trusting in the process, and knowing that the best is yet to come."

Chapter 22: Pagan Holidays: Hanukkah, Solstice, Yule, Christmas

Section: Faith, Religion, and Spiritual Reflections

1. "Hanukkah, Yule, Solstice, and Christmas are all about the same thing: sun worship—light returning, life enduring, hope reborn. We worship on SUNday."
2. "The lights on your tree are like the stars in the sky, a reminder of the billions of lights that have guided humanity for centuries."
3. "As we reflect on these blended traditions, let us see the beauty in their diversity."
4. "Despite our modern distractions, we are still connected to these stories, still bound to the sun, the moon, the stars, and the earth."

Chapter 23: "Insha Allah": God's Will? Bless You?

Section: Faith, Religion, and Spiritual Reflections

1. "One major problem in the world comes from fundamentalist religious views which lead to major harms being perpetuated."
2. "The idea of blessings has often been intertwined with the notion of some being chosen and others not."
3. "God's will can also be about letting go knowing that some things are beyond our control."
4. "God's will can also be interpreted as 'goodwill' toward all because we know all are wrestling with existential concerns."

Chapter 24: Tipping Point (Shifting the Paradigm)

Section: Unitarian Universalism

1. "Transformation means change, conversion, renovation, and revolution. It's about becoming something new and better."
2. "Malcolm Gladwell's book shows how small things, when in the right hands, can make a huge difference."
3. "By doing the small things–the small 't' transformations, we set the stage for the BIG 'T' Transformations that can reshape us into true reflections of the Beloved Community."

Chapter 25: Decolonizing Our Spirituality: A Return to Earth-Centered Roots

Section: Unitarian Universalism

1. "Daniel Quinn, in his seminal work, reminds us that hunter-gatherers were 'leavers'—taking only what they needed from the earth. In contrast, agrarian societies became 'takers,' cultivating and expanding their reach in ways that often exploited the land."
2. "When we pray, 'Thy kingdom come, thy will be done on earth as it is in heaven,' we are calling for a reality where heaven and earth are united—where the spiritual and the physical coexist in harmony."
3. "Our work is to reclaim what has been lost—to understand why we do what we do, to find the deeper meanings behind our rituals, and to embrace a spirituality that celebrates our connection to the earth and the cosmos."
4. "Let us remember that the kingdom is not some distant hope; it is here, now, in every act of wholeness and connection."

Chapter 26: New American Transcendentalism:

Section: Unitarian Universalism

1. "As Unitarian Universalists, we are part of a transcending faith—a tradition that stretches us to define our understanding of the divine, or even to embrace the absence of it."
2. "We are moving from a world defined by 'either/or' thinking—where we separate ourselves by race, class, gender, and more—to a 'both/and' reality."
3. "Quantum thinking asks us to look beyond linear equations and see the interconnectedness of all things. It's about shifting perspectives and embracing the unknown."
4. "As you consider your personal journey, think beyond traditional boundaries. Dare to do something different, just as our Transcendentalist ancestors did."

Chapter 27: Heretics Faith: Prayer, Meditation, Contemplation:

Section: Unitarian Universalism

1. "We, Unitarian Universalists, call ourselves heretics because we are not orthodox–among the accepted traditional protestant faith traditions. I'm left-handed, that's not orthodox either and that's just fine by me. Ours is a living tradition that is non creedal."
2. "Our goal is unity consciousness, not separation. The old ways we ran from often remind us of division."
3. "For me, these [prayer, meditation, and contemplation] are fundamentally the same spiritual practice."
4. "When you see life as a prayer, every moment becomes an opportunity to connect deeply, to live beyond randomness, and to find calm perspective."

Chapter 28 : Why I am a Unitarian Universalist:

Section: Unitarian Universalism

1. "I went from being a religious fundamentalist to a religious, liberal free thinker. I went from condemning my first girlfriend's dad to Hell to not believing in a literal Hell at all."
2. "This faith saved my life, so I feel called to give back —to offer my time, talent, and treasure because, with 'great freedom comes great responsibility.'"
3. "When I lost my religion, I knew I wasn't a traditional, literalist Christian. I knew I was something 'divergent.' There were many dark nights of the soul back then, but they were precursors to many bright days of transformation."
4. "I chose it because I needed affirmation of my humanity; I needed a beloved community to raise my family and to grow my soul."
5. "Unitarian Universalism at its core is a quintessential American Religion. We are both a spiritual and secular faith, an institution grounded in democracy and a sacred system of belief."
6. "I am a Unitarian Universalist because this faith has changed me. It challenges my assumptions, allows me to let go of fear-based narratives, and calls me to be my best self."

Chapter 29: Chaos or Community: Dr. King, Oppenheimer, and Barbie

Section: Social Justice and Cultural Critique

1. "Dr. King would say, 'The means by which we live cannot outdistance the ends for which we live.' The bombs brought a false peace—one rooted in fear and domination, not in justice or reconciliation."

2. "Oppenheimer's most famous quote is from the Hindu Upanishad: 'Now I am become Death, the destroyer of worlds.' When you play with weapons of mass destruction, you cannot control how that power will be wielded."

3. "Barbie, directed by Greta Gerwig, who was born and raised in a Unitarian Universalist congregation, challenges societal norms and flips traditional paradigms on their heads."

4. "Chaos arises when we deny the humanity of others, when we allow fear and hatred to rule. Community is built through collaboration, humility, and the recognition that we are all interconnected."

Chapter 30: You Throw Like a Girl: Toxic Masculinity:

Section: Social Justice and Cultural Critique

1. "Being a man is good. Being male, embodying masculine energy, is inherently good. But like all things, there are aspects of masculinity that can become off-balance and harmful, and that's what I'm naming today."
2. "I grew up in a hyper-masculine time, where showing toughness was a survival mechanism. In my community, we were still unlearning the brutal legacy of chattel slavery, and many of us learned toxic lessons about manhood: 'Be tough,' 'Man up,' and 'Don't throw like a girl.'"
3. "This imbalance between masculine and feminine energies disrupts our ability to nurture, collaborate, and heal. It perpetuates a cycle of harm that affects everyone—fueling violence, inequality, and disconnection."
4. "A real man does not measure his value by his ability to dominate, but by his capacity to uplift, nurture, and collaborate. He embraces vulnerability as a strength, not a weakness."

Chapter 31: Caste and America

Section: Social Justice and Cultural Critique

1. "We are all victims of destructive psycho-social programming. These are the stories we've been told, stories that have seeped into our institutions and our minds, and they drive much of the division and discord we see today."
2. "This is THE GREAT WORK of our time: to free ourselves from these mental and physical tyrannies."
3. "Caste isn't personal. It's not necessarily about hating someone or even consciously thinking they're inferior. Caste is insidious because it's woven into the very fabric of society. It's those unspoken rules we all follow without even realizing it. It's the boundaries we accept as 'the way things are.'"
4. "Caste is the root, and racism is the flower. It's like a play—caste assigns the roles, and racism is the script that tells us how to treat each other based on those roles."

Chapter 32: Hacking the Brain & Race

Section: Social Justice and Cultural Critique

1. "To change this world, it's going to take a revolution of the mind and a transformation of the heart. Getting beyond racial prejudice, systemic racism, and cultural biases will take everything we've got."
2. "We live in a reality that's been constructed for us—where whiteness is seen as rightness. Think about how many of our systems, especially law enforcement, are rooted in this."
3. "Our minds have been hacked. We've been programmed from birth to see the world through this false lens. And we need to rewire our brains, our thinking, and our hearts."
4. "Hack your brain. Commit to reprogramming how you see the world. This is the greatest work you can do—for yourself, for your faith, and for the world."

Chapter 33: MLK: 90 Years Later

Section: Social Justice and Cultural Critique

1. "We are living through a repeating 50-year cycle of racial and cultural tension, and it will keep returning until we reconcile it."
2. "Today feels very much like the 1960s, when a new consciousness, voiced by Dr. King, disrupted the old order. The result? Bloodshed, violence, resistance. We're seeing the same resistance today because we still haven't learned to stop 'othering' one another."
3. "We are part of the global 1%, and we have a hand in shaping the systems of injustice we're fighting against. As Gandhi said, 'Change yourself and you change the world.'"
4. "We can remain awake during this great revolution, knowing that we are not powerless but empowered to be the change we wish to see."

Chapter 34: The Poor People's Campaign Revisited

Section: Social Justice and Cultural Critique

1. "The Poor People's Campaign was about more than just feeding the hungry and clothing the naked. It was about demanding systemic change. It was about justice."
2. "Dr. King knew that poverty isn't just about a lack of money—it's about a lack of opportunity, a lack of justice. Poverty, he said, is violence. It's a violence against the soul, a violence against the spirit, a violence against our shared humanity."
3. "Charity addresses the symptom, but justice addresses the root. And we, as a people of faith, are called to be agents of justice."
4. "This is not just about the poor. This is about all of us. Poverty dehumanizes us all. It cheapens the soul of a society. And if we allow it to persist, we are complicit in the injustice."

Chapter 35: Power Over or Power With: Shaping a Just Humanity

Section: Social Justice and Cultural Critique

1. "As Dr. Hogue states, power as potestas is the power we know all too well—it dominates, controls, and imposes. It's a hierarchical power rooted in scarcity, fear, and the relentless belief that power must be wielded over others to maintain order and security."

2. "Professor Hogue teaches his seminary students that potentia represents a fundamentally different approach. It is a relational power that emphasizes connection, collaboration, and shared potential. This power is transformative because it encourages us to act together, leveraging our diverse strengths to create new possibilities."

3. "Our struggle lies between two opposing forces: the entrenched power of domination and the emerging power of collective action. To engage with these dynamics, we must be vigilant and intentional."

4. "Let us be bold and unwavering in our commitment to this vision. By embracing our interconnectedness and acting with purpose, we can help shape a future where justice, equity, and compassion are not just ideals but lived realities."

Chapter 36: Justice is Love in Action

Section: Social Justice and Cultural Critique

1. "Justice is love in action. Justice is not just in what we say, it is in what you're willing to do."
2. "We can collectively speed up the day to beloved community, but first we have to dedicate and rededicate ourselves to this work."
3. "There has to be a moral imperative that holds us captive and moves us from hibernation to participation."
4. "We are religious liberals, that's what we do. We evolve and resolve. We embrace, not erase."
5. "Sometimes we have to go against the norm so that the circle of privilege can be widened and shared by more people."
6. "I believe that we have the power to change human history to something that is truly welcoming and affirming."

Chapter 37: You Are the Earth: Transforming Our Thinking About Nature

Section: Nature, Science, and Philosophy

1. "Humanity is in crisis, but we have the power to heal ourselves. The key lies in transforming how we think about our relationship with nature—from something we conquer and subdue to something sacred that we must protect."
2. "We are not separate from nature; we are nature. We are it, and it is us."
3. "You cannot destroy what is sacred. You cannot exploit it, oppress it, or harm it. When you understand that we are all part of the same web of existence, it changes you."
4. "To heal, we need to transform our thinking. We must move away from the old narratives of domination and exploitation."

Chapter 38: The American Buffalo: A Lesson in Hubris

Section: Nature, Science, and Philosophy

1. "The lesson I hope to share is that human hubris—our exaggerated pride and unbalanced ego—can lead to great destruction if not guided by a theology of interdependence, reverence, and compassion for all living beings."
2. "What we pay attention to can grow and thrive. When we meet the world with compassion and empathy, we can create beauty and preservation."
3. "Interdependence means trust and support between and among all living beings, not just humans. It is a sacred, holy trust that includes animals and the earth itself."
4. "We cannot bomb into dust what we are truly connected to. We cannot starve what we love. We cannot destroy what we hold sacred."

Chapter 39: Evolution: Are We Devolving?

Section: Nature, Science, and Philosophy

1. "We are not bound by dogma or the past. We are free to adapt, to change, to grow. This is what it means to be part of a living faith. And it is also what it means to be human."

2. "Our higher consciousness allows us to transcend those base instincts and move toward a more compassionate and peaceful existence."

3. "We are evolving. We are moving from competition to collaboration, from either/or to both/and. We are transcending the rigid binaries of race, gender, and power."

4. "As we evolve, we will look back on this time and wonder: How did we ever live like that? How did we ever believe that one race was superior to another?"

Chapter 40: Civilizations: Collaboration, Cooperation, Conquest

Section: Nature, Science, and Philosophy

1. "We've become experts at self-promotion, often without stopping to think about the impact this has on those around us. What's sold to us as self-empowerment is, in many ways, a distraction from something deeper—our communal responsibilities, our shared well-being."
2. "The problem isn't the desire to collaborate; it's the way collaboration has historically played out. Too often, 'collaborating' has really meant dominating."
3. "We can grow beyond the cycle of conquest, moving from destructive creation to constructive creation."
4. "The new story is about safe connections, egalitarian cooperation, compassionate engagement, and bold collaborations."

Chapter 41: 2: The Power of Yin/Yang (Left/ Right Brain Balance)

Section: Nature, Science, and Philosophy

1. "The left brain is all about the 'I,' and this is good. The 'I' says, 'I AM.' 'I am somebody.' 'I exist. I have agency.' That's beautiful! But in our current world system, which is left-brain dominant, all these virtues can become vices if they're not balanced by the creativity and expansiveness of the right brain."

2. "The right brain is where the 'I' disappears, and the 'we' emerges. It's the side where oneness is the norm, where we find rhythm in music, and where living in the present moment becomes natural."

3. "We are born into duality—into tension, drama, and angst. But the grand spiritual game is to take the two and make them one again. This is the secret that both nature and spirituality have been teaching us all along: balance."

4. "All the '-isms' and inequities we see today—racism, sexism, patriarchy, and environmental degradation —are a result of imbalanced left-brain processing. The right brain embraces unity consciousness, expansiveness, and collaboration."

Chapter 42: Fibonacci, Ahimsa, The Buddha, and You

Section: Nature, Science, and Philosophy

1. "Buddha realized the middle way was the best path —the path of balance. He had been wound too tightly, and the extremes could not be sustained. His message became the first humanist and moderate one the world had ever heard."

2. "We are both—black and white, yin and yang, good and bad, joy and suffering. When we understand this, we stop clinging to rigid views and embrace the complexity of life."

3. "Life is math. It is a set of patterns and cycles that continually unfold, guiding everything toward balance and growth. From the micro to the macro, this pattern is woven into the very fabric of existence."

4. "When we move beyond duality, when we step into the gray, we enter divine spaces of compassion, nonviolence, and unconditional love. We come into acceptance—acceptance of life's highs and lows, of its beauty and brokenness."

5. "ALL will become buddhas in due time."

Chapter 43: Beloved Community Explained

Section: Society, Conflict and Human Behavior

1. "Beloved community isn't just an idea we aspire to—it's a reality we live into, moment by moment. It's the ground we stand on when we commit to love, justice, and equity."
2. "When love is truly at the center of beloved community, everything changes. We start asking different questions. We don't just focus on what's fair for us—we look at what's just for everyone."
3. "Justice in beloved community means we don't just settle for surface-level fairness. It means we roll up our sleeves and get to work dismantling the systems that keep people from thriving."
4. "In beloved community, we recognize that we're all connected. What happens to one of us affects all of us. We understand that our well-being is wrapped up in the well-being of others."

Chapter 44: Sex & War

Section: Society, Conflict and Human Behavior

1. "Two forces—sex and war—have shaped our societies, our structures, and our stories since the beginning of time."
2. "Men, in particular, have inherited what Potts and Hayden call 'war genes'—a behavioral predisposition toward violence."
3. "This aggression, this drive for dominance, it doesn't serve us in the world we're trying to build. It may have had its place in the Stone Age, but today, it causes more harm than good."
4. "Instead of celebrating domination and violence, we should be lifting up qualities like compassion, collaboration, and emotional intelligence."

Chapter 45: Fanatics (Extremism)

Section: Society, Conflict and Human Behavior

1. "We all worship something, don't we? It doesn't matter what you believe about God or religion. At the core of human nature, we are drawn to something bigger than ourselves."
2. "Fanaticism isn't just passion—it's when we cross the line from healthy zeal into something that consumes us, shaping our lives in ways we don't even realize."
3. "The most important kind of freedom isn't the freedom to do whatever you want. It's the freedom that comes from attention, awareness, and discipline."
4. "We all worship something. The only choice we get is what to worship. Choose wisely, my friends."

Chapter 46: Our Civil War —A War for Civility

Section: Society, Conflict and Human Behavior

1. "We are still engaged in a Civil War in this country— a war that didn't end in 1865. The Civil War might have physically concluded then, but spiritually and mentally, it continues."
2. "This war has always been mental and spiritual —about what kind of country we want to be. We've been struggling ever since to define who 'all' includes."
3. "Freedom for some is not true freedom. This great sin of 'othering' is part of our national DNA, and it runs through every problem we face today."
4. "This ongoing Civil War is not fought with guns, but with a lack of civility. This is a war on civility. Can we put aside our tribalism for the higher cause of community, peace, and justice?"

Chapter 47: Tattoos From the Heart

Section: Spirituality in Practice

1. "True transformation happens when we move beyond words and into action—when we actively engage in seeing and uplifting those around us."
2. "When we spend time with people who are different from us, we start to truly see them. Once we see them, our fear disappears, and we can engage in real relationships."
3. "Faith isn't just what we believe; it's what we do with that belief. It calls us to live out our principles in real, tangible ways."
4. "The world has many dark places, but together, we can turn the world around. We build a new way by imagining a planet where people, regardless of culture, gender, race, or sexual orientation, can pursue happiness in a fair and equitable way."

Chapter 48: Invitation as Spiritual Practice Section:

Spirituality in Practice

1. "Being inviting is not just about being polite or friendly. It's about embodying a generous spirit that says to others, 'I see you. I hear you. You are welcome here.'"
2. "Spiritually, being inviting means recognizing the inherent worth and dignity of every person. It's about lowering our walls and widening our circles because when we all feel included, we all thrive."
3. "When you live a life of invitation, you recognize that no one is a stranger; we are all journeying together through the peaks and valleys of life."
4. "Invitation is a radical spiritual practice because it calls us to be courageous, vulnerable, and authentically ourselves."

www.uuannapolis.org

jcrestwell@uuannapolis.org